BIN LADEN

BIN LADEN

BEHIND THE MASK
OF THE TERRORIST

ADAM ROBINSON

ARCADE PUBLISHING • NEW YORK

FIRST U.S. EDITION 2002

There is still significant variance among news sources for the times of key events on September 11, 2001. For these events, the author has relied on the *New York Times*, the *Christian Science Monitor*, msnbc.com, cnn.com, bbc.com, the FBI, and the public relations offices of United Airlines and American Airlines. In addition, the times of impact at the two World Trade Center towers and of their subsequent collapse were verified by records from the Columbia University seismograph as reported in the *New York Times*. The author thanks the New York Public Library for bringing this article to his attention.

ISBN 1-55970-640-6
Library of Congress Control Number: 2001134043
Library of Congress Cataloging-in-Publication information is available.

Published in the United States of America by Arcade Publishing, Inc., New York
Distributed by AOL Time Warner Book Group

Visit our Web site at www.arcadepub.com

10 9 8 7 6 5 4 3 2 1

EB

PRINTED IN THE UNITED STATES OF AMERICA

Contents

An eight-page section of photographs
falls between pages 154 and 155.

Preface

'The high-minded man does not bear grudges, for it is not the mark of a great soul to remember injuries, but to forget them.' Twenty-four centuries later, these words of the classical Greek philosopher Aristotle may still ring true as a formula for living harmoniously with our fellow man. The unspoken assumption, the civilising factor, is that this is what everyone wants.

What if there are some who do not?

The events in New York of Tuesday, September 11, 2001, have scarred the world irreparably and indelibly. Over and over, we hear that the world we knew will never be the same again. This we understand. What we do not understand is who . . . how . . . why . . . and the greater tragedy, in the midst of so much sensible, sensitive and honest reporting and writing, is that far too many of us cannot comprehend these answers even when we hear or read them. We cannot grasp that there is another world view at least as potent as ours, a separate reality represented by the furtive figure of Osama bin Laden.

The danger presented by Bin Laden and his minions is considerable and the greatest part of it is our ignorance. We ask many imponderable questions: how is it possible that his rage could have been fuelled to such a degree? How is it that, once recognised, his anger has managed to fester, to manifest itself in plots and deeds and to spread like a virus? How has a man declared persona non grata even by his own homeland remained at liberty? How has his doctrine infiltrated the hearts and minds of good men and turned them into monsters capable of flying themselves and innocent fellow human beings into the side of a building and certain oblivion? These questions and others demand that we stop and listen to the answers. If we do not, then Osama will not be the last of his ilk.

For more than a year prior to September 11, I had been discussing this biography with members of the Binladin family. Speaking on such a subject is no easy matter. Their estranged relative Osama is responsible for some of the worst, most callously executed atrocities in recent history. The Binladins, who altered their name in an attempt to distance themselves from their terrorist relative, are as helpless as everyone in reaching out to those whose families and lives have been shattered. They have their own burden to carry: Osama was born one of their own.

To put them in context, the Binladins are like the Rockefellers of Arabia – equally known for their success in business and their philanthropy. With more to lose than most, they have been tarred by association with the evil deeds of a man they have consistently disowned and tried to remove from their lives. After September 11, however, word reached me that there was perhaps something the family felt they could contribute: a knowledge of what made Osama into the antithesis of his peace-loving kin; a better understanding of what goes on inside his head. For the family, these are old wounds that have caused agony for many years. Reopening them has been painful. They did so knowing of the personal jeopardy in which it might place them, but also knowing that their discomfort will have helped to illuminate the psyche of Osama.

Other individuals have also come forward to help us shed light on Osama's years in Beirut, Khartoum and in Afghanistan. Most asked for their identities to be kept off these pages for fear of reprisals. We thank them for their support and efforts on our behalf.

The production of *Bin Laden: Behind the Mask of the Terrorist* is the result of the collective memories of many people. Thanks to their efforts, what emerges is an extraordinary picture, radically different from the one that Osama seems to be painting of himself. His past is littered with alcohol and prostitutes, grudges and contradictions. He courts self-publicity and will sacrifice men's lives – and perhaps ultimately his own – without a second thought in order to feed the personality cult he craves. While much has been made of his commercial management capabilities, in reality his success has come in environments such as Sudan where influence and kickbacks are normal practice and ensure that the rich stay rich and the poor stay poor.

Most damning are the revelations that he and his organisation have knowingly benefited from revenues generated by the opium and heroin trade in Afghanistan, which may be Osama's final sanctuary. Much of this heroin finds its way onto Middle Eastern markets and into the veins of fellow Muslims. Osama and his Al Qaeda organisation must shoulder a fair share of the responsibility for the drug problem and spiralling AIDS and HIV infection rates in many Islamic countries. The United Nations Office for Drug Control and Crime Prevention says that some nine million people worldwide were addicted to heroin in the late 1990s. Afghanistan produces nearly three-quarters of the world supply of opium, the basic ingredient of heroin.

The enigma of Osama is undeniable. He is a hero or villain, depending on perspective. Tall, aristocratic in appearance and well-spoken, he might have become a legitimate statesman of some significance, and certainly his birthright would have given him every chance to do so. Instead he is Public Enemy Number One of the civilised world, a man without conscience or pity, the embodiment of evil vengeance. This is the story of his slide into the abyss, and a story that will not end with the fall of his hosts, the Taliban, but will continue beyond even his capture or death.

CHAPTER ONE

Family Ties That Bind

Imagine for a moment that you awoke one morning to discover that your relative – brother, cousin, uncle – was a mass murderer. Imagine that it was September 12, 2001, and the pendulum of guilt for the destruction of the twin towers of the World Trade Center in New York was swinging in the direction of a member of your family. Imagine, if you can, the revulsion and helplessness that you might feel – almost as strongly as those who lost friends and loved ones in the tragedy. Imagine your exemplary past crushed beneath the weight of those tragic towers.

This numbing reality is what the Binladin family of Saudi Arabia faced. On that morning, on the other side of the world, the responsibility for this callous act of terrorism was being laid squarely at the door of one of their own clan, Osama bin Laden. Years of frustration at his outspoken, invective and extremist views had isolated the family from him; they had disowned him and even changed the name of the family business to distance themselves from him, but nothing could have prepared them for this.

Typically, the family's thoughts were for others. 'This is a tragedy for humanity,' said Harvard Law School-educated Abdullah Mohammed bin Laden, a younger brother of Osama, only later adding: 'This is a tragedy for our family. How will people look at our family?'

Other family members were equally horrified. 'All life is sacred,' said another brother, Yesalam, a Geneva-based banker. 'I condemn all killings and attacks against liberty and human values.' His uncle, Abdullah Awad bin Laden, said: '[We issue] the strongest denunciation and condemnation . . . Our family has no connection with his works and activities.'

Friends have rallied round the Binladin family just as they have rallied round countless others less fortunate than themselves ever since their revered father established a tradition of charitable and humanitarian work. One friend, Mouldi Sayeh, quoted in *Newsweek* magazine, said the family 'feels shattered, feels abused, feels tortured'. Official support even comes from the Saudi Arabian government. Prince Naif ibn Abdul Aziz Al Saud, brother of King Fahd and Minister of Interior stated that the family 'should not be blamed for the deviation in the behaviour of one of them. We will not accept that.'

Osama bin Laden was born in 1957 into luxury that most of us can only imagine. He had every opportunity – perhaps too many opportunities. Where did it go so horribly wrong?

By all accounts his father, Mohammed bin Laden, was a wonderful man, a self-made billionaire, an entrepreneur of rare skill and genius and a philanthropist on a scale seldom seen in the developing world. He had a reputation as a kind, generous man. His company grew to employ thousands and, it is said, he knew the names of hundreds of them. His office door was always open, even to the lowliest immigrant worker with a problem.

He poured millions of dollars each year into charitable causes. Mohammed was one of the first businessmen to finance schools for the underprivileged in Jeddah, and later added several small hospitals and clinics for the poor to his payroll. Outside of Saudi Arabia, he sponsored orphanages, schools and clinics. Every year he paid for hundreds of poor Muslims from all over the Middle East to perform Hajj, the pilgrimage to Mecca. In every sense he was a humanitarian.

Mohammed brought up 54 children at a time of great upheaval in Saudi Arabian society. The Gulf region was going through a period of unheralded economic change on the strength of petro-dollars. Tremendous strains were being placed on the socio-cultural base of Saudi society, one of the effects of sudden, massive wealth.

For the most part, the Bin Laden family were held together by Mohammed. He insisted that his offspring honour their Islamic heritage but, at the same time, used his time and wealth to ensure a rounded upbringing. Youth, being youth, some of his children went through a period of rebellion but by and large returned to the straight and narrow.

Osama was the one who did not. From the start he was an outsider. The only son of a mother who immediately fell out of favour with his father; the urge to please, to impress, to be accepted were driving forces in his childhood. His father's death when he was ten years old seems to have unhinged him and, from then on, he swung crazily like an ever-more dangerous wrecker's ball from one obsessive attachment to another.

At first the only person he damaged was himself: living in the world of books, he cut himself off from the world that his brothers and sisters inhabited. Then he swung in the opposite direction, losing himself in hedonistic pleasures abroad as only one with unlimited funds can do. Back in the family fold, he once again embraced his religion but with a fervour that rebelled against orthodoxy and, in hindsight, was a portent of things to come.

The years following the death of Mohammed bin Laden had been good to a family that had been left his billions. His sons for the most part were highly educated, motivated professionals who created wealth, jobs and prosperity for Saudi Arabia.

First Salim Mohammed bin Laden took charge of the company, but was himself killed in an ultralight plane accident in Texas in 1988. Later, Bakr Mohammed bin Laden and Yahia Mohammed bin Laden went about building a formidable conglomerate. The Bin Laden Group's areas of activity included engineering, design, and construction of large-scale turnkey projects such as highways, bridges, tunnels, airports, public sector buildings, high rise structures, industrial and power plants; petrochemicals and mining; real estate development; and maintenance and operation. Its operations spread around the Middle East and wider afield.

Bakr, Yahia and others also maintained Mohammed's principles of giving to the community. The family poured money into philanthropic causes and even maintained a department to manage charitable work at its headquarters in Prince Abdullah Street in the Al Rawdah District in Jeddah, and through its London headquarters in Berkeley Street in the heart of London's West End.

From these offices and others, the Bin Laden group invested millions of dollars each year in infrastructure projects around the Middle East. They donated to disaster relief, built low-cost homes for the poor and invested in poor countries. They funded programs to bore wells that provided reliable, clean water sources to remote villages. They built and maintained orphanages and schools in some of the remotest and poorest areas of Pakistan, Egypt, Jordan, Yemen and elsewhere.

Mohammed's sons also followed in their father's footsteps by continuing to pay the expenses of tens of thousands of poor pilgrims. They gave the community in Jeddah a multi-million dollar mosque in 1988. Named the Bin Laden Mosque, it stands like a monument to the charity that the family have shown to good causes the world over. And these examples are just the tip of an iceberg of charitable giving.

What was more, for the most part, it was a process that was entered into without fanfare or publicity. Since 1970, the companies that Mohammed bin Laden founded, and the corporation of diversified interests that his sons have sculpted, have invested millions of dollars annually in charitable causes simply because it was their duty as human beings.

While a family can tolerate a certain amount of dissent and errant behaviour and forgive, the Bin Laden family members found themselves increasingly pained by what Osama bin Laden was saying and doing. It was not enough for him to be a hero after the successful fight to rid Afghanistan of the Soviet invaders. In the years that followed, it became clear that he wanted to be nothing less than the saviour of the world, and that he would resort to whatever means he felt were necessary – including annihilation of everything that mankind had achieved over millennia of development – to achieve it.

Reeling at the evil their infamous relative was inflicting upon the world, the family nevertheless time and again tried to reach out to him and curb his excesses. Each time they were rebuffed.

During the 1990s, a family conclave led to a decision to alter the family business name to Binladin to distance themselves from Osama. The family business was rebranded the Saudi Binladin Group and the family attempted to construct a life away from his dark shadow. It has not been an easy task. Events such as the Khobar Towers bombing, attacks on the US embassies in Kenya and Tanzania and the USS *Cole* inevitably brought his memory back to life and media attention back into theirs. 'The Binladin family and

14

the Saudi Binladin Group have no relationship whatsoever with Osama or any of his activities. He shares no legal or beneficial interests with them or their assets or properties, and he is not directly or indirectly funded by them,' stated Abdullah Awad bin Laden, brother of the founder.

It is not easy living a proper life when your brother is a despised terrorist, avowed to overthrowing the government of the country in which you are living, ruled over by an Al Saud family with which there has been an ongoing, close personal relationship. It is even harder when Osama has murdered innocent Western citizens. In a world of globalisation the Binladin family and companies have spread across the globe. Many live respectable lives in the United States; as many as 11 in the Boston area alone. Binladin clan members can be found in most western European countries, throughout the Middle East, even in the Far East. Wherever they are they lead normal lives, with jobs, paying taxes and living quietly.

In the world of business, the Binladin Group remains a corporation of global importance. Osama's brothers have also made determined if low-key attempts to try and build some of the bridges that their brother's actions have demolished, particularly with the United States.

The Saudi Binladin Group is a member of the US–Saudi Arabian Business Council, alongside the likes of IBM, AT&T, the Ford Motor Company, General Electric, 3M and Pepsi Cola International. This body brings together business leaders in both countries to increase trade and investment by promoting broader understanding. It has offices in Washington DC and Riyadh. Its co-chairmen are Sheikh Abdulaziz Al-Quraishi, former governor of the Saudi Arabian Monetary Agency, and Alfred C. DeCrane, retired chairman and chief executive officer of Texaco.

In commercial terms, too, the group works to boost international ties as its vast industrial interests bring it into close contact with some of the world's biggest firms. The Saudi Binladin Group, working with US giant General Electric, won a $57.1 million contract to expand electrical facilities in the holy city of Medina. The US–Saudi consortium undertook a 33-month overhaul of Medina's existing electrical system, adding two 50-megawatt gas turbines for additional power generation. In June 1995, GE's local affiliate Saudi American General Electric (Samge) and its local partner, Saudi Binladin, won a $1.4 billion turnkey contract to further extend power-generating capacity in Riyadh.

These were just two of the multi-billion dollar contracts that Saudi Binladin have undertaken, along with foreign partners, in Saudi Arabia over the years. The company is responsible for much of the Kingdom's modernisation and as a by-product, has created wealth and jobs to boost the Saudi Arabian national economy.

As one of the most successful corporations in the Middle East, the Saudi Binladin Group has worked hard to reach its success. The sons of Mohammed bin Laden are highly respected; Bakr sits with the Prince of Wales on a UK Arab–English committee. Others are revered in their social and commercial circles as intellectuals, philanthropists and well-equipped businessmen. Despite their association with Osama, they had survived, worked harder to overcome and hardened themselves to the evils wrought on the world by their infamous relative.

Then came September 11, 2001 . . .

CHAPTER TWO

The Manhattan of the Desert

The Arabian Peninsula and its population exist in the minds of most of the world as a mysterious, romantic stereotype, wrapped in legends, fables and half-truths. The hardy Bedouin who have eked a living from this unforgiving environment for thousands of years share a stage with the characters of the *1,001 Nights*. The great Rub Al Khali, the 'Empty Quarter' that lies at the heart of the peninsula, is quite possibly the most remote and desolate location on earth. If ever there were a land that time truly passed by, this is it. Only in recent times, with the rush to exploit the region's vast oil deposits, has Arab society begun to emerge worldwide.

The region's distinct culture has not, however, simply evolved during the seven decades since oil production began. Away from the inhospitable deserts, particularly in coastal and mountain areas, pockets of society have thrived, occasionally making an impact on the outside world. One such area is the Hadramawt. Situated on the southern tip of the peninsula, today it is a province in Yemen. In ancient times it was a mystical land ruled in turn by many of the world's great civilisations, all of which left their mark on the people and their culture. Legend may link the Hadramawt with the Queen of Sheba, but fact shows that its mountains cradled the largest and, in places, most fertile wadi or mountain valley of the Arabian Peninsula and this is what has given it its place in history. The region had the ideal climate and soil to grow a variety of trees whose dried resins have a number of valuable properties, not least the strong and pleasant odours that they give off when burned. The best known of these are frankincense and myrrh; both had such enormous ritual value for the ancient Egyptians and later for the Greeks and the Romans that for many centuries, the Hadramawt enjoyed an enviable wealth and prosperity.

To the south of the Hadramawt is the Arabian Sea; its riches of sea life and ocean crops giving life to the coast of what is now Yemen and providing employment and food for large swathes of the population. Part of the ancient Sabaean kingdom from 750 to 115 BC, the area was later ruled by the Himyarites, Romans, Ethiopians, and Persians. The one thing all these conquerors failed to do was to set the region on a course toward any real social or economic evolution. The country was conquered by Muslim Arabs in the seventh century AD, and in the sixteenth century it became part of the Ottoman Empire.

While the regional capital of the Hadramawt is Mukalla or the 'Bride of the Arabian Sea', many of the region's important settlements are located in the hot and dry interior. These include Ash Shihr, Dowan, Seyun, Shibam and Tarim.

The latter, Tarim, is one of the oldest towns of the Hadramawt valley. For hundreds of years, it has been an influential scientific and religious centre. Its scholars are acknowledged to have played a role in spreading Islam to East Asia, the Indian islands, the African coastal belt and several other areas of the world. Today, the town is famed for its large number of mosques and religious places — a rare tourist destination in modern Yemen — while the town's Library of Manuscripts boasts a collection of rare and ancient parchments that are said to be unmatched in the world. Scattered around the Hadramawt are further sites of interest to the Islamic tourist, notably the grave of the prophet Hood and some of the prophet's companions.

Other parts of the Hadramawt are internationally renowned for their architecture. The best example of this is at Shibam where, 500 years ago, settlers constructed the world's first skyscrapers. The UNESCO World Heritage List carries a description of Shibam, where 'impressive tower-like structures rise out of the cliff and have given the city the nickname of "The Manhattan of the Desert".' Built of clay, the houses of Shibam rise as high as 130 feet, and vary between five and sixteen floors. The walls on the ground level are between one and a half and two yards thick. Higher levels are usually painted with thick layers of white alabaster. For defence, the residents of ancient Shibam constructed a wall reaching, in places, a height of over 20 feet.

Aden, at the southern tip of the region, came under British control in 1839 when Captain Haines of the East India Company landed a party of Royal Marines in order 'to put an end to the Adeni pirates who were harassing British merchant ships on their passage to India'. For the next 95 years a posting there was to be a bleak prospect for any soldier, sailor or airman sent to what had become known as the Aden Protectorate. The British also made a series of treaties with local tribal rulers in a move to colonise the entire area of Southern Yemen. British influence eventually covered the Hadramawt and a boundary line, known as the 'violet line', was drawn between it and Turkish Arabia in the north.

In 1849, the Turks had returned to Yemen. Their power extended throughout the whole of the region not under British rule, and for some time this included the Hadramawt. The Turks ruled with a heavy hand, which led to insurrections from all quarters of the community, even the peasants. After a protracted conflict that claimed many lives on both sides, autonomy was finally granted in 1911. By 1919, at the end of the First World War, the Turks had retreated from the Yemen for the last time and the country was left in the hands of Imam Yayha, who became the country's king. Yemen's independence was recognised by Britain in 1925.

In the early 1900s, a farmer named Awad bin Laden lived near Tarim, eking out a living through odd jobs in rural communities near the family home, only on occasion holding down long-term employment. Simple survival dictated that every able-bodied person contributed to the family's well-being, so while Awad worked elsewhere, his wife and other family members tended a small herd of goats and grew subsistence crops on a small plot of land – probably no larger than an acre in size – near the family home. Little information exists within the family today about this land. However it is thought that Awad's ancestors had been granted it by the king of Yemen in recognition of their participation in the Yemeni struggle against the Turks.

In such a hot, dry climate it would have been all the family could do to coax their barley, maize, potatoes and wheat to harvest. Theirs was a hard and precarious existence and in this respect, little has changed in Yemen. The family's largest source of income was from its honey bees. Bee-keeping had been a significant industry among rural agricultural communities in the Hadramawt and Yemen for hundreds, possibly thousands, of years. Honey and its many uses were mentioned in the Sumerian and Babylonian cuneiform texts, the Hittite code; the sacred writings of India, the Vedas and in the ancient writings of Egypt. The Old Testament book of Exodus refers to Palestine as 'the land of milk and honey' and in Greek and Roman mythology, honey was the food of kings and gods. Taxes were paid in honey, and many a Roman and Greek chef became famous for his honey recipes.

But it was in Egypt that honey first became fashionable and widely used. In ancient Egypt, honey was offered to the gods, buried in tombs with the dead to provide food in the hereafter, given to new-born babies to ward off evil spirits and bestow the gifts of health, poetic inspiration and eloquence. Almost all Egyptian medicines contained honey. Highly valued, honey was commonly used as a tribute or payment. Mead, a sweet wine made with honey, was considered the drink of the gods.

Bees were able to adapt well to conditions in the Hadramawt and since time immemorial Yemenis have been producing and using honey as a revenue generator. Indeed, the Hadramawt became famed throughout the region for its honey, and bee keeping became vital to the local economy as well as a significant part of the local diet. Bee-keeping was for many a full-time profession, with holdings up to several hundred hives. The Bin Ladens ran a medium-sized operation, but Awad was known in his locality as something of an expert and added to his income by advising wealthier families on how to run their hives.

Borders in Arabia were ill defined in the early part of the twentieth century, and subsequently whole pockets of population were free to migrate – which they did, time and again – in search of better opportunities. Yemen held little promise, and with the Bin Ladens' subsequent shift to Saudi Arabia, today's family has no direct recollection of Awad. What descriptions there are have been passed down from older generations in the time-honoured oral tradition of Arabia. These suggest that his face was like leather, deeply lined and tanned by years of outdoor toil in the harsh climate. His clothes were said to be little better than rags. He had one wife who is described as small of stature and fine of feature. Nothing is known of her except that she was a Yemeni from a local tribe.

For all the peasants of Yemen, life was cruel: a hard daily struggle to survive, punctuated by little in the way of happiness or joy. Though devout Muslims, like most people the necessity of their daily toil precluded the possibility of becoming overly fervent in their beliefs. There was simply no time.

Despite the uncertainty of the Yemeni resistance to the Turks and the economic hardships of the day, what is known is that the Bin Laden family was expanding steadily during this period. Awad had several children. His first son had been named Mohammed. A second son, Abdullah, followed soon after, while several girls were already playing at their father's feet.

When he was crowned king of Yemen, Imam Yayha had an extraordinary task before him. Centuries of stagnation and conflict had taken a catastrophic toll on his country. His people were backward, uneducated and had few prospects. The land itself has no discernable assets, only minimal mineral wealth and an agriculture sector that hardly produced enough to feed his subjects, let along produce exports. With few resources at his disposal to affect a change, there seemed little hope that the cycle would be broken. Support for the new monarch was widespread, but ordinary Yemenis quickly began to look elsewhere to better themselves. For Awad, this meant that he was to lose his eldest son.

Mohammed was a handsome boy who worked hard on the family plot even before reaching his teens. When Awad was working elsewhere, he assumed responsibilities as man of the house, tending the family's goats and taking care of their beehives. But, as Mohammed grew into his teens, Awad became increasingly aware that the boy's future did not lie on the family farm. Better opportunities lay elsewhere in the region, opportunities that might allow Mohammed to send money home and make a life for himself away from the abject poverty of his childhood.

The late 1920s were times of tremendous change on the Arabian Peninsula. The history of modern Saudi Arabia had begun in 1902 when 21-year-old Abdul Aziz ibn Saud and a band of his followers captured the city of Riyadh, returning it to the control of his family. His daring and bravery in this key historical event remains the stuff of legends throughout the peninsula.

With 40 tribesmen, Abdul Aziz had left his family's sanctuary in Kuwait in December 1901, where they had lived in exile since being ousted by the powerful Rashid tribe. He reached Riyadh one month later where he set about planning his assault on Masmak fort, home of the ruler. Under cover of darkness, Abdul Aziz quietly approached a part of the city wall that he judged his group could scale with the help of grappling irons. Abdul Aziz and a small group of men then made their way to an empty house close to the residence of Ajlan, who had taken over as amir of Riyadh after Abdul Aziz's father had been deposed. Then they waited.

At dawn, after prayers, Ajlan emerged from the mosque into the street. With his enemy exposed, Abdul Aziz gave a battle cry and attacked. Ajlan fled, with Abdul Aziz and his companions in hot pursuit. Quickly cornered, Ajlan defended himself briefly but was killed by the sword of one of Abdul Aziz's men. This unexpected attack and the death of their leader caught the large Riyadh garrison of Ajlan's tribal supporters by surprise. Assuming that such an assault could only have been mounted by a large and well-equipped force – and perceiving that the population of the city welcomed the return of the Al Saud – they surrendered without further resistance.

After the capture of Riyadh, Abdul Aziz spent the next 12 years consolidating his conquests in the area around Riyadh and the eastern part of the country through a combination of military prowess and calculated Islamic fervour. Like their cousins in Yemen, the northern Arab tribes had never liked the Turks and they were only too willing to listen to a new ruler whose ambitions were aided considerably by the internal troubles of the Ottoman Empire. In rallying the tribes in the region to throw out a common enemy, he succeeded where others had failed and in so doing created the first unified state in greater Arabia, giving it his family name.

Jeddah, in what would become Saudi Arabia's Western Province, was one of the peninsula's most important seaports and the only major city on the Red Sea. The original gateway to Mecca and Medina for pilgrims arriving by ship, it was a bustling, cosmopolitan place whose thriving docks employed many men of Yemeni extraction and a large number of first generation settlers from the Hadramawt. Awad bin Laden immediately recognised it as a place that offered an opportunity for his eldest son.

Awad had visited Jeddah in 1928 or 1929 on the Hajj, the pilgrimage that forms one of the chief tenets of the Islamic faith. As directed by the teachings of the holy Koran, a Muslim, if financially and physically able, should make the pilgrimage to the holy sites at least once in his lifetime. The centrepiece of any pilgrimage is a pilgrim's prayer at the Dome of the Rock, the first Muslim masterpiece, built in 687 AD, half a century after the death of the Prophet Muhammad. Muslims believe that the rock marks the site of the Prophet's ascension, known as the *Miraaj*, or night journey into the heavens. Travellers and pilgrims have compared the cupola of the dome to a mountain of supernatural light. The atmosphere of beauty and intensity of religious feeling that prevails in the Dome of the Rock can have a profound effect on the faithful.

After fulfilling his religious duties, Awad spent some time on the dockside and secured from a Yemeni official at Jeddah the promise of a job for Mohammed. Several months later, according to family members probably late in 1929 or early 1930, Awad purchased passage for his son on a cargo boat that was scheduled to travel from the Hadramawt port city of Mukalla to Jeddah. On his departure, the family grieved as though Mohammed were dead, such was the loss that they felt.

Mohammed himself was keen to start a new life. He had listened hard when his father told stories of the bustling town he had visited, of the jobs that were to be found in Jeddah and of the wealth that could be seen there. It was all in stark contrast to the poverty and stagnation of Tarim and its outlying areas. Even during an era when most people lived and died within a few miles of where they were born, Mohammed had set his sights higher than farming and bee-keeping.

The Jeddah at which Mohammed Awad bin Laden disembarked was an extraordinary place. It was undergoing expansion on a colossal scale. After the completion of the Suez Canal in 1869, Jeddah had become one of the main ports on the trade route between the Mediterranean Sea and the Indian and Pacific Oceans. As a result, it and its merchants were prospering. European diplomatic legations were established on the northern side of the city, and rich merchants had begun to build their family homes here. Pilgrims often brought goods from their native lands to sell in Jeddah, and those who could not afford the homeward journey often stayed on. The city that had begun its life around 2,500 years ago as a tiny fishing settlement was then the fastest-expanding conurbation in the Middle East.

Awad bin Laden's groundwork was successful, and Mohammed

was quickly employed on the quayside as a porter — a low-paid job, but nevertheless a step in the right direction. He revelled in Jeddah's energy and found himself attracted to Islamic learning in a way that would have been impossible at home. Soon he also found his feet socially, falling in with many of his young Yemeni colleagues working in the port. During rare days when he was not working, he explored the city, walking the narrow, labyrinthine streets of Old Jeddah in the shadows of closely-packed buildings. He mingled with other strolling inhabitants, water carriers and street vendors. Along wider thoroughfares he saw the camel caravans, some of which would have passed through his native Hadramawt, piled high with trade goods.

Here too Mohammed learned the elements of commerce that were to transform his life. Despite his restricted upbringing, he was clever and an adept communicator and used these skills to learn, engaging merchants and pilgrims from all over the world in long conversations. His thirst for knowledge was insatiable, and quickly helped him gain an understanding of the world well beyond his years and limited personal experience.

But it was not idle chat that Mohammed sought. He knew there was more to life than loading and unloading vessels in Jeddah port. His key was finding the opportunity that would allow him to pursue his dreams. He listened to the experiences and advice of others, all the while plotting his own path.

Mohammed bin Laden had been in the country for three years when Abdul Aziz ibn Saud finally completed his mission to unify swathes of the Arabian Peninsula. On September 23, 1932, the country was named the Kingdom of Saudi Arabia, an Islamic state, with Arabic designated as the national language and the Koran as its constitution. The unification of the kingdom brought new stability everywhere. In Jeddah, the high, protective city walls became obsolete and were torn down, with the rubble then used as fill for a new pier in the harbour, built to enable larger steamers to use Jeddah's facilities. The rocks once used to discourage invading forces were now helping visitors to come ashore.

Through much of this evolution, Mohammed was an onlooker. But unlike his Yemeni counterparts working in the port, he was already planning his escape from low wages and back-breaking toil. In addition to sending money home to his family in the Hadramawt,

Mohammed had saved hard, being prudent to the point of spending nothing more than a bare minimum on food. During the three years following his arrival, he amassed a nest egg, waiting to be invested in the opportunity he was sure would come.

In 1932, he found his opportunity. One morning, as he was unloading a vessel, he was approached by a passenger who had arrived on the boat. A Jordanian, the passenger said that he wanted to buy a property in Jeddah and asked Mohammed if he could recommend an agent to help him. The young dock porter, with his rapidly expanding network of contacts, knew an agent and engineered an introduction. A purchase was subsequently arranged which brought him a commission, and it was this catalyst that opened the door for the ambitious young Yemeni.

With Jeddah going through its most astonishing period of expansion, housing and office property prices were skyrocketing as demand was far outstripping supply. Such was the speed of growth, the few construction companies in Jeddah were hopelessly stretched. Mohammed jumped in by locating and hiring some obsolete construction equipment, and immediately scored a coup by using his contacts to win himself a major construction contract for the Jeddah government. He resigned his post as a porter, and went from lowly employee to one of Jeddah's major employers in a matter of months.

Mohammed went from strength to strength during 1934 and 1935 as Jeddah's construction boom continued unabated. The returns from his initial contracts were reinvested in new equipment, which in turn brought in more profit that was invested in further expansion of Bin Laden Construction. In a matter of 24 months, his intrinsic understanding of the market exploded into a construction firm that employed hundreds of labourers. Within the same time frame, he engineered an expansion out of Jeddah into Taif, Mecca, Medina and across much of the new kingdom.

By 1940, an extraordinary decade after arriving in Jeddah, the one-time porter had risen to become a businessman of considerable substance. Through an astonishing mix of unlimited ambition, successful expansion of his empire and the massive development in Saudi Arabia, he was now a multi-millionaire. Without doubt Mohammed had been lucky to hit a wave of development and even within the family it has been suggested that he would not have been equipped to handle anything other than a booming industry in a market that was itself booming. Nevertheless, it was an astonishing achievement. Mohammed made his own luck.

He now did his networking almost exclusively in palaces: his own and that of the ruling Al Saud dynasty. He was known to King Abdul Aziz himself, and counted several of the monarch's elder sons as acquaintances. Crown Prince Saud was an associate, as was Prince Faisal, future king and one of the most intellectually gifted individuals at the top of the Al Saud hierarchy and therefore a natural friend of the construction magnate. Other family members whom Mohammed befriended included future king Prince Khalid; Prince Nasir, the governor of Riyadh; and Prince Mansour, the kingdom's first Minister of Defence, from 1944 until his sudden and untimely death in 1951 at 29 years of age.

Bin Laden Construction and other companies that Mohammed had set up received a great deal of defence business through the office of Prince Mansour. It is supremely ironic that some of the very sites and installations from which the family firms amassed fortunes should in later decades become the targets of a rage fuelled by unparalleled hatred from their own flesh and blood.

After the Second World War, Bin Laden Construction had been commissioned on several occasions by Prince Mansour to carry out work at Dhahran Airport, one of the kingdom's largest aviation facilities, located close to the Arabian Gulf coast. Between 1945 and the early 1950s, the company constructed new airport administration buildings, was responsible for an extension to the main terminal and worked to extend and improve a runway.

This work helped Dhahran cope with an increase in passenger traffic and larger civil aircraft, but also to deal with traffic generated through one of King Abdul Aziz's key foreign and domestic policy decisions. In 1985, President Ronald Reagan would comment that 'the friendship and cooperation between our two governments [US and Saudi Arabia] and peoples are precious jewels whose value we should never underestimate'. By the time of Reagan's comments, the two states had been moving closer through a relationship that had been evolving over a period of nearly 50 years. This relationship dated back to a meeting during the 1930s between King Abdul Aziz and President Woodrow Wilson. In the 1940s, ties grew closer when King Abdul Aziz and President Franklin D. Roosevelt were politically close. In 1945, at the end of the Second World War, the pair held a historic first summit between the leaders of the two states when Abdul Aziz and Roosevelt met aboard the heavy cruiser USS *Quincey* in the Suez Canal. The United States had opened its first diplomatic legation in Jeddah in 1942, while two years later a Saudi Arabian embassy was inaugurated in Washington.

This evolution in political ties was part of a burgeoning overall relationship. Economic ties were understandably strong, the US being one of the prime destinations for much of Saudi Arabia's oil exports. But cooperation also began to extend to the military sector. In the wake of the Second World War, the Saudi monarch agreed that the US Air Force could continue its use of Dhahran Airport as a staging post. On occasions, when US strategic interest required, an agreement between both governments allowed the US to use Dhahran as a semi-permanent base.

Later again, under the reign of King Saud, the monarch subscribed to the so-called 'Eisenhower doctrine' and renewed the Dhahran agreement in return for $180 million in economic and military aid. Once again, in the wake of this agreement, Bin Laden Construction was the preferred contractor in preparing Dhahran Airport for an expanded and greater US presence.

Throughout the 1940s, Mohammed bin Laden's star grew inexorably, both commercially and politically. It was his relationship with Crown Prince Saud that finally saw the Yemeni farmer's son arrive in the big league, informally at least, as private builder of choice to the most senior members of the Al Saud family.

His first major commission from Prince Saud came several years before the prince succeeded his father as king. Al Nariyah Palace in Riyadh was Prince Saud's gift to himself. He wanted something spectacular, a home that reflected his status and a show of opulence and style that would impress friends and visitors to the kingdom.

Prince Saud mentioned his plans for a new palace to Bin Laden in 1948, on an occasion when the latter visited his *majlis*, the regular open forum for discussion among senior members of the community. He had already taken quotes and personally overseen the drawing up of some plans, to his own specification. Now he sought Mohammed bin Laden's opinion as a builder.

Despite now being a multimillionaire and walking the corridors of power, Mohammed had not gone soft. He saw an immediate opportunity. Without a moment's hesitation, according to family members, he offered to take on the job for half the price of the lowest quote that Prince Saud had received. It was a startling gambit, but one that would entrench Mohammed bin Laden's status within Saudi Arabia's royal elite. In a bid to impress Prince Saud further, Mohammed threw the best architects and designers within the Bin Laden Group of companies at the project, incurring further losses on the project as new improved blueprints were given a green light by his client.

Within 18 months, shortly before the turn of the half-century, Prince Saud was able to survey a remarkable development on a patch of barren desert outside the capital that he had designated as the site of Al Nariyah Palace, his new home. The gates of the palace opened into a half-mile avenue of tamarisk trees, bordered by vast flowerbeds and grass-covered lawns. A 200-room Mediterranean-style palace sat centre stage, flanked by a blue-tiled Olympic-sized swimming pool and smaller kidney-shaped pools. Dotted liberally around the palace and its grounds, huge aviaries stocked with songbirds generated a chorus of natural song. Each evening, 25,000 coloured light bulbs illuminated the entire complex. One writer described the scene as a 'vast sparkling patchwork mantle . . . the vast compound shimmered magically in the darkened desert as though dropped down by some passing genie . . . '

Prince Saud was pleased, and with a $6 million price tag it had been a bargain. For his part Mohammed lost perhaps $3 million on the project, a vast sum in the late 1940s. But it was an investment that soon paid huge dividends as it was followed by a plethora of new contracts. He was now the Al Saud's favourite and most fashionable contractor, and that reputation was worth billions.

Among dozens of projects for the Al Saud family and Saudi Arabian government the Bin Laden Group subsequently took, the most surprising was another for Crown Prince Saud. Al Nariyah Palace had been fine for a Crown Prince but, in 1953, on succeeding his father as king, Saud believed his new status called for something better. Less than half a decade after it was completed, the $6 million palace was torn down and Bin Laden Construction commissioned to build a $15 million replacement. Again Mohammed personally supervised the project, and he did not take a loss on this second Al Nariyah Palace. He sourced the best in international architectural talent from Lebanon, used only the finest materials and made it clear to all his own senior employees that their jobs depended upon King Saud's approval.

28

Even by the standards of Arab taste, which to the Western eye can appear garish and ostentatious, King Saud's new palace was something that visitors would not forget. A seven-mile blush-pink wall was the starting point, standing out starkly from the largely whitewashed or sandstone buildings one would see in Riyadh and even more from the few Bedu settlements on the outskirts of the Saudi capital. Entering a gate not dissimilar to the Arc de Triomphe in Paris, the new Al Nariyah Palace came to be known as the 'Disneyland of Nariyah'. But this mattered little to Mohammed bin Laden. King Saud loved it, and that was all that counted.

Saudi Arabia began exporting oil in May 1939 when the first tanker load left a terminal at Ras Tanura on the Arabian Gulf coast. Already it was clear to world leaders that this huge part of the Arabian Peninsula was going to be a global economic power due to its vast oil reserves. The industrial world was hungry for oil, and the Al Saud family could turn its supply on and off like twisting a tap, almost at will.

But while the kings of Saudi Arabia enjoyed a seat at the top table of world leaders, at home the petro-dollars that made them global statesmen would bring much disrepute. Many businessmen, such as Mohammed bin Laden, would be in the right place at the right time and make millions, even billions, and in so doing create a whole new wealthy middle class. But generally, super wealth became a source of discord within the kingdom. It took a generation or more for the largely Bedu population — the Al Sauds included — to come to terms with their new-found wealth and to understand the implications and responsibilities associated with it. Meanwhile, vast amounts were squandered; the Al Nariyah Palace saga was not an exception during this period.

Mohammed bin Laden was by now a citizen of the country. He was the foremost, but hardly the only, Yemeni of Hadramawt extraction to have made this transition. Familiar Saudi commercial dynasties such as Al Amoudi, Baroum and Binzager could all trace their roots back to Yemen. Mohammed was closer to the Al Sauds, however, and after becoming the kingdom's premier and most fashionable palace builder he found his business doubling and trebling year after year. His group operated throughout the kingdom, counted on a significant proportion of government contracts for its turnover, and had emerged as one of the leading developers of private housing and office space in a booming economy.

Mohammed was a wealthy man. But those who worked for him during this period recall that success had hardly changed him. He counted the Al Sauds as friends, but was seldom not in his spartan office by 8 a.m. He dealt with many projects personally, and when visiting sites always made a point of stopping to speak with the workers. 'Treat the men right, and they will treat the company right,' he often instructed family members and managers within his companies. It was not lip service either. Despite its size, the Bin Laden Group was considered one of the best employers in the kingdom and, as a result, never had a problem recruiting quality staff, from its management down to the shop floor.

For all his wealth and influence, Mohammed bin Laden remained a committed Muslim, praying five times a day and making a pilgrimage to Mecca and Medina at least once a year. His interest in Islam also extended to sponsoring mini-conferences called *halqas*, where the kingdom's leading scholars and best-known mullahs would meet to discuss the history of Islam and ruminate over its future direction.

Mohammed was also a generous man to family and friends, donating large amounts to charities and good causes. He was the first merchant to sponsor schools in Jeddah for the children from poor families. He also paid the expenses of thousands of poor pilgrims from neighbouring Arab states, enabling them to make the Hajj.

Nor did he fail to recognise or to deny his roots. Relatives in Yemen were offered the chance of moving to Saudi Arabia, where they were found jobs in the family firm, or of staying in Yemen and receiving generous allowances. One of those who moved early on to Saudi Arabia was his brother Abdullah, who became a highly-respected member of Saudi society and a pillar within the family firm.

Although Mohammed's father, Awad bin Laden, had died before the start of the 1950s, his mother lived well into the decade. The old lady refused any attempts to shift her from Yemen, or even away from the dusty plot of land on which Mohammed himself had toiled as a child. However, she lived out the remaining years of her life in a new house, attended by a handful of servants and surrounded by family – great luxury by Yemeni standards.

Mohammed bin Laden reacted to his meteoric rise in status in the time-honoured and traditional way of Arabia, by creating his own dynasty. A custom born of the harsh environment and precarious nature of life, Islam allows four wives at any one time. The father of the nation, King Abdul Aziz, used marriage as a way of cementing tribal alliances and reportedly always made sure when he began a campaign that he could marry another wife should circumstances dictate. In this state of affairs, divorce was by necessity a relatively straightforward procedure, but such was the family ethos of the culture that ex-wives and their children remained part of the larger family group. King Abdul Aziz produced 43 sons, officially, and an unknown number of girls and illegitimate offspring. His successor, King Saud, was even more prolific, reaching an official figure of 53 sons and 54 daughters.

From the 1940s, Mohammed bin Laden took one new wife every couple of years, so that by the beginning of his dotage, he had ten or eleven wives and ex-wives. Included among them were Saudi Arabians, a Yemeni, Syrian and a Palestinian. Fifty-four children were born to his wives, most notably in 1957 a son named Osama.

CHAPTER THREE

National Politics, Childhood Scars

The oil revenues that drove the Saudi Arabian economy into an unprecedented boom – catapulting Mohammed bin Laden from dockside porter to multi-millionaire construction magnate – also provided the central challenge to successive Saudi rulers. Inevitably petro-dollars set in motion a modernisation process that challenged everything that had seemed fundamental to the monarchy. The religious fervour that had swept the Al Sauds to power in the lean decades was out of step with the Al Saud family that inhabited $15 million palaces, owned private jets, took extended holidays in Europe, were waited upon by hundreds of servants and kept harems of bejewelled concubines.

History is littered with examples of what happens when religious conservatism is swamped by great wealth. The two are incompatible. For Saudi Arabia, there was no shortage of critics, both within the kingdom and across the Red Sea, to point out the shortcomings of an antiquated Bedouin monarchy awash in money and self-indulgence.

That King Abdul Aziz ibn Saud came from the background of a poor Bedu tribesman made the adjustment to handling billions of dollars extremely difficult. Many are the anecdotes that purport to highlight the consequences of this clash; they also serve once again to illustrate the fundamental differences that existed – and continue to exist – between the West and Arab culture, particularly in the higher echelons of the ruling family.

Much is made in Arab culture of the exchange of gifts. Each offers according to his means. In earlier times, when the population was small and the national treasury travelled with the king in a single wooden chest, it was a convenient if haphazard way of distributing what little wealth there was. But times change.

In the latter years of his life, on a visit to the hot springs at Hofof, King Abdul Aziz was presented by a citizen with a grey Arabian mare. Although the monarch had long since given up riding, he knew his Arabians and this was a fine animal, worth perhaps 100 riyals. In response to such a fine gift, it was his nature to offer a gift of his own. He summoned the aide responsible for his expenses and wrote in his leather financial ledger that the former owner of the horse should be given a gift of 300 riyals, three times the actual value of the mare. While writing, however, the king inadvertently dug the nib of his fountain pen into the paper and sprayed a row of ink blobs along the column in which he was writing. In Arabic, the figure for zero is written as a dot. The aide, confused, pointed this out to the king, who studied the page carefully. After some time he stated: 'By God, this ledger is telling me that my hand wrote 300,000 riyals. This is the gift I must offer – and immediately. I will not hear anyone say that my hand is more generous than my heart.' With that, a 100-riyal gift horse was rewarded with a gift of 300,000 riyals.

This also illustrates the monarch's attitude toward money. In 1946, Saudi government revenues, including oil exports, were $19.1 million, while expenditures hovered around $25.4 million. 'The Lion of the Desert', as he was known, patently did not understand the most rudimentary aspects of economics. Indeed, the demands of office as a whole gradually drew the life out of King Abdul Aziz ibn Saud. He was a warrior, and the transition to administrator never sat well. The last time Mohammed bin Laden met the monarch was at one of the last times the king convened a majlis, in his palace in Riyadh, in the autumn of 1952. By mid-1953, his health was failing. He was flown from Riyadh to the cooler climate of the mountain city of Taif during the summer and never returned. He died in Taif on November 9, 1953.

The new king, Saud, had been born in Kuwait in 1902, the same year in which his father recaptured the city of Riyadh. Moving with other members of the Al Saud family from Kuwait to Riyadh, as he grew he took a role in both politics and war. In the meantime he learned government and administrative methods, preparing himself for the responsibility that would come when he succeeded his father.

By the time of the new monarch's accession late in 1953, Mohammed bin Laden was established as a regular in Saud's majlis and someone on whom the king could rely for good advice. At 51, King Saud was popular throughout the kingdom and big things were expected from him. With men like Mohammed bin Laden around him, who could read the population and advise, King Saud's reign started with great energy and good intentions.

Government expenditure was a major bone of contention. His father's state expenditure in 1946 had included items such as around $3 million for the royal garages and $1.5 million for hospitality. By contrast, just $225,000 was spent on the national education system. Mohammed bin Laden and other majlis figures had made it clear to King Saud that his people were growing restless, that the minimal, privately-funded education system could not be maintained, that health care was a concern. The monarch took note and in November 1953 stated: 'My father's reign may be famous for all its conquests and its cohesion of the country. My reign will be remembered for what I do for my people in the areas of welfare, their education and their health.'

It was a promise from which he never backed away, and ordinary people all over the country, in time, felt the benefit. Mohammed, who genuinely cared and used his time to encourage the king in this direction, was elated. It was also a profitable new development for the magnate. Throughout the vast country, 200 new schools sprang up in 1954 and 1955 alone, along with a dozen hospitals, two dozen grand new buildings for freshly-established public ministries, and thousands of miles of paved roads spread out from Riyadh connecting the kingdom's major conurbations. It was a vast and overwhelming period of national construction. Mohammed bin Laden, of course, one of those closest to the king, was well placed to pick up the juiciest contracts that became available.

However, things quickly began to go wrong. King Abdul Aziz had been generous to a fault and had also spent lavishly on himself. Without the demands of a multi-million dollar construction and social development program to drain his funds, he could have just about afforded to. King Saud threw his government into an entirely worthwhile new spending program, but then he too stumbled. He proceeded to stop one of the kingdom's major sources of revenue. He announced the rescinding of the taxes that pilgrims paid when visiting Mecca, stating: 'Let the pilgrim come and I will pay his tax, because God has given me money from oil.' What was more, King Saud then handed Bin Laden Construction the lion's share of a contract valued at $4.5 million to add new facilities in Jeddah and Mecca in order to modernise the Hajj.

The family name quickly became linked with work on Islam's holiest places, an auspicious honour in a country where religion is such a part of everyday life. It was a gift from God, his errant son Osama was later to tell an Arabic television interviewer. His father 'built the holy Mecca mosque where the holy Kaabah is located and at the same time – because of God's blessings to him – he built the holy mosque in Medina for our Prophet.

'Then, when he found out that the government of Jordan had announced a tender for restoration work on the Dome of the Rock mosque, he gathered engineers and asked them to estimate the cost price only, without profit. They said to him: "With God's help, we will be awarded the project and make some profit as well." He said to them: "Calculate only the cost price of the project."

'When they did, they were surprised that he reduced the cost price in order to guarantee that God's mosques, and this mosque in particular, are well served. He was awarded the project. Because of God's graciousness to him, sometimes he prayed in all three mosques in one single day. It is not a secret that he was one of the founders of the infrastructure of the kingdom of Saudi Arabia.'

All this new spending in Saudi Arabia was, however, complete folly, particularly because King Saud's private generosity outdid even that of his father. The king was in the habit of carrying with him, at his feet, two large bags of gold and silver coins whenever he left the palace. When his Rolls-Royce travelled the roads of Riyadh and its surrounds, the vehicle was mobbed by peasants and children as the monarch handed coins to his subjects individually out of the window. To the Bedu tribes of the interior he also became a legend, surpassing even his father.

King Saud delighted in hearing his own praises being spoken and his generosity being eulogised. As time went on, his vanity extracted an ever-greater price, and his extravagant spending sent the country directly into a financial crisis. Members of the Al Saud family quickly became aware of the downward spiral, but King Saud would not hear of financial constraint. Steadily, over the course of 1954 and 1955, he retreated from the emerging crisis and into a world that was inhabited solely by yes-men.

Among those now shunned was Mohammed bin Laden. The king's trusted friend had made millions from the monarch's spending spree, but cared deeply for Saud as a man and even more for his adopted country. Time and again he attempted to speak gently with him, avoiding the fights that had cost so many good men their seats in his majlis. But King Saud only had ears for sycophants. The king's sons also fêted him and indulged his fantasies in order to maintain their own places at his table. Even more scandalous was the elevation of Eid ibn Salim, who rose from being the king's chauffeur to head of the royal garages and then to manager of royal budgets. His secret was to agree with everything that the king said, and never to say no to any request. The monarch's majlis became stocked with Eid ibn Salim clones, all hoping to catch a seat on the gravy train before it went off the rails.

Throughout these unhappy years of the mid- to late-1950s, Mohammed bin Laden remained at the service of the king, while growing closer to the crown prince, Faisal. In Prince Faisal, Mohammed found a personality that more closely mirrored his own. While the heir to the throne was just as prone to fits of generosity and moments of weakness when it came to spending money on himself, his vision of Saudi Arabia's future, carved from a basis of balanced spending, matched the merchant's own hopes. The two men grew close.

The consultative process at the heart of traditional Arab government – a factor little understood or appreciated by Westerners – allows for critical give and take among major political figures and prominent citizens within a structured forum – the majlis. This ensures that the consensus essential for progress is reached among the most influential members of society. Prince Faisal had the experience and respect to effectively utilise the consultative process to accelerate the modernisation of Saudi Arabia. King Saud did not, and what little good faith he had enjoyed was quickly evaporating.

The heir to the throne was the perfect bridge between the old and the new because, though he was steeped in traditional Bedouin ways, he clearly understood the requirements of the modern world. Mohammed bin Laden appreciated this fact and, as he grew closer, took on a private role for Prince Faisal that was unprecedented: he was neither a member of the Al Saud dynasty, nor even an indigenous citizen.

King Abdul Aziz had known that his two eldest sons were different in character and perhaps even foresaw the problems that each would face. On his deathbed, he reportedly called both to his side and ordered: 'Join hands over my body and swear that you will work together when I am gone. Swear too that if you quarrel you will quarrel in private. You must not let the world catch sight of your disagreements.' Saud and Faisal readily promised, but years later tension began to build between them. This was where Mohammed bin Laden came in. As the crisis deepened steadily throughout the second half of the 1950s, he was one of the few in a position to prevent a dangerous split in the royal family becoming a chasm.

During this period Mohammed reached his zenith in terms of political power. His business empire was worth hundreds of millions of dollars and his personal wealth was nearly as great. The Yemeni economic refugee was now a rich and powerful man, with palatial homes in Riyadh, Jeddah, Tabuk and Dammam. For all that, he retained his common touch and, among family, showed glimpses of a self-effacing humour. He was proud of the bag he had used when he was a porter in Jeddah and kept it as a trophy in the main reception room in his palace in Jeddah. He enjoyed pointing this out to visitors and friends, in addition to reminding family members of their humble origins.

However, Mohammed bin Laden was also a strong and dominating personality. His complex household remained ensconced, for the most part, within a large compound that surrounded his main palace in Jeddah. He insisted that all his children, born to 11 mothers who lived in separate homes dotted around this complex, lived together, so that he could watch over them personally. This complicated family structure was organised and watched over by Mohammed's first wife, the kind and beloved matriarch Al-Khalifa.

Mohammed also insisted on strong discipline and was adamant that all his children adopted the same strict religious and social code that he followed. But, just as he was sometimes a bully, Mohammed adored all his children. Releasing himself on occasion from the pressures of politics and business, he would relax by taking his offspring for sailing trips on the Red Sea or Arabian Gulf, while at least once a year the extended family headed into the desert for a camp.

Osama bin Laden was born during the summer of 1957. He is Mohammed's seventeenth son of a clan that would ultimately number 24 boys and 30 girls.

Little is known of Osama's mother, Hamida. While visiting Damascus, Mohammed had come across her, the daughter of a Syrian family with whom he had business links. Although Mohammed usually married Saudi women, entrenching himself within a society that he always felt looked down on him for his Yemeni roots, Hamida was stunning and her family were happy to marry her off quickly.

Mohammed kept four wives, three of whom were 'permanent'. But his fourth wife, he was in the habit of marrying and divorcing fairly frequently. This is normal within upper levels of Saudi society. Mohammed certainly did not abandon his ex-wives; the mothers of his children usually continued to live within the family compound in Jeddah indefinitely.

Osama was Hamida's only son to Mohammed. His infatuation had soon worn off. She was beautiful but had her own mind and was not the suppliant, unquestioning sort of woman to which Mohammed had become accustomed. She had lived a normal life for a Syrian youngster, enjoying shopping trips into Damascus with friends and family. Married at the relatively late age of 22, she was vivacious and had a strong personality. Life within the tightly controlled walls of Saudi society was a shock to her. She struggled to get used to covering her face with a *burka* and attracted scorn from Mohammed's wives and ex-wives for her independent ways. She was later ostracized by some who were pleased by her subsequent fall from grace.

Faced with a woman who had her own mind, Mohammed dug in his heels. He was the man of the house; his word was law. Even before Osama was born, a deep rift had opened between his parents that would never heal, and would overshadow the first and most painful chapter in Osama's childhood. By the time he was born, Hamida was isolated and ostracised. Within family circles she was spitefully nicknamed 'Al Abeda' (the slave) and Osama was soon cruelly branded 'Ibn Al Abeda' (son of the slave). It cut him like a knife.

As a result of Hamida's estrangement, almost from his birth, Osama's mother was forced into a background role in his life, unlike the mothers of his siblings. In the place of his mother, he knew the care of nurses and nannies retained by Mohammed. While Osama spent most of his childhood in Jeddah, his mother resided either on the verges of the family unit or at some far-flung home, such as one retained by Mohammed in the distant northern town of Tabuk. Wherever she was, Mohammed wanted her out of his sight.

As he became older, this was a situation that Osama felt deeply, the hurt and anger growing inside him. The youngster came to realise that the affections of a nanny or nurse were hardly the same as the permanent and deep love of a mother. Children being children, his siblings found this Achilles' heel and teased him constantly about his parentage. The taunt 'Ibn Al Abeda' was bandied around often in Jeddah.

His only close family attachment was with his stepmother Al-Khalifa. Like his mother she was another strong personality, but was comfortable within the confines of Saudi society. Adept in family politics, Al-Khalifa was cherished by Mohammed and the entire family held her up as a mother figure. She was, in every sense of the word, the matriarch of the family. In addition to her own sons and daughters, she loved and cared for all of Mohammed's children as her own. Most would remain just as close to Al-Khalifa as they did their own birth mothers.

After the death of his father in 1967, Osama did make an effort to get to know Hamida properly. But the memory of what had gone before hung heavily over him like a cloud. Some of the family today explain that Osama came to resent both his father for removing him from his mother, and his mother for not attempting to bridge the gap with his father for his sake. The wounds healed but the scars remained.

Mohammed bin Laden, meanwhile, was in the business of building character among his boys. He dealt with them as though they were men and demanded they show confidence at a young age, while also taking pains to ensure that all were treated alike. When they were old enough, he put some of his sons to work on a company construction site for several weeks alongside ordinary employees. Mohammed would not tolerate slacking and, before any of his sons would be whisked from building site to a cosy managerial position within Bin Laden Construction, they needed to prove that they were ready and willing to work on the ground floor of his company. Osama was only ten when his father died and therefore was not one of those who grabbed his father's notice by the way they handled the challenges of this adult world.

However, according to family members, despite being low in the pecking order, Osama had his own means of building a reasonably successful relationship with his father and attracting his attention. Tall and gangly, he was the son who shone during his father's desert camps. Most of his siblings tolerated the desert in order to appease their father, while yearning for the luxury of palace life. But for Osama, the freedom of the desert was an opportunity to throw off the shackles of a gilded cage in which he felt an outsider. Mohammed, perhaps himself reliving the simpler days of his childhood while working on his father's farm in Yemen, revelled in the once- or twice-yearly trips into the sand dunes and stony plains of the Saudi countryside. Osama stood out from his less-adventurous, mollycoddled siblings. He loved nature, riding horses and camels, shooting and playing among the dunes. This drew him closer to Mohammed than he might otherwise have been, but ultimately these trips were too short and too infrequent in themselves to build any lasting relationship between the two, and he returned home the same shy and increasingly introverted boy.

Mohammed bin Laden's program for preparing his boys for the responsibilities that lay before them was one of his most endearing traits. He himself had simply been placed on a boat by his father, Awad, and sent to Jeddah. Left to sink or swim, Mohammed had risen to the challenge. But all around him on the docks of Jeddah were ordinary young men like him, most of whom ground out a basic living until they were too old to continue. And many times since leaving the docks, Mohammed had also seen men who were ill-equipped and ill-prepared fail at all levels of society. Indeed, one wonders if he drew the same parallel from his old friend King Saud, who was failing in his job too.

On occasion, the preparation of his boys for later life would lead the 'merchant king' to allow one his youngsters to accompany him to see the real king. This was how Osama bin Laden came to sit on the knee of King Saud ibn Abdul Aziz during an informal majlis in the late 1950s.

By this time, King Saud was in serious trouble. His sycophantic advisors had allowed him to lose millions investing in a failed plan to develop a Saudi Arabian oil tanker fleet, a project that placed him in jeopardy with the Americans who hinted that they might attempt to engineer a coup. He was also embroiled in a failed attempt to scupper a proposed unified Egyptian–Syrian state. But what was perhaps worse than both these tremendous and damaging faux pas were King Saud's finances. He continued to fight with anyone who dared suggest that the kingdom was bankrupt and that he should stem his spending. Mohammed bin Laden was practically the only individual allowed to bring up the matter with King Saud personally, and then only because he was careful with his choice of words and because the monarch knew his friend was also close to his largely estranged brother, Crown Prince Faisal, and therefore a vital conduit.

But King Saud did not listen. Now when he drove through Riyadh, he hurled handfuls of gold and silver coins from the window of his car, leaving peasants to fight in his wake over this bounty. This is also a useful metaphor for the state of Saudi Arabia during the reign of King Saud: a monarch throwing titbits to his impoverished people while he continued his journey aboard a Rolls-Royce.

By the second half of the 1950s, the riyal had plummeted against the dollar from 3.75 riyals to 6.4 riyals as the head of state ordered millions of new banknotes printed to support his spending habits. King Saud had also borrowed heavily to finance his personal extravagances and the national construction program. He owed America's Chase Manhattan Bank some $92 million and even more to a variety of other US banks. More worryingly, the Saudi government was increasingly finding it difficult to pay the wages of the armed forces. Civil service salaries were sometimes months in arrears. Government contractors found themselves facing huge delays in payments, and this, in turn, was beginning to damage the whole economy.

This danger did not go unnoticed by other members of the ruling family. Prince Faisal, who spent nearly a year in America for medical treatment and surgery, resisted calls from within the Al Saud family to openly move against his brother. From his New York hospital, he utilised Mohammed bin Laden as a go-between. At one point in the emerging power struggle, Mohammed was asked by the Crown Prince to inform the monarch that his continued intransigence would certainly cause open rebellion within the family. This message was delivered in late 1957.

But either King Saud was unwilling to temper his spending, or was unable to grasp the situation in which he was placing the kingdom. As 1957 gave way to 1958, Mohammed bin Laden saw his friend on a handful of occasions. Despite an atmosphere of depression that had even pervaded the coterie of yes-men in the majlis, the king was still impervious.

During much of 1958, Mohammed bin Laden left his family in Jeddah while he spent most of his time in Riyadh doing what he could to help stave off the collapse of his adopted country. With a genuine sadness, he reported to Prince Faisal by telephone that there was simply no hope of finding a solution. King Saud ignored the warnings – and the fiscal realities. In part, his information led to an unprecedented meeting of nine of the sons of the late King Abdul Aziz. The gravity of this gathering at Prince Talal's Fakhriyah Palace – built by Bin Laden Construction – was underlined by the attendance of Prince Abdullah, today Crown Prince of Saudi Arabia, and then one of the most influential figures within the family. Prince Talal was dispatched as an emissary to speak to the king, who brushed his younger brother off with the same dismissive attitude he showed Mohammed bin Laden.

Sensing serious trouble ahead, Prince Faisal checked himself out of his hospital and hurried home for a showdown with his elder brother. Within days, on March 22, 1958, a statement issued by the king announced that he was placing government in the hands of Prince Faisal.

The events of previous months had moved the Bin Laden family close to the seat of power, Mohammed playing an unprecedented role in internal Al Saud family politics. But the weeks following Prince Faisal's appointment as prime minister showed the extent of his loyalty. Predictably, considering the imminent fiscal collapse of Saudi Arabia, the prime minister also took on the role of finance minister. What he discovered in the Treasury shocked him, and has become the stuff of Saudi legend. The Ministry of Finance, in late March 1958, held 317 riyals, less than $100. Civil servants and military personnel were months behind on their wages, and to make matters worse the Islamic holy month of Ramadan was approaching, when all government employees were due a bonus of one month's salary.

In order to stave off collapse and possibly even civil unrest, Prince Faisal needed 25 million riyals immediately. Several banks refused to help, including several owned by Saudi Arabian families brought to prominence by patronage from the Al Sauds. Some records suggest that Mohammed bin Laden stepped in at this point to pay civil service salaries for several months, but family members say this is wrong – he was never asked. Instead the government was propped up by a loan from the Riyadh Bank, and through Aramco, the Arab American company set up to run Saudi Arabia's oil industry, guaranteeing deferred debt repayments to a consortium of American banks. Where Mohammed bin Laden did step in was to support the royal household privately.

During proceeding years, King Saud had given $32,000 plus expenses to every male member of the family, each year. But 'expenses' were liberally interpreted and many received more than $200,000 in additional monies. The extended Al Saud family was draining the kingdom, most living a lavish lifestyle at the outer limits of their funding that fed the tabloid image of playboy Arab princes. Without regular expense payments, great swathes of the royal family would have become major debtors overnight, which in turn would have caused political troubles among many who were concerned only with their own narrow self-interest.

Even if he cut back on the amounts paid to his kinsmen, this was not an expense that Prince Faisal could legitimately take to either local or foreign banks seeking support. Instead he turned to Mohammed bin Laden. In 1958, less than three decades after he had arrived in Jeddah penniless, the former Yemeni peasant was funding the Al Sauds to enable them to live in the style to which they had become accustomed.

Over subsequent years, the outrageous lifestyles of the Al Sauds were tempered somewhat by fiscal restrictions, as the government attempted to bring down the cost of maintaining the extended royal family. From the outset Prince Faisal set a new tone personally. He dispensed with a chauffeur and drove his own car, often had no bodyguards, rarely threw parties, lived in modest palaces and brought his own children up like normal people. His behaviour was quite a scandal! With the ongoing support of his friend Mohammed bin Laden, Prince Faisal managed to balance Saudi Arabia's books for the first time since the kingdom was founded in 1932. He never forgot the favour.

In the four years following Faisal's promotion, King Saud and his named successor often sparred over the powers of government. It was now the turn of the king to be out of the country through ill health, seeking expert medical treatment elsewhere. Mohammed bin Laden drew closer to Prince Faisal and became a fixture in his innermost circle. This was a period when Prince Faisal needed all the support he could get, not simply of the financial kind but business advice as well. Fiscal sense had dictated that the kingdom stop spending money it did not have on social and infrastructure development. But the country still needed modernisation and the input of a hardened, successful businessman was vital.

Mohammed also drew close to Prince Faisal's closest allies in the Al Saud family, the future king Prince Fahd and Prince Sultan. Mohammed was particularly fond of Prince Fahd. The two men socialised together a great deal and it was not uncommon for the prince to visit Mohammed bin Laden's palaces in Riyadh or Jeddah during the early 1960s.

Mohammed bin Laden also consulted and involved himself in some of the most radical changes in the kingdom during this period, a ten-point program announced by Prince Faisal in November 1962. This included a constitution based upon the Koran, a reorganisation of government, welfare system and – most controversially – a provision for home-based entertainment that permitted the introduction of television. The latter horrified the religious right and led to riots in the streets; indeed one of Prince Faisal's brothers, Musaid, was shot dead by riot police during anti-television violence in 1965. Ever the modernist, Mohammed bin Laden had pressed Prince Faisal to include in his plan one of the most controversial points in the statement of intent – the abolition of slavery. Mohammed had long since considered his faith and found that references to the practice did not relate to the modern world. He had released all slaves from his service and re-employed most as paid servants.

The stability that the Prince Faisal premiership heralded was good for the country as a whole, and Mohammed bin Laden consolidated his reputation and fortune during this period. But he continued to be involved in a see-sawing situation between King Saud, now largely sidelined, and his powerful brother Prince Faisal. In between bouts of treatment or recuperation in the United States, southern France, Austria and Switzerland, King Saud periodically arrived back in his homeland with his batteries charged for a renewed political struggle. This generally did not go down well. By September 1963, the family even tried to prevent this destabilising factor by sending a delegation to visit the king in Vienna, seeking his acquiescence in an agreement that he would remain on the sidelines. Despite promising, King Saud returned and sought to rally the people behind him. It was a fatal mistake that lost him the remnants of his support within the royal family.

Three months later he barricaded himself into the gaudy Al Nariyah Palace, behind its seven-mile pink wall, surrounding himself with 2,000 members of the Royal Guard. It was a time of polarisation, when many men were forced to make a choice between Saud and Faisal. Ever the diplomat, Bin Laden unofficially moved between both, seeking to maintain a dialogue, while many in Riyadh headed for the countryside or their holiday homes elsewhere in the country in case of trouble.

By early in 1964, Mohammed's efforts brought about a partial easing in the crisis. King Saud emerged, and it was agreed that he would represent his country at an Arab Summit in Cairo, partly to appease Saud and partly to show the world a unified front. But this too backfired. Buoyed by a warm reception in Egypt, Saud returned home again seeking a fight. It was his last mistake as monarch.

Both circumstances and family went against him, as pressure mounted for him to become a ceremonial monarch with all powers sitting with Faisal. Again, Mohammed bin Laden was called upon to deal with an increasingly bitter Saud and the construction magnate shuttled between many palaces around Riyadh. 'They think me a decoration,' complained Saud to his old friend. 'I am not Queen Elizabeth. I am the king of Saudi Arabia, and the king exercises power.'

During the remainder of 1964, the constitutional crisis continued until, in the winter, the Al Saud family was prompted to act decisively. A delegation was set to Prince Faisal, proposing to depose Saud and make him king. And when Faisal finally agreed – he was always reluctant to usurp his elder brother – Saud was notified that his family wished him gone.

Once again Saud barricaded himself in Al Nariyah Palace and refused to talk. For three days he declined to discuss the matter and denied many intermediaries access. Each day, his old ally and friend, Mohammed bin Laden, entered King Saud's majlis. He argued that events had gone too far, that the king could no longer hold on to his position and that it was better to go swiftly than hang on and damage both himself and the country further. It was a painful duty, but the kingdom's paralysis could not go on indefinitely.

After three days of marathon talks, Saud realised that there was nowhere to go. Through Mohammed, the family offered the olive branch of a well-funded retirement in exile. The final act of King Saud's reign came on November 3, 1964. Mohammed bin Laden notified family heavyweight Prince Mohammed that the monarch was ready to abdicate. The same day he flew from Riyadh to Dhahran and from there into exile.

His successor, King Faisal ibn Abdul Aziz Al Saud, according to those who knew him, was the most dedicated and hard-working monarch one could imagine. Outside the family circle, no man was closer to the new head of state than Mohammed bin Laden. With Faisal on the throne he would be rewarded as the king threw his country into an age of planned and sustainable development and growth.

What no one could have foreseen was that at the same time the kingdom was stabilising, at home in his Jeddah palace, Mohammed bin Laden was inadvertently moulding one of his sons into the man who would see Saudi Arabia eclipsed. Osama bin Laden's fragile psyche was on the brink of collapse.

CHAPTER FOUR

Son of the Slave

By the time that King Faisal acceded to the throne of Saudi Arabia in 1964, Osama bin Laden was seven years old. Brought up in his father's Jeddah palace, he was suffering a motherless upbringing surrounded by siblings who, quite naturally for children, recognised his weakness and exploited it mercilessly. The 'Ibn Al Abeda' tag was one that never left him.

As a result he was shy – a characteristic some interpreted as weakness. He isolated himself and was reluctant to participate in family life. Because of this he was both unpopular and shunned as a playmate by his brothers. Confused and hurt, he sought attention through silly childish antics and mischief. But, when his father was nearby, Osama was clever enough to transform himself into a dutiful, well-behaved son. Mohammed bin Laden cared little for whining and tantrums, the sort of behaviour frequently associated with privileged children. So the Osama he encountered suited him immensely.

During the early 1960s, Mohammed criss-crossed the country. Already one of the richest men in Saudi Arabia, indeed the Middle East, he was extending his considerable empire. He was often absent from his main home in Jeddah, fulfilling a political role in the capital, Riyadh. As a new era dawned under King Faisal, he knew that his star was still very much in the ascendant.

The future monarch Fahd was also very close to the Bin Ladens. During the 1960s Prince Fahd, then the powerful Saudi Interior Minister, and the construction magnate spent a great deal of private time together. Their children mingled on many occasions, Fahd's boys even joining in on winter desert camps. These were the bedrock of the Bin Laden family's year, as Mohammed bin Laden attempted to stay involved in his children's upbringing, despite his demanding personal schedule.

Osama stood out in the desert as a high-octane child, full of energy. Mohammed delighted in the change he saw in an otherwise pallid and uninspiring boy who at this age was neither intellectually notable nor socially adept. He preferred his own company to that of his siblings, or formed attachments to a nanny or one friend and tended to focus on this single relationship.

In the open air, however, Osama bloomed like a desert rose. In 1966 or 1967, shortly before Mohammed's death, Fahd and his sons joined the camp. Prince Fahd, who was even then seen as a future king, was on a fast-track career within the administration of King Faisal, his half-brother. The Interior portfolio was, of course, a key position in the national cabinet, but few were closer to Faisal personally than Mohammed bin Laden. In a culture where *wasta*, influence, is of paramount importance in most matters, from business to marriage to political decision-making, even senior Al Saud family members and government ministers were keen to stay on the right side of the 'merchant king'. Joining the Bin Laden family on one of its trips into the untamed interior was just such an opportunity, and Prince Fahd brought with him several of his sons.

While the two powerbrokers remained in quiet discussion for most of the trip, their offspring played. And it was here that nine-year-old Osama, a natural in this environment, had his first opportunity to escape the small circle of his everyday life. He quickly befriended Fahd's sons Abdul Rahman, Abdul Aziz and others; the aforementioned pair being slightly older than him.

Given his age, the young Prince Abdul Rahman was a natural leader for the group, but his royal upbringing had hardly prepared him for the rigours of play in the desert. He fell in behind Osama, and his brothers did likewise. The five or six children formed their own gang, almost to the total exclusion of the others, exploring the surroundings of the Bin Laden camp on their own.

Osama revelled in finding peers who either did not know or did not care about the emotional problems that he carried like a heavy weight. Coming from the higher levels of the huge Al Saud family, King Fahd's sons grew up in an intensely masculine environment. They knew a life where the harem, the home of all the women in the family including their mothers and sisters, was entirely separate from the palace where the males lived. Their father Fahd, in his mid-forties at this point, was surrounded instead by Arab concubines and western prostitutes. He saw no point in hiding this from his sons, who from an early age learned and perpetuated their father's approach to the opposite sex.

Osama and his royal playmates were inseparable. They rode camels together and travelled in Mohammed bin Laden's Land-Rover when he and Fahd went hunting. One of Fahd's sons, believed to be Abdul Aziz, became close to Osama and this camp marked the beginning of a friendship that would endure for some time. But that year the childhood playmates were more preoccupied with discovering the wildlife near their base, such as lizards, snakes and small mammals. On one occasion recounted by a family member, Osama and his gang caused a stir at camp after they discovered and hauled back a full-sized dhub, an indigenous lizard that can grow as long as four feet. Dhubs look fearsome but are essentially harmless vegetarians. If provoked or scared, however, they can take a chunk out of a leg or arm, or remove fingers with their strong jaws. Amid screams of protest from retainers and other children, Osama and his small gang manhandled the lizard to the feet of Prince Fahd and Mohammed bin Laden. The two men, tickled by the antics of their offspring and the panicked reaction of the rest of the camp, howled with laughter.

At the end of this sojourn, Osama and Abdul Aziz, heading for opposite sides of the country in Jeddah and Riyadh respectively, resolved that they would stay in touch. It was a friendship that both fathers would encourage in order to foster their own political and commercial interests.

Back at home in the stifling surroundings of the family's main palace in Jeddah, Osama once again withdrew into himself. Having turned ten in 1967, he was being tutored privately at home and also attending a small and exclusive private school named Al-Thaghr near the palace. At home, an entire wing was turned into a school and Mohammed's children were separated into classes reflecting their ages and ability. He had hired the best private tutors available and had brought many well-qualified teachers from abroad to educate his offspring. Poverty had denied him schooling while teaching him the value of education. Almost illiterate, he himself had been secretly tutored as a mature man. During his early years in business, Mohammed had often locked himself in his office while his secretary read all correspondence, as he simply did not have the skills. This made him determined that all his children – his modernist Islamic outlook meant that this also included his girls, at a time when most were denied the opportunity – be given the best start in life. Although it was expected that girls would marry and live out their lives in sleepy luxury, the forward-looking Mohammed understood clearly the emancipation he felt at being able to write letters and read newspapers. Even today Mohammed bin Laden would be considered liberal in many ways.

He placed great emphasis on his children receiving a well-rounded grounding in Islam. Local clerics and learned Islamicists were employed to teach in the family home. They took large classes and also had private individual sessions with each child several times each week.

Mohammed's generosity extended to sponsoring a number of 'poor schools' around the city, and indeed paying much of the expense involved in maintaining Al-Thaghr school. There, Osama and other pupils were tutored in English grammar and comprehension and some English literature. In Arabic they received one-hour lessons in geography, history and the sciences. Also on the curriculum was Islamic studies.

Family members recall that Osama was far from obviously the brightest in any of his classes. He never spoke unless called upon and instinctively attempted to be seated as anonymously at the rear of a class as possible. Brian Fyfield-Shayler, an English teacher at the school, was quoted many years later as recalling that Osama was 'quiet, retiring and rather shy. He was very courteous – more so than any of the others in his class. Physically he was outstanding because he was taller, more handsome and fairer than most of the other boys. He also stood out because he was singularly gracious and polite . . . he was very neat, very precise and very conscientious. He wasn't pushy at all. In fact he was quite reticent. Many students wanted to show you how clever they were, but if he knew the answer to something he wouldn't parade the fact.'

But he was, nevertheless, considered a bright child. One area where he did well was Islamic studies. The shy child was transformed in this class. His was the first hand in the air when questions were asked. The anonymous student in mathematics, geography and sciences was most eager to participate in Koran memorisation and reading.

This key area of learning, however, Mohammed bin Laden was not content to leave just to outsiders. When in Jeddah he liked nothing better than to sit in his vast majlis, surrounded by his children, and talk religion, expanding on his following of Wahhabism, the doctrine followed by the Al Sauds. Like most Saudi Arabians he followed the Sunni form of Islam, and wound into these beliefs were a great number of political themes, the oppression of the Palestinians and hatred of Israel being just two.

There was much to confer over. At the time Saudi Arabia was essentially in Islam's driving seat. The ultra-conservative regimes that came to power around the region in the 1970s and 1980s were still a long way off. Saudi Arabia, with its control over most of Islam's holiest sites, and its money, exerted considerable influence over the currents of Muslim thinking worldwide. The kingdom was the unchallenged home of Islam, although it was a thinly disguised secret that many of the Al Saud princes were investing their slice of Saudi oil revenues in a life of debauchery. Their names appeared regularly in European newspaper gossip columns for the wrong reasons. Many did little to endear themselves with King Faisal, wrapping sports cars around lampposts in London and Paris while inebriated on alcohol, while others frittered away fortunes in the casinos of Monte Carlo. But for the most part, despite its new access to a fortune, the Al Saud family retained its goodness and a sense of religious purpose and principles instilled by Abdul Aziz.

Mohammed bin Laden wished his children to be prepared for a life following the teachings of Islam as their guide. He had enjoyed a successful life by the edicts laid out in the Koran and saw no reason why his children could not do likewise. In his majlis, he would discuss at length the lessons he had learned from life and how his approach to these had been guided by the Koran. His sons now recall a man convinced in his faith and the way it had helped him succeed. He had seen great wealth and its corrosive effect on weaker personalities and was determined that the same would not happen within the Bin Laden dynasty.

Islamic thinking and discussion was an area in which Osama shone before his father. He was far ahead of those of a similar age in Koranic studies. But more than this, the youngster was not simply memorising chunks of the Muslim holy book, but thinking about the contents and interpreting what he read. When Mohammed paused for breath during one of these marathon sessions with his children, it was more often than not Osama's hand he saw raised with a question.

Some of Osama's enthusiasm for the subject was probably competitiveness and the desire to hold his father's attention, to be the special one, if only for a few seconds. And he appreciated the value of the subject to his father, playing on his advantage in asking questions and making comments that his father warmed to. This undoubtedly genuine enthusiasm for the subject enabled him to debate with his father in a way that helped bridge some of the distance that existed between them.

Osama bin Laden was just ten when his father disappeared from his life. Mohammed bin Laden was travelling home when the helicopter in which he was flying developed problems and crashed in the desert. He died on impact. When news of the accident reached Jeddah, his household erupted in mourning: wives wailing in anguish, children sobbing and, apparently, servants quietly pilfering ornaments and silverware in anticipation of losing their jobs if the household were to break up.

The afternoon of the crash, Mohammed's body was flown across the country and preparations made, in accordance with Arab and Islamic custom, for burial the following morning in a family plot. Shortly after dawn and the completion of morning prayers, his body, wrapped in a simple white cloth and laid on an open bier, was brought from the house. Osama joined his uncle, Abdullah, who would soon assume the role of patriarch of the family, and several brothers in carrying his father's body to its final resting place.

Outside the gates of the family palace, news had spread quickly. Mohammed bin Laden had lived the sort of life he had preached to his children. He had helped many families and given jobs in his empire to just about anyone who found their way into his presence and asked. In the mould of his long-time friend, the deposed King Saud, he had also been a philanthropist, supporting worthy causes and charities throughout his lifetime. Osama later said in a television interview: 'King Faisal was still alive when my father died. King Faisal cried. He said upon the death of my father that "Today, I have lost my right arm".'

The death of arguably Jeddah's most prominent citizen was a

cause for citywide mourning. Observers of the spectacle say that as many as 10,000 men were gathered between the gates of the Bin Laden residence and the nearby cemetery. It was an emotional occasion and greatly affected Osama. A great tide of people swept along with the body. To the side, from inside their homes came the sound of women crying and wailing, a strange backdrop to the silence of the large crowd in the street.

Several hours later, Osama returned to his room and shut the door. The events of the day had shattered him, but his grief was deeper than simply the loss of a loved one. Beneath the surface, he had long repressed a deep gouge in his psyche caused by the partial loss of his mother and a relationship with his father shared with so many siblings, a handful of wives and the pressures of a vast business empire. Before this tragic death, his interest in Islam had drawn him closer to his father. It was a paternal relationship he craved, yet Mohammed's sudden death had robbed the youngster of a chance to enjoy anything other than fleeting moments of satisfaction. Family members recall him reeling emotionally. In the months following Mohammed's death he drew further into himself.

The death of Mohammed brought change to the whole family. Others now had the Bin Laden Group of Companies under their charge. The central home, an environment that was an anchor for young Osama even if he resented and disliked much of what it stood for, could not continue without its head. Gradually, the pool of Mohammed's children was broken up and dispersed elsewhere among the many nooks and crannies that was the extended Bin Laden family.

For Osama this could have been an opportunity for a fresh beginning. One morning without warning he was told by a servant to pack his bags and prepare for a journey. He was leaving the place that had been his home for all his ten years. No one bothered to explain where he was going or why. Without a father to dictate his son's fate according to his own wishes, Osama was shifted to a home that he had never visited in Tabuk, a city in the north-west of the kingdom. After a long, bumpy journey by car and plane, he and an attendant reached their destination. Ushered inside to a large, enclosed garden, he was greeted with tears and a warm hug by a woman whom he had hardly had the opportunity to get to know. It was his mother, Hamida.

Losing a father had been a blow to Osama. Suddenly gaining a full-time mother was something for which he was neither ready nor prepared. He did not know how to react and initially shunned the woman whose complete presence in his life he had craved for so long. Although he cried in his mother's arms, it was not from relief at seeing her, or joy, but pure emotion: a child's reaction to the sudden end of the life he had known and the uncertainty of the unknown. He had only occasionally shared quality time with the woman who now held him so tightly, although there had been times, mainly family celebrations, when the two had been together for an extended period. But these had been group moments, not the one-on-one into which he had now been unwittingly thrust.

The pain was too much to bear. As soon as Osama could politely extricate himself from his mother's embrace he asked calmly to be shown to his new room. He closed the door and cried once more.

After the death of Mohammed bin Laden, his most precious child, Bin Laden Construction, remained largely intact. Abdullah, the brother Mohammed loved more than perhaps anyone else in the world, was now the patriarch of the family. Mohammed's eldest son, Salim, would later take charge of Mohammed's business affairs and those of his siblings.

Faced with a large, unruly household, a decision was made to sensitively scatter the many children and mothers around Saudi Arabia into more manageable groups. For most, escape from the inevitable political undercurrents and infighting of the larger body was something that they cherished. They had lost a father, but most were still young enough to need their mothers and the umbrella of servants and nannies that went with them. The break-up of Mohammed's super-nursery was no great loss to most. With only one notable exception, the sons and daughters of Mohammed bin Laden grew up to be well-rounded and well-educated people. A majority still live in Saudi Arabia, where most of his sons are respected members of the commercial sector. Others have spread across the world and have become bankers, lawyers, doctors and landed senior positions in industry.

The only victim in the family break-up was, in his own mind, Osama. He fought to escape the political undertones of the Jeddah complex, and his detested nickname. But in the final analysis he came to see that, in the absence of reasonable parental relationships, being surrounded by family was a powerful anchor around which to build a stable life. The loss of this anchor, added to the backdrop of all his other problems, was the scenario that would set him on the road to becoming what could be described – at best – as the black sheep of the family.

Over several months, in 1967, Osama genuinely worked at settling into his new situation in Tabuk. If he and his siblings had not been so in awe of their father, perhaps Osama might even have plucked up the courage to ask for the opportunity to spend more time with his mother. But he had shied away from falling out with his father and remained silent. With the permanent reunion he had imagined as a youngster forced upon him, unprepared, he became almost mute in front of his mother.

Hamida had also wished for nothing less. Fleeting moments with Osama as a youngster had not allowed her to settle for a life without his permanent presence and news that her son could now live with her had been a thrill. But the bright young boy, a little shy but nevertheless polite and upstanding, was not the child she now encountered. Despite her efforts, Hamida, now 32, struggled to reach out to her son, their conversations remained brief and hard work. Osama was simply aloof and preferred to remain either in his room, or to have one of the servants follow him as he miserably explored Tabuk. The monuments and mosques of Tabuk were perfect escapes for a boy whose interest in religion was mounting. They were also an excuse to be absent from home.

The city holds historic significance for Saudi Arabia and Islam. In September 629, the Battle of Mootah had been fought nearby, a disastrous campaign in which the Muslims had been defeated. This had opened the way for the Romans to attempt to take Medina. A year later, the Prophet had begun a campaign against the invaders, in which he was ultimately successful. His 'Expedition to Tabuk' was the first success in a long war, and it was there that the Prophet made one of his most celebrated addresses to the people.

After only a couple of months, Osama had withdrawn almost completely from his mother and interaction between the two became virtually non-existent. He had tired of Tabuk and wished to return to the more cosmopolitan Jeddah. He sent a note to his uncle and received the answer he had hoped for.

Those who know her say Hamida is a fine person, warm and kind – just as much a victim of this scenario as Osama. It would take time for Osama and his mother to build the relationship that they had been denied. Indeed, perhaps it was because of the tribulations of early times, and the few all-too brief years that they had to rebuild their relationship before he went off the rails, that a bond later formed. This is the reason that she endured with the Osama of recent years when others cut him off, attempting to bring him back from the abyss.

Back at home in Jeddah in the last years of the 1960s and into the early 1970s, the central family home was a much quieter place. Osama returned feeling bitter and disillusioned. His father was dead. He did not know his mother and found that he had nothing in common with her. The only real sense of family he had ever enjoyed was with his siblings, and now even this part of his life had been partly removed.

There were moments of joy, group holidays and family events. On one memorable occasion the sons and daughters of Mohammed holidayed in Sweden; another time many travelled to Paris and other European capitals. Ironically, in light of his hideouts of recent years in the highest mountains in Afghanistan, Osama is recalled as suffering from vertigo and developing a nosebleed after climbing the Eiffel Tower. While visiting Sweden, Osama, who was known for a stomach unable to handle anything but the most bland of foods, was persuaded to try a favourite Swedish dish known as *stekt falukorv med senap och potatis*. The 14 year old eagerly attacked his plate of dried slices of thick German beef sausage with mustard and boiled potatoes, but the mustard did not agree and he was forced to miss one precious day of his holiday in bed with an upset stomach.

During the summer of 1971, he joined several of his older brothers in a month-long study sojourn to a language school in Oxford. He felt at home anywhere outside of his native city, and life in Oxford seems to have suited him. Having arrived in Britain with a broad grasp of the English language courtesy of his studies in Jeddah, he settled well and became infatuated with the cinema. As often as possible, the young Osama would either drag one of his brothers with him, or slip off alone to visit the local movie theatre. As later revelations have hinted, his elder brothers had more mature diversions in their minds than the cinema. Osama appears to have been in awe of the opposite sex, but never had the opportunity to lose his virginity until paying for sex much later in Beirut.

At other times groups of Mohammed's brood stayed closer to home to visit the great Arab cities in search of holiday fun. Osama loved Cairo and never missed an opportunity to visit Egypt. He explored the metropolis and revelled in its unique atmosphere, in particular finding himself drawn to Ibn Tulun, Al-Azhar, Sultan Hasan and Muhammad Ali, four of the city's famed mosques.

Now that the intensity of lobbying for Mohammed's attention was removed as a factor, Osama believed that he would be more accepted by his siblings and he readily accepted offers to join in. This may be what he chose to believe, but family members say in retrospect that little had changed except Osama's attitude. He had always been oversensitive, choosing to misinterpret the childish squabbling among the large group as vicious personal attacks. Much of his early isolation was self-imposed while the wounds to his immature pride had been largely self-inflicted.

Aside from these brief moments of respite he remained a generally unhappy youth, however, going through the motions of attending school. He completed his secondary-level education at the age of 16 in early 1973. During these bitter years, Osama did at last begin to reconstruct a bond with his mother. For his sake, Hamida had returned permanently to Jeddah, which had its own bitter memories for her.

One silver lining for Osama might have been the only true personal friendship he had ever really enjoyed, his relationship with Abdul Aziz ibn Fahd, kindled during the desert camping trip and nurtured sometime after that by their respective fathers. As events allowed, Osama and Abdul Aziz had seen each other in a variety of situations since then. When not in the same place, they remained in touch by telephone – a rare luxury in Saudi Arabia – and letter. But the death of his father changed the dynamics of the Al Saud–Bin Laden relationship. Mohammed might have been the man who had extended private help to King Faisal in the kingdom's darkest hour, and who was personal friend to seemingly every major player in Saudi Arabian politics, but *wasta* by its nature cannot simply be transferred like a title or even a crown. While the Bin Laden family would remain – and still is – highly respected in Saudi Arabia, even enjoying special status, things could never be the same. It was another lesson for Osama to learn the hard way.

Within months of his return from his exile in Tabuk, he heard news that delighted him: Prince Fahd was coming to Jeddah and

Abdul Aziz would be with him. When news filtered though to the Bin Laden household that his Al Saud friend was in the city, he telephoned Prince Fahd's residence repeatedly over several days. He never got past the gatehouse. He sent written messages to Abdul Aziz with a delivery boy, to no avail. Finally, he went to the door of their home. He was turned away.

To a ten-year-old boy, having just lost, physically and emotionally, both his parents, the subtleties of a brush-off were not easy to spot. Indeed, he prepared with great excitement to see Abdul Aziz for several days. But after a dozen attempts at making contact, over three to four days, gradually the implications of what was unfolding began to sink in. A few days later, Prince Fahd and his family moved on. Abdul Aziz had not bothered even to speak to his friend. Osama never heard from Abdul Aziz again.

For a shy boy of limited emotional strength, 1967 was a turning point. He grew bitter and angry. By all accounts, the next few years were spent in a sort of survival mode. With no real friends to speak of, he sought refuge in books. His appetite for reading was insatiable. Returning home from school, within minutes he would be safely ensconced in his room, deep in a book.

If Osama's room was a refuge from a world that had rejected him, books were an escape from the room itself. His appetite for reading was voracious, and this passion was happily indulged by all around him simply because the sulky child would remain in his room as long as there was something to read. Steadily, though, books began to have a further effect on him. Replacing people with books was a diversion that worked in the short term, but in the longer term his social skills suffered still further. He became an outcast, only the obligation of attending school preventing a complete introversion.

In 1973, aged 16, Osama completed his secondary schooling. All that reading had not been in vain as his exam results were excellent. But now the family had a problem. He patently needed a sense of purpose and direction. The family's solution was a spell abroad furthering his studies, away from its bosom. The destination chosen would set Osama on one of the stranger twists in his extraordinary life.

CHAPTER FIVE

Off the Rails

For three decades following independence from France in 1943, Lebanon was a model ecumenical society. Its inhabitants embodied a unique blend of Eastern and Western cultures, speaking Arabic, French and English and enjoying the benefits of both Islamic and Christian traditions in a climate and environment that remains today, at least by reputation, the finest in the world. In the early 1970s, Lebanon's capital, Beirut, had a sense of life and energy that was almost palpable. It revelled in its dramatic location on a great promontory jutting into the blue sea with fabulous beaches stretching mile after mile on the one side and dramatic mountains rising behind it.

Thanks to its strategic location at the eastern end of the Mediterranean Sea – the crossroads of Asia, Africa and Europe – and relatively stable government, Lebanon had become a major trade and financial centre: the country's free exchange system, strict secrecy laws and strong currency all served to attract regional and international financial institutions and customers. Through the dynamism of its entrepreneurs and the development of a strong service economy, it had become the principal intermediary between the developed countries of the West and the developing countries of the Near and Middle East. And where there is money, there is the urge to spend it. During this period, Lebanon's banking and hospitality sectors were both booming.

Beirut was the focal point for most of this activity and grew into the Middle East's answer to the world's great tourism centres, more than living up to its nickname as the 'Paris of the Middle East'. At the top end of the scale, downtown Beirut was awash with classy bars and nightclubs and the only casino in the Middle East. At the other end of the scale, less salubrious establishments had no shortage of customers.

But this was not all the city could legitimately claim to be. Beirut was also the cultural and learning centre for the Arab world, a cradle of high-quality education and cross-cultural pollination. During this, its greatest era, the Lebanese capital nurtured an entire generation of Arab intellectuals and saw tens of thousands of well-educated, well-rounded students graduate from its institutes of learning. Thirty years later, in every level of every Arab government, and in most company boardrooms around the Arab world, one will find a senior official who studied in Lebanon.

It was this side of Lebanon that encouraged his family to enroll Osama bin Laden in school in 1973. They chose the most prestigious and reputable educational facility in the country, Broumanna High School, set high on one of the many mountains that dominate the skyline behind Beirut.

With not a little trepidation and a great deal of reluctance – he had never left Saudi Arabia before for longer than one month – Osama flew into Beirut International Airport aboard Middle East Airlines in late August 1973. Through contacts in the city, the family had arranged a plush apartment for him in the village of Broumanna. The apartment came with a maid and a cook. He would receive a generous weekly allowance through the Beirut branch of a Saudi Arabian bank and, in common with a handful of the pupils from wealthier families attending the Broumanna facility, he even boasted a car and chauffeur. As he was driven across the city in a top-of-the-range silver Mercedes-Benz 350 SE, the young Osama looked very much the part he quickly adopted – that of the Saudi aristocrat.

But liberal and open Lebanon was a strange and alien place to a boy from the restrictive society of Saudi Arabia who had only limited experience of western ways through short holidays to the continent. First and foremost, Osama was shocked by the women. Growing up largely in the company of his brothers and other male relatives, at the age of 16 he had hardly mixed with adult women with arms or legs not covered. Nor were women in the kingdom permitted by the strict religious edicts that governed their lives to wear make-up or perfume. In Lebanon, by contrast, fashion consciousness among both men and women was a way of life, a means of displaying wealth and, by inference, power and success. If hemlines in Europe that year were well above the knee, in Lebanon they would be several inches higher.

This was not the only shock that Osama faced over his initial days and weeks away from home. He was not keen on taking lessons in mixed-sex classes, and horrified to find students arriving at the school aboard buses crammed with both boys and girls together. But, as he later explained to classmates, this was not because of his own tastes, but because he had been brought up to believe in preserving the modesty of girls and women, and that segregation was one means of ensuring this. To find such permissiveness in a Middle Eastern country was a revelation.

Osama settled in well considering the misery and loneliness of the preceding years. Overall an intelligent boy, one benefit of his isolated reading in Jeddah was that he was considerably advanced in his studies. He impressed several teachers as a good student and one surprisingly without the usual superior attitude encountered in upper-class Saudi Arabian children. His initial worries quickly gave way to happiness. All of the misery that had afflicted his life over the preceding years had been left behind. The possibility of a fresh start enlivened him.

From descriptions of Osama given by fellow students at his school, it is hard to recognise him as the same teenager he had been in Jeddah. It had taken a radical transformation in circumstances to shake him out of his lethargy and back into the world of the living. In fact, if anything, in the lurch out of his long depression he went to the other extreme. For a time at least, the very proper, God-fearing, Koran-quoting young Saudi took on a persona that would have had his father, Mohammed bin Laden, turning in his grave.

In academic terms, Osama excelled. An intelligent boy with an inquiring mind, he threw himself into his studies. According to one who was at the school during the same period, he was considered something of a 'grind' and a teacher's pet. If after his years of isolation, he wanted to be liked and appreciated, this was the way to do it. To classmates he was friendly and affable; some remember him helping with homework. Because of his warm demeanour, the smiling youngster quickly entered a world that he had previously only dreamed of. Now he was popular, always surrounded by friends and acquaintances from his various classes.

Osama and his new-found friends found plenty of distractions in Beirut. Just 15 minutes by car from their school, the Lebanese capital had everything to enthral a youngster from the staid and boring confines of Jeddah. They went swimming and boating, and made frequent visits to the cinema, something of an illicit delight as cinema was banned in the kingdom.

As well as drawing him into a world that he had not even imagined, Lebanon gave Osama a taste of acceptance and friendship that he had hankered after all his life. But Beirut was also well-stocked in forbidden fruits that would inevitably test the moral fibre of the inexperienced and unworldly son of a Saudi merchant. In this he was no different from the innumerable sons of rich families from every culture who, given half a chance away from the shackles of their own traditions and family influence, will test their wings. The emotional and physical wreckage of those, like Osama, who choose to soar has given many a family and nation cause to mourn.

In the mountains around Beirut, the city's swinging lifestyle was not quite as apparent, but Broumanna, like nearly all cosmopolitan villages close to the capital, was itself crammed with small, family-run bars. Broumanna had long been the summer playground of the upper classes in Lebanese society. Along the twisting main roads, cafés jostled with fashionable shops for prominence. Three- and four-storey sandstone apartment blocks hugged the edge of mountain sides, empty for much of the winter when most people lived in Beirut, but full during the summer when society shifted toward the cooler climate found in the mountains around the capital.

In this mixed Christian-Muslim society, the consumption of alcohol was more than tolerated. Indeed, bars existed all over Beirut in all neighbourhoods, Christian-dominated or otherwise. Although the staff at the school would issue warnings, the facility itself could no more control its hundreds of pupils after school hours than could the parents of foreign children from thousands of miles away. It was a matter of trust. There was an unwritten, unspoken understanding that most would drink, at least at some point, but that trouble would only ensue if the after-hours social side of Broumanna life affected academic hours.

At 16, Osama bin Laden tried alcohol for the first time. Most students were not sophisticated enough to try spirits or cocktails, so it seems likely that he began with a bottle of beer, probably the Dutch-brewed Heineken that was favoured by students because it was cheaper than other imported beers. He seems to have enjoyed his beer, or at least the social environment surrounding it, because during his first year in Lebanon Osama and his friends became fixtures in the Broumanna student drinking scene.

It was a raucous, but entirely peaceable fraternity and within it Osama socialised and mixed with a wide circle of nationalities, races and creeds. Amid a natural plethora of Lebanese, his circle included a handful of students from the Gulf states, Syrians and Jordanians. The facility also attracted the cream of European students in Lebanon, most of those the children of foreign diplomats and high profile names in the commercial sector. It was a mixed group, but one that Osama was a natural dealing with. While others chose to remain largely within national, religious or ethnic cliques, he was one of those who befriended anyone who shared a similar mentality or humour, regardless of where they were from or the colour of their skin.

Perhaps not surprisingly given the good manners taught him at home, his obvious money, and his open, fun-filled personality, it was not long before Osama had his first girlfriend. She was the daughter of the Christian owner of one of the bars in Broumanna; the family had owned small businesses in the village for generations, as they do today. Prior to the civil war, the family maintained a small bar and it was here that Osama met the girl, known as Rita. Although she was one or two years older than him, his strict upbringing had given him a maturity and social graces beyond his years. He was more polite and charming than the students who normally frequented such places. Tall and well built, he was never short of female company.

As there were no prejudices in Lebanon during those pre-war days, there was no problem with Osama and Rita striking up a friendship: the Saudi Arabian Muslim courting the Lebanese Christian. Osama was introduced to her parents and brothers and spent time with them, often being driven in his smart Mercedes-Benz 350 SE for dinner in the family home. It seems that the two were considered an item for months. During the winter of 1973–74, the pair frequently went skiing at a resort in the mountain village of Faraya. Despite being a product of the desert, Osama took well to the slopes and quickly found his feet on snow after several lessons.

Predictably, the revelations of life in Lebanon became a Pandora's box. Within a few short months, Osama had broken out of his shell, begun socialising in mixed company, frequenting bars and generally understanding something of the world that had passed him by in Saudi Arabia. As more thrills came within reach, the more he strived for new experiences and tastes.

His platonic affair with Rita ended during the summer of 1974 when suddenly something better came along. Osama had integrated himself completely into the life of a student until this time, but he was hardly typical. Most of his Lebanese friends lived with their parents and existed on a meagre allowance. Fellow Gulf Arab students were slightly better off, but those he befriended did not come from such wealthy families; they could not hope to match the generous spending allowance paid each week to Osama.

For his first year, Osama was content to immerse himself in the routine of daytime study and evenings getting tipsy in the bars of Broumanna. The weekends meant greater freedom and on Friday evenings Osama and his friends invariably bar-hopped around the village until they were too drunk to continue. Saturdays Osama reserved for Rita and his chauffeur would drive the two of them to restaurants in nearby villages or on longer jaunts into Beirut.

This was the pattern of life he adopted for nearly a year after his arrival in Lebanon. During this time he changed dramatically. Influenced by more liberal Muslims around him – and Christian friends – he took a more liberal attitude toward religion, adopting what would perhaps most accurately be described as a pacifist approach. Despite the abundance of mosques, he was lax about praying five times a day.

Osama's first academic year had been a success. He was thriving and happy, and this showed in his work, which, despite his evening exploits, seemed not to have suffered. Nearing the end of the school year, plans had originally been made for him to return to Saudi Arabia for the summer break, before flying back to Lebanon in the autumn. But things were different now, and after only a little thought he cabled Saudi Arabia requesting permission to stay on. To his relief, the family agreed.

The summer of 1974 was a turning point for Osama bin Laden. He had planned to pursue his relationship with Rita while enjoying the convivial atmosphere of the village bars, punctuating that with a little time on the beach, boating and similar leisure pursuits. But his plans quickly changed.

Pre-war Lebanon was a magnet for Arabs; beautiful, developed, civilised and relaxed, it had everything to offer that a European capital had but with the advantage that Arabic was spoken. For the Arab inclined to seek them out, the country was also knee deep in the sort of pleasures and vices denied to them at home.

In the wake of the Arab-Israeli War of 1973, the subsequent Arab Oil Embargo and steep rise in the price of oil, the petro-dollar-infused economies of the Gulf were booming as never before, and the effect spilled over into neighbouring countries. In the summer of 1974, Lebanon was full. Never before had the country experienced such traffic. Each plane into Beirut International Airport brought with it the rich and powerful – and the newly rich and newly powerful – from all over Arabia, many attracted like children to a ice-cream vendor by the availability of gambling, drinking and prostitutes.

From his base in the mountains, Osama was well aware of the goings on in Beirut, but had his own preoccupations in Broumanna during his first school year. Indeed, he might never have been introduced to the fleshpots of the capital had he not stayed on that summer. The catalyst was a trip to Casino Du Liban – the only casino in the Middle East in the 1970s. He had been to the casino several times during his initial 12 months in Beirut but had not been impressed. Indeed, once he had been turned away for looking too young, despite arriving in his Mercedes. On the occasions he had obtained entrance he had played a little roulette, but did not like the speed at which his money disappeared and quickly retired to one of the excellent bars on the premises. But in the summer of 1974, Osama accompanied a couple of his roulette and blackjack-loving friends to Casino Du Liban. The gaming rooms and bars were packed with Saudi Arabians and he joined in the conversation. Given their natural hospitality and the ease with which most Saudis strike up acquaintances, bar conversation quickly led to an invitation to Osama to join his compatriots the following evening for a night on the town.

The next evening he made his first visit to a nightclub that was to become almost a second home for the remainder of his time in Lebanon. The Crazy Horse remains a legend to this day, especially among Lebanese old enough to remember it. Part Moulin Rouge and part brothel, even by Beirut's bawdy standards at this time, this was a place that stood out. Whatever a patron made of the many diversions on offer, the Crazy Horse was all the more remarkable for the fact that it was in Arabia. With its high roof, glittering chandeliers, raucous atmosphere and room for hundreds of tables, in 1974 this was the pinnacle of clubs. The cream of Lebanese society – and some of the worst – rubbed shoulders with wealthy foreigners. Government ministers and – discreetly – not a few clergy were patrons. Arabian sheikhs patronised the Crazy Horse extensively, along with business leaders from all over the Middle East.

That first night in the Crazy Horse was one that turned 17-year-old Osama's head. Not even his months living in Lebanon had prepared him for what he saw. His older companions, knowing exactly who he was, were eager to impress and gain a foothold in his affections. The champagne flowed freely as Osama took in the dancers, the hostesses and the prostitutes who were attracted to a table of well-to-do Saudi Arabians. It was a wild night at the Crazy Horse and a revelation to a boy from a sheltered background.

By September 1974 and the beginning of Osama's second term of school at Broumanna, a different young man seemed to have taken the place of the one who had impressed so many the previous year. Gone was the smart dresser with his tidy, pressed shirts, good manners and conscientious participation in his work. The boy of the year before had become a man. This was not unusual in itself in Osama's school, which likes to believe it helps its teenage pupils through a period of great change, especially its foreigners who were away from their families. But in Osama's case, it was an overnight metamorphosis, a transition driven by temptation and fuelled by money.

With some disappointment, teachers quickly registered the change in his demeanour. He was still obsessively polite and courteous to a point of embarrassment toward female members of staff and classmates. But he was no longer shy and childlike in his ways. Instead he had quickly matured into a confident individual. And it was his attitude toward school and his schoolmates in general that raised cause for concern.

He now did little to disguise the fact that he felt attending school was somewhat beneath him. One of his strengths had been his eagerness to participate in group discussions. Now he sat as close to the back of the class as possible and gave only faint signals that he registered what was going on around him. Within weeks of the beginning of term, there was murmuring among staff that Osama's work was well down on the previous year – that is, when indeed any was being done.

Away from the classroom, people who had earlier counted the irrepressible Saudi a friend now saw a shift in his allegiances. He became a rare sight in the bars and taverns of Broumanna, preferring to pursue the nightlife in the city. Nor did he have time any more for Rita. His smart Mercedes-Benz 350 SE was now joined by a sporty Mercedes-Benz 230 and, instead of hanging out in jeans and an open-top shirt, he adopted the playboy look of flared suits and kipper ties that was then in vogue.

A glitzy, glamorous world had now appeared before him; this was something far too attractive not to explore. To a handsome young man of excellent financial means, Beirut was an open book. Doors opened easily and, if there were doubts about his age, his arrival in a chauffeur-driven Mercedes was usually enough to dissuade any embarrassing questions. Gradually his appearances at school became less frequent to the point where he was no longer even missed. Now café society, as much as nightclubs and bars, became his focus. Lebanese from his age group naturally warmed to this stranger in their midst, especially one with obviously impeccable breeding and funding. Osama the socialite did not want for friends.

This included lady friends. By now having shaved his beard and sporting a more image-conscious slick moustache, he was rarely without a companion. He favoured European blondes, but whether Lebanese, Arab, European or American, it meant little to him. He was there to sow his oats. That was all that mattered.

With his sycophantic friends and a lady in tow, Osama then set out to explore the city in which he had now established himself. The Crazy Horse was his base, but there was plenty of competition among the clubs in Beirut. Several were his favourites. The Casbah, an expensive and quieter nightclub than the Crazy Horse, was one such. Osama befriended the owner, who doted on the Saudi Arabian as he invariably outspent and out-tipped even the richest and most lavish Lebanese patrons. An exclusive front table near the stage was always Osama's, despite the Casbah being perennially full. Should he arrive unexpectedly, the manager would think nothing of offending other customers to clear space.

A relative of the owner explained that there were customers that one would want at the Casbah for political reasons, and customers that one would want for financial reasons. Prominent in the latter category was Osama. He and his friends drank only top brand whisky and champagne. Osama puffed determinedly at a Cuban cigar and rarely departed at the end of an evening without leaving a generous tip.

Between the Crazy Horse and the Casbah, Osama also had a penchant for the well-known nightclub Eve's. What it lacked in class, Eve's made up for in other ways. The stage show was not the best, the service less noted, food rather plain and the clientele not as discerning. But Eve's was more open in terms of which women it permitted to enter. In between girlfriends, Osama was a much welcomed and generous patron.

Throughout this period, the Crazy Horse above all others was the place that welcomed Osama as one of its most cherished customers. The owner of the club was a big man in every way. He was a millionaire himself by the mid-1970s, but rarely missed an evening in his showpiece club. Always dining with guests, he remained the heartbeat of life in the club, monitoring events and standing politely as guests made their way to his table to pay their respects.

There were only a few patrons – Lebanon's elite – whom he took the trouble to meet personally at the door of the Crazy Horse. In addition to senior Lebanese political figures and a sprinkling of Arab singing stars, a VIP welcome was reserved only for a few high-spending guests and in 1974 and '75 this included the 'Saudi Arabian prince', as Osama enjoyed being called.

At least two or three nights a week, Osama and an assortment of friends and freeloaders would descend on the Crazy Horse. His table was one of the finest in the house, and when he arrived it was already well-stocked with Dom Perignon and Black Label in anticipation. Through a typical evening Osama, debonair in his sports jacket and neat black trousers, or alternatively a handmade suit, was the perfect host. No one was allowed to want for anything; no expense was spared.

Only occasionally did the management have reason to regret his presence. While Osama's guests seldom stepped out of line for fear of being dropped, his own heavy drinking did sometimes become a concern. Periodically he would switch from whisky to champagne, back and forth, and in doing so get hopelessly drunk. The Saudi was not a loud drunk, but with his inhibitions removed, the suave, sophisticated man became a sex pest, given to sending bottles of champagne to attractive women at nearby tables, most of whom were usually accompanied. Invariably this led to confrontation and on at least two occasions, punches were thrown. While Osama's good reputation as a gentleman playboy was often whispered, so was the footnote that he could sometimes attract trouble.

Unfortunately for Osama this way of life could not last, if only because circumstances around him would not allow it. Civil war destroyed more than a beautiful country; it destroyed an entire way of life. The spark that ignited civil war occurred in Beirut on 13 April 1975 in the neighbourhood of Ain Al Roumaneh, 20 minutes by car from the Bin Laden residence in Broumanna. On that warm, sunny spring day, unknown gunmen killed four Christian Phalangists during an attempt on the life of Pierre Gemayel, their leader. Believing the assassins to have been Palestinian, the Phalangists retaliated later that day by attacking a bus carrying Palestinian passengers as it passed through a Christian neighbourhood, killing about 26 of the occupants. The following day fighting erupted in earnest, with Phalangists pitted against Palestinian militiamen. The layout of Beirut's various residential quarters facilitated random killing. Most Beirutis stayed inside their homes during these early days of battle, and few imagined that the street fighting they were witnessing was the beginning of a war that was to devastate their city and divide the country for decades to come.

President Frangie saw it as a conspiracy to break down law and order in Lebanon and fought over successive days and weeks to stem the brutal fighting, but to no avail. It was spring and the tourist season was already in bud, like the city's flowering trees; the number of foreigners on the streets of Beirut was spiralling. Within days, however, the city emptied, Lebanese and non-Lebanese alike crowding the airport seeking passage abroad.

Ordered home despite his protests, Osama packed a few of his belongings and bade farewell to his maid, entrusting her with the care of his apartment in Broumanna. He expected to be back within weeks when the situation calmed, and to pick up his life where he was leaving it. Most of his possessions, including his beloved wardrobe of fashionable clothes, were left behind. It was the beginning of a long, long war of attrition that devastated Lebanon. He would never return.

CHAPTER SIX

Alcohol and Redemption

From his adopted home in Beirut, Osama had been preoccupied with his hedonistic lifestyle and unconcerned with events at home. But the Saudi Arabia he returned to in April 1975 was under a cloud of despair unlike any other it had experienced. Only a month before Osama's flight from Beirut touched down in Jeddah, his father's closest friend, King Faisal, had been assassinated.

Even in a nation that lionised its monarch, King Faisal had been special. During his years as crown prince, Faisal had prevented the financial collapse of the kingdom, and as king he had ruled wisely. It would be fair to state that the people of Saudi Arabia loved him.

Just as the Bin Laden family had been embarrassed by the wild behaviour of its indolent youth, so had the Al Sauds. One such rebel was the king's nephew, Faisal ibn Musaid. He had been sent to study at Berkeley, one of America's finest universities, but there he had been seduced by all the temptations that were available, as had Osama in Lebanon, but worse. He had become addicted to LSD, drank heavily and more than once stretched the State Department's ability to keep him out of jail. For these indiscretions, King Faisal had decreed that his nephew be brought back to the kingdom and not allowed to leave.

Unlike Osama, who would eventually pick himself up and buckle down, Faisal ibn Musaid continued to drink heavily: finding smuggled whisky is not a problem for those with wealth and connections. From the depths of an almost permanent stupor, Faisal resolved to take revenge upon his uncle. On April 25, 1975, Faisal paid a call to King Faisal's office. It was unusual, because family

73

business was normally reserved for the monarch's evening majlis. But the determined Faisal slipped into his uncle's office among a handful of officials from Kuwait. As King Faisal stood to embrace his nephew, the boy pulled a gun from beneath his robes and fired three shots at the king from point-blank range. The first bullet entered King Faisal's chin, the second entered his ear and a third narrowly missed his forehead.

The king was rushed to hospital still conscious and received seven pints of blood by transfusion as doctors worked to repair the massive damage to an artery caused by the first shot. But the injury was so extreme that they could do little. Within an hour, King Faisal slipped into a coma and died soon after.

One month later, Osama flew into a country that was still in shock. Flags stood at half mast, while soldiers remained in the streets, where they had been positioned within hours of King Faisal's death. The authorities feared an organised coup, but none was discovered.

Most Americans of a certain age can recall where they were the moment they heard that President Kennedy was shot, and it is much the same for Saudi Arabians and King Faisal. One of the few exceptions would likely be Osama who, occupied at the time by clubbing, alcohol and prostitutes, did not seem to realise what had befallen his country until he arrived in Jeddah.

During the 18 months Osama had been absent 'pursuing his studies' in Lebanon, little else had changed in Saudi Arabia other than the accession of King Khalid ibn Abdul Aziz Al Saud. But this did not concern Osama. After all, he reasoned, this was only a temporary absence from his beloved Beirut. When things settled down, probably in a couple of weeks, everything would return to normal.

Being home in Jeddah was initially a pleasurable experience for Osama. Now 18, he stood well over six feet tall and had matured. Seeing some of his siblings again pleased him immensely. Most, he thought, were the same one-dimensional slaves to tradition that he had been. He pitied them, believing that the experiences and life he had enjoyed would never be theirs.

Although not in a desperate hurry to leave, Osama nevertheless quickly began a vigil for Lebanon. He pored over newspapers, and listened endlessly to the radio, praying for good news. But in his adopted homeland events were turning from bad to worse. In fact, the writing had been on the wall for some time if Osama had only been able to disengage himself from his worldly pursuits long enough for such things to register. The international help that Lebanon had hoped for was already patently not going to come. America, its policy steered by Secretary of State Henry Kissinger, was eyeing the potential carcass of Lebanon to solve its problems with Israel and the Palestinians. In early 1975, Lebanese President Sleiman Frangie had met with Kissinger, seeking US support to end the bloodletting in Lebanon. He discovered that the American solution to the Lebanon problem neatly matched their solution for the Palestinian problem. Kissinger planned to resettle Lebanese Christians outside Lebanon, in a country of their choice, and in their place to settle the Palestinians permanently in Lebanon. President Frangie rejected outright the American plan, declaring: 'We are prepared to defend our homeland to the death. We will never abandon Lebanon.' His sentiment would become a reality with the death of tens of thousands of people in Lebanon.

During the remainder of 1975, all the news that reached Osama in Jeddah was bad. Occasionally a friend would call from Beirut and offer a relatively neutral view of what was happening. But from wherever he got his information, Osama could see only gloom.

Despite the urgent need to control the fighting, the political machinery of the government in Lebanon became paralysed during the initial months of the spreading civil strife. The inadequacies of the political system, which the 1943 National Pact had only papered over, reappeared more clearly than ever. The government could not act effectively because leaders were unable to agree on whether to use the army to stop the bloodletting. As various other groups took sides, the fighting spread to other areas of the country, forcing residents in towns with mixed sectarian populations to seek safety in regions where their sect was dominant. The political hierarchy, composed of the old *zuama* and politicians, was still incapable of maintaining peace, except for occasional, short-lived ceasefires. Most ominously, the Lebanese army, which generally had stayed aloof, began to show signs of factionalising and threatened to bring its heavy weaponry to bear on the conflict.

By the summer of 1975 Osama realised that memories were all that remained of his halcyon days in Lebanon when he discovered that the Crazy Horse, the Casbah and Eve's were all closed. Suddenly it was clear that he would not see Lebanon again for a long time.

Osama had earlier made it perfectly clear that he had no intention of leaving Lebanon and, indeed, the family had sanctioned his wishes the previous summer by allowing him to stay. If the civil war had not intervened, it is likely, however, that he would soon have been summoned back to Jeddah anyway. Word had reached the kingdom of the behaviour of the 'Saudi Arabian prince' nightclubbing, drinking, carousing in public and spending his allowance on the attentions of dubious blondes. Osama's mother was horrified to hear of her son's predilection for prostitutes.

Osama was the only one of Mohammed bin Laden's sons to go off the rails. Many scattered across the globe seeking a fresh start and the family was never forced to recall other errant offspring. In several European capitals and throughout the United States, they went on to become respected business leaders, advocates of law and decent citizens. With Osama back in Jeddah, control was seemingly restored, and the family had another decision to make. The process of family decision-making eventually decreed that he would not be allowed to go abroad simply to pick up where he had left off, and that the youngster should now prepare himself seriously for a future role within the family firm. Although conservative Saudi Arabia as a whole offered few top-class scholastic opportunities, it was decided that Osama should remain close to home and resume his studies.

The oldest university in the kingdom is King Saud University in Riyadh. When it first opened in 1957, there were only nine teachers and twenty-one students. A decade later King Abdul Aziz University in Jeddah was founded by a group of national businessmen who understood the importance of education in driving national development. Among them was Mohammed bin Laden, who donated funds to build schools not just in Saudi Arabia, but throughout the Middle East. It was said that every year 100,000 children throughout the region passed through schools supported by Mohammed.

That first scholastic year, 68 men and 30 women were admitted to King Abdul Aziz University. But the university developed so rapidly that in 1971 – four years after Mohammed's death – the founding fathers could no longer cope with the financial demands placed upon them and petitioned the Saudi government of King Faisal to assume responsibility for its operation. Since then it has expanded considerably and, today, has over 2,000 teachers and more than 39,000 students enrolled in undergraduate and graduate programs in various fields of study.

As is often the case for youths in the autocratic Saudi family hierarchies, and indeed Arab society, Osama was given little room for input into decisions regarding his life and found himself studying economics and Islamic economics – he detested both. The latter was emphasised as a distinct field of study at King Abdul Aziz University for the first time in 1976. The course aimed to spread an awareness of economic thought and considerations based on Islamic principles. One aspect of its activities is cooperation with banking institutions for the purpose of exchanging and obtaining expertise and information through visiting lecturers, so as to widen the base of scientific research and provide students with a practical application of what they learn of the theory of Islamic economics.

For Osama the adjustment was hard. But he was in no position to fight the family and risk being cut off from the flow of cash. Kowtowing before his uncles and elder brothers and other senior members of the Bin Laden clan was something that Osama detested. His resentment began to build.

Staff and pupils at King Abdul Aziz University have little recollection of the future terrorist in their midst during the second half of the 1970s. Indeed, practically the only thing that made him stand out was his pride and joy, a canary yellow Mercedes SL 450 convertible. With its smart, burnt-orange interior, air conditioning, cruise control and electric windows, the SL 450 was top of the range and everyone knew it.

The Mercedes was the single luxury countenanced by his family. Aside from this Osama was forced to toe the line. He attended his classes without fail, but he was anonymous. Instead of the quiet yet conscientious schoolboy who had left the kingdom for Lebanon, he was now concerned with getting by with as little effort as possible. Osama had other things on his mind.

Saudi Arabia under King Khalid remained much the same as it had been under his brother. The conservative regime followed Koranic doctrine as its basis, and there was little room for discussion. Even something as basic as television was still not accepted by the religious right; cinema was outlawed and men and women were segregated in workplaces, schools, restaurants and on public transportation. Such restrictions were now alien to Osama the liberal. He hated the mentality that forced women to wear the face mask called the *burka*, or the *abaya* – a black garment covering the head, face, and body. Just as his mother before him, Osama could not comprehend the need for these, no matter what Islamic doctrine said.

Though physically in Jeddah, Osama's mind remained in Beirut. He receded to the edges of mainstream Saudi society. While the consumption of alcohol was a serious offence under Saudi law, in the higher reaches of society whisky and other intoxicants were easy to get hold of. The children of the rich and powerful, brought up in luxury and often tasting western-style freedoms, found it increasingly hard to reconcile existing within such a stifling, restricted society. In every city around the kingdom, this small but significant group formed its own private elite. Away from prying eyes, behind the high walls of a villa, or in the remote desert, these groups got together for drinks parties and to air forbidden talk of a gentler, more-open Saudi Arabia. While these groups remained out of sight and out of trouble, the authorities turned a blind eye, particularly as these were the spoilt children of the kingdom's most prominent and influential families.

Unable to escape the prison in which his family had placed him, Osama retreated into this world. By day he was an average student. Most evenings he would drive his Mercedes to a friend's villa and drink himself into a stupor on Johnny Walker Black Label whisky.

A person's perspective of Jeddah is framed by his mental state. Writings on the city are varied. One writer has called it 'the city surrounded by walls with beautiful markets and teeming with buildings' while another described it as a 'small city on the Red Sea coast crowded with pilgrims and cluttered with mankind'. Certainly the dour pessimistic view of the latter was closest to the thinking of Osama, trapped in the city that was almost his prison for several years.

Between the boom years of 1974 and 1980, the population of Jeddah doubled. In general, construction appeared to run amok. The pious atmosphere of the graceful mosques was disturbed by ugly new buildings, which overwhelmed the skyline. For one so inclined there is, however, much to see and enthuse over. In addition to its Islamic sites, Jeddah's past dates almost from the beginning of the human race, according to an old tradition. One of the meanings of the name of the city itself (Jadda) is grandmother, which refers to the mother of mankind, Eve. Tradition says that after Adam and Eve were expelled from Paradise, Eve lived in Jeddah, and was buried there. Her tomb – or supposed tomb – withstood the ravages of the ages up until only half a century ago when it could still be seen. Sadly the monument was destroyed inadvertently when the city walls were pulled down in the 1930s. But Eve's Graveyard, as it was known, had been venerated for many centuries, and people still stop to stare at the place where the tomb used to be.

Aside from private drinks parties, the best-kept secret in Jeddah – and one which many Saudis remain unaware of and would probably deny if asked – is that there is a Christian cemetery in the city. It is in a street in the old city named, with predictable Arab pragmatism, 'the Street of the Cemetery of the Foreigners'. The cemetery itself is no longer in use, the last burial having taken place in the 1950s, but it continues to be maintained by several of the foreign consulates in the city. It is walled and there is a large, heavy gate preventing any view, but the curious can peer into it from some of surrounding buildings.

Osama ignored the culture and colour around him. Between university and his evening binge drinking, the sulky youth joined others from the upper classes to cruise Al Malek Road (the King's Highway) or Sultan Street aimlessly. He became a familiar sight, speeding up and down the length of Al Malek Road, the roof removed from his Mercedes SL 450. It was a pointless way to pass the hours, but for Osama and those like him, the only option available.

Religion was largely absent from Osama's life during this period. Indeed, considering that Jeddah was a city that thrived as the gateway to Mecca, he might as well have lived in New York considering the attention he paid to his faith. Before the death of his father, Osama had warmed to Islam. He had read the Koran cover to cover and, even at a young age, had grasped many of its nuances and been able to debate them articulately with adults. But the collapse of his family had led him to grasp for something palpable and more immediate. The something he found had been sycophantic friendships, alcohol and prostitutes. For over two years, between the spring of 1975 and into 1977, he maintained as similar a lifestyle as he could in his home country, albeit within the confines of the Saudi Arabian state's restrictive society. For their part, family members gave Osama a wide berth. His drinking was beyond the pale as far as many were concerned, and even his family now considered him too far gone to salvage.

However, as so often before, his life swung through another surprising 180-degree turn. An unexpected lifeline was provided by his older brother, Salim. Of all the sons of Mohammed bin Laden, Salim was considered closest to Osama – perhaps 'least distant' would be a better description.

Salim was around 25 years old in 1977 while Osama was 20. The former had passed though his teens without the streak of rebellion that affected many of his generation. A handsome and charming man, he had completed his education and joined the family business. Even at such a young age, and considering his status as son of the firm's founder, he had enjoyed a meteoric rise. Some sources later claimed that Salim was disparaging toward his younger brother, due to his supposed lowly status within the family, but this is untrue. While some of those around Salim were happy to avoid Osama because of what he had become as a youth, Salim was unwilling to write off the troubled youngster.

The catalyst to Osama's redemption came in 1977. Salim, although not dogmatically religious himself, had made plans to perform the Hajj pilgrimage and invited Osama to join him. Of all the teachings of the Koran, one of the most important is the requirement of every Muslim who can afford it to perform Hajj at least once in his lifetime, or more often as his means will allow. The Hajj is important because it allows the believer to come to the place that is both the centre of the world, as well as the site where the divine revelations collected in the Koran took place. But most important, the Hajj is a continuation of what, according to Islam, is one of the oldest religious rituals. What the believer does during Hajj is to recall events that shaped important persons in Muslim history. For believers, the entire two-week Hajj process is a moving experience. Family members recall that Salim and Osama embarked on the ritual out of a sense of duty rather than enthusiasm. Even before the problems and tragic events during the Hajj of recent years, with hundreds of thousands of people sharing the same space, it was a dusty, hot and often difficult ritual to follow.

Despite their lack of enthusiasm, the boys had rejected the luxury motor-homes and red carpet Hajj reserved for royals and VIPs. Osama, showing rare backbone, dismissed this five-star version of Hajj as being elitist and against the very principles of pilgrimage, which insisted that all men should be the same. With admirable gusto, the two departed on Hajj from their home in

Jeddah, expecting to return days later, their religious responsibilities taken care of. What happened remains a subject of debate within the Bin Laden family, but what seems to have occurred is that Osama experienced his own personal revelation.

The Prophet Muhammad had habitually visited a cave at the top of a mountain near Mecca to reflect and meditate. According to his story, during one of those visits the Angel Gabriel appeared and conveyed the divine assignment of prophethood and gave him the first revelation from the Koran. Later the angel visited him again and again, until Mohammed agreed to pursue the mission that he had been set by God.

Visiting the site of the Prophet's revelation, Osama was moved. He had read the Koran as a child and visited the site before, during earlier pilgrimages. But the energy he felt on this occasion stunned him. He would never be the same again.

It was an entirely different Osama bin Laden who arrived home in Jeddah at the end of Hajj. He now prayed five times a day, something that he had not done since his early days in Lebanon. In the days following his return he made a fresh start and did everything within his power to effect an immediate change of direction. First, he rid himself of the symbol of his old life, his yellow Mercedes SL 450 convertible. His drinking friends were similarly dispatched from his life, with a sermon on their sins, and Osama visited the mosque to deliberate with God over his loss of faith.

Within weeks Osama was growing his beard long as an indication of his piety; he threw himself into his studies at King Abdul Aziz University and immersed himself in the religious studies he had shunned for so long. The Bin Laden family celebrated Osama's return to the fold. Sadly, however, the instability that had seen him come off the rails the first time would ultimately see him lost altogether to the family and its values.

CHAPTER SEVEN

Fighting for Islam

On April 27, 1978, the People's Democratic Party of Afghanistan (PDPA), a Marxist organisation led by well-known poet Nur Mohammed Taraki, seized control of Afghanistan. Babrak Karmal and Hafizullah Amin, key figures in the unfolding drama, also assumed prominent posts in the revolutionary government. Although Marxist, the new leaders insisted that they were not controlled by the Soviet Union and that their policies did not deviate from the principles of Afghan nationalism, Islamic justice and non-aligned foreign policy. The PDPA also promised to respect all agreements and treaties signed by previous governments.

Soon after seizing power, the Taraki regime announced a traditional Marxist-Leninist reform program, including the establishment of full women's rights and the implementation of land reform. Although the reforms threatened to undermine Afghan cultural traditions, widespread resistance did not begin until the summer of 1978 when revolts spread throughout Afghanistan's provinces and cities.

On March 28, 1979, Amin became prime minister, although Taraki retained some of his political posts. When anarchy continued to spread through the country, Amin asked for, and received Soviet aid. Conditions continued to deteriorate, and on September 14, Taraki died in a confrontation with Amin's supporters.

Early in the evening of December 27, an explosion in Kabul crippled the country's communications system. Three days earlier, the Soviet Union's minister of communications, a guest in Afghanistan, had been shown the country's communications hub.

The Afghans were hoping this visit would help them obtain technical assistance from the Soviet Union. The minister's mission however was to pinpoint the centre of the system to ensure that a single act of sabotage could disrupt the system when the Soviet invasion began. After darkness set in, about 5,000 Soviet soldiers, who had been landing during the previous three days at Kabul International Airport, headed toward the presidential palace. Just after seven, the palace came under rocket fire.

That evening, under a clear sky, the region became a scene of carnage. The Alpha antiterrorist squad of the KGB, dressed in Afghan uniforms, had gone in firing and killed hundreds. Their aim was to capture strategic centres in and around the capital city, from which immediate opposition could be expected. Occupying them would ensure immediate success.

When the Soviet forces started operations in Kabul, Babrak Karmal was in Dushanbe, the capital of the Soviet republic of Tajikistan bordering Afghanistan. Using a radio frequency close to that of Radio Afghanistan, he broadcast a message in which he said: 'Today the torture machine of Amin has been broken.' In the name of the Revolutionary Council of the Democratic Republic of Afghanistan, he urged Afghans, especially the security and army officers, to remain vigilant and maintain security and order.

At 3 a.m. the news of the formation of a new government headed by Karmal was broadcast. He took up residence in the old palace in the city. Later in the morning came a second official announcement that shocked the independently-minded Afghans: 'The Democratic Republic of Afghanistan earnestly demands that the USSR render urgent political, moral and economic assistance, including military aid, to Afghanistan. The government of the USSR has accepted the proposal of the Afghan side.' It was a case of words catching up with actions as the Soviet Union had already supplied the military aid now requested – it had made the declaration possible in the first place. It was an astonishing coup de grâce by the Soviets.

In a series of live radio broadcasts over ensuing days, Karmal gave hopeful promises. He said that henceforth there would be no executions and that a new constitution would be drawn up, providing for the democratic election of national and local assemblies. He also promised that political parties would function freely and that both personal property and individual freedom would be safeguarded. In particular, he stressed that soon a government representing a united national front would be set up and that it would not pursue socialism.

Meanwhile, in Jeddah, Osama bin Laden was ensconced in a plush office getting a taste of life in the family business. Having completed his studies at King Abdul Aziz University, he had joined the family firm just months before the Soviet incursion. Life was becoming a series of tepid meetings and dreary routine. He recalled later: 'I studied economics at Jeddah University, or the so-called King Abdul Aziz University, and then worked at an early age on roads in my father's company.'

But his involvement in the company ran far deeper than simply road building. The family set aside their differences, so pleased were they to have him finally back in the fold. Osama was brought into the company at senior management level, negotiating contracts and overseeing projects at the highest level in a variety of different sectors. What was more, he seemed a natural and moved effortlessly through a transition after joining the company. His brothers were delighted and believed that their reborn sibling's ability, rather than simple nepotism, warranted putting him on a fast track into the boardroom.

He had, by now, put his life back on an even keel and exorcised the demons that had carried him into a life of vice. The new Osama spent much of his time in the mosque. He now attended many *halqas*, debating with clerics and religious scholars. One of the foremost issues of the day related to his old home, Beirut. The fact that the Lebanese had seen their country slide into civil war, Islamic scholars said, was proof that God was punishing them for their sins. Osama agreed and shared this nugget of wisdom with anyone who cared to listen. Typically, one obsession had given way to another. He found the new 'drug', religion, altogether more intoxicating and surprised his family a second time with an evolution toward a more conservative doctrine.

But even so, he was not yet disposed to being a radical. Had he been, he might have reacted differently on November 20, 1979, when 300 armed religious extremists occupied the great mosque in Mecca. During the occupation, the extremists made their message clear by berating the Saudi royal family and the country's rush to modernisation. This siege occurred just months after the Islamic revolution in Iran, in which a radical Islamic regime overthrew the Shah, a western-oriented leader. The occupation of the mosque was a message from the people to the government warning the regime of what awaited if it did not remain sufficiently conservative.

The smell of a great plot wafted around Saudi Arabia for some time. Many Middle Eastern countries were implicated while the nationals of others were involved in the action. For a time there was confusion and not a little panic in Saudi Arabia.

Osama did not condone the action. To his family in 1979 he expressed dismay and bewilderment at men taking up arms against a legitimate Saudi Arabian leadership. More than this, he roundly condemned acts of violence.

However, it was just a matter of time before his own bland, comfortable existence in the family business would pale into insignificance beside some cause. Perhaps he was subconsciously looking for a way to prove his piety, redeeming himself in the eyes of God and a deceased father whose memory he felt had been slighted by his actions. Today, family members believe that if Afghanistan had not appeared, another cause célèbre would have fired his imagination.

Whatever his reasons, overnight the fate of Afghanistan became his new obsession. He had never been there and had no ties to the country. But he was outraged: for the first time since the Second World War, non-Muslim forces had occupied a Muslim country. 'When the invasion of Afghanistan started, I was enraged and went there at once,' he told an interviewer. 'I arrived within days, before the end of 1979.'

Although his family members were startled, Osama certainly took with him the best wishes of the whole dynasty. Freeing Afghanistan was a noble Islamic cause around which the entire Arab world rallied. For the Bin Laden clan in particular, seeing their lost sheep not only return but then go on to join such a noble effort was a cause for celebration, if not a little worry for his safety. Before he departed from Saudi Arabia, Osama had been summoned by the family's senior figures. His uncle, Abdullah Awad bin Laden, had offered support. 'By God, it is our duty to support you, Osama. Anything you need for this noble cause, do not hesitate to ask.' His brothers, many now in senior positions within Bin Laden Construction, added their voices to that of Abdullah, telling their brother to contact them as soon as he could ascertain what was required.

★

For a time after the Soviet invasion of 1979, most of Afghanistan was willing to adopt a wait-and-see attitude. Around the world, diplomatic pressure was brought to bear on the Soviets, but to no avail. It was not long before trouble erupted and resistance to the invasion quickly spread nationwide.

By contrast with earlier resistance movements in Afghanistan, which had been headed by traditional leaders, resistance leaders in the late 1970s emerged from among the modern, educated members of Afghan society. They had been organised in political parties set up in the 1960s, a by-product of the transition from a traditional to a modern society. Following the overthrow of the monarchy and subsequent corrupt government rule, the parties inside the country were suppressed. Some carried on their activities from neighbouring Pakistan. Soviet invasion stirred the parties into action once again.

New resistance groups also mushroomed. In 1980, a total of 84 resistance groups of all sizes were set up in Peshawar, the main city of the remote and mountainous region of northern Pakistan that borders Afghanistan. Inside Afghanistan, about 20 militias were active by July 1981, including Islamic, nationalist, leftist and some regional.

Islamic groups constituted the backbone of the opposition movement. Some were traditional while others claimed to be fundamentalist and revolutionary. They aimed not only to oppose the invasion but also to reorganise the state and society on the basis of Islamic ideology.

Islamic fundamentalist thinking is generally traced to Sayyid Qutb, one of the most influential Muslim thinkers of the last century. An Egyptian, he spent two years in Europe and the United States between 1948 and 1950, a trip that opened his eyes to what he felt was the rot of western culture and non-Islamic ideologies. After his return to Egypt he devoted himself to the idea of bringing about a total change in the political system. Arrested by the Egyptian government, he wrote a book while in jail in which he laid out his dream of establishing an Islamic state in Egypt. Sayyid Qutb recommended that a revolutionary vanguard impose Islamisation on an Egyptian society that had deviated to Arab nationalistic ideologies. Then, he said, the movement should actively export the same system. His ideas were rigid about the many prevailing social, political and economic injustices and the need for Islamic reform.

In 1965 Sayyid Qutb published his book, *Mallem Fittareek* (Milestones). This led to his re-arrest with the accusation of conspiracy against the Egyptian President Gamal Abdel-Nasser. He was hanged on August 29, 1966. His work included 24 books, but he is most remembered for clearly defining the basic ideas of 'oneness' and sovereignty of Allah, the distinction between pure faith and the association of partners with Allah, and of Islam as the only hope for salvation of humanity.

In Afghanistan, as elsewhere in the Muslim world, Islamic fundamentalism grew in response to the transition from the traditional to the modern that set the state on the road to secularisation. The overriding concern of Afghan Islamists was to defend Islam from the encroachment of atheism in the form of the Soviet Union, and to install a fundamentalist regime in Kabul.

If the Soviets thought in 1979 that a heavy-handed approach was what was needed to subdue the population, they were badly mistaken. Indeed, it was the catalyst for the opposition. Until the invasion most Islamic organisations were more or less dormant. The Soviet invasion enabled them to come to the forefront of politics. Over the course of 1979, several moderate Islamic organisations were formed. These included the Front for National Liberation, the Revolutionary Islamic Movement, and the National Islamic Front, which were created and led from Peshawar.

Situated about 96 miles west of the Pakistani capital Islamabad, Peshawar is the spiritual home of the proud Pathan people and the capital city of Northwest Frontier province. It is the meeting place of the subcontinent and central Asia. Here ancient traditions jostle with those of the late twentieth century; the bazaar in the old city has changed little in the past hundred years except to become the neighbour to a handful of more modern buildings. Wild-looking tribesmen carry guns openly, beggars line the gutters and there are few educated souls to be found.

The outrage of the Soviet invasion immediately attracted hundreds of Arabs and Muslims from around the world, vowing to protect Islamic land, and it was to Peshawar that most began arriving at the end of 1979. Peshawar was the entry point and staging post for most 'non-Afghans' wishing to join in the war.

Even by the standards of the time, the arrival of Osama bin Laden by helicopter from Islamabad was dramatic. Where most volunteers arrived by road, those who came by air landed at the airport on the outskirts of the city. Osama touched down at the edge of the bazaar, in the centre of Peshawar. The noise and dust kicked up by the helicopter's blades sent dozens of people running for cover. If his arrival made an impression, he would continue to do so throughout the struggle against the Soviets. When a comprehensive account of the Afghan resistance and the mujahideen is published, the vital input of Osama bin Laden could fill a chapter, say loyalists. But in typical self-effacing fashion, he has commented: 'Yes, I fought there, but my fellow Muslims did much more than I. Many of them died and I am still alive.'

Osama found the resistance in disarray in Peshawar, but he was determined to join the fight and use what influence he could to help organise it. He was at least partly driven by his need to atone for his own past, as his subsequent comments in an interview with *Time* magazine suggest. 'In our religion,' he explained, 'there is a special place in the hereafter for those who participate in *jihad* [holy war]. One day in Afghanistan was like 1,000 days of praying in an ordinary mosque.'

The Afghan opposition was fractured and led by several dozen men of little standing, all attempting to use the conflict to bolster their own careers. Each was jealous of the other and worked hard not only to bloody the Soviets' nose, but also to discredit his rivals. Groups worked independently, sometimes planning attacks on the same target. To make the campaign a success, a coalition of the resistance forces was needed. This was the objective of a series of secret meetings held in Peshawar in 1980. Osama attended several as an observer and was not impressed, predicting that unity would not last. He was correct. These meetings led to a coalition of three Islamic and three moderate organisations, called the Islamic Union for the Liberation of Afghanistan. Its leader was Abdul Rasool Sayyaf, a founder of the Islamic movement who had arrived in Peshawar after being released from prison in Kabul. Osama had a lot of time for Sayyaf and responded to a plea for funds by telephoning home to ask for several hundred thousand dollars to be wired to an account in a bank in Peshawar. This was the first of tens of millions that he would plough into the Soviet resistance over the next decade.

Sayyaf also wished to keep ordinary people in Afghanistan informed of the efforts of the emerging military opposition and to wage a propaganda war. He again asked the support of Osama, who helped prepare, print and organise secret distribution of several *shabnama*, or propaganda leaflets.

One *shabnama*, of which some 100,000 copies circulated around Kabul in February 1980 – much to the anger of the Soviets – stated: 'Do not accept the orders of the infidels, wage jihad against them . . . The Muslim people and the mujahideen of Afghanistan, with the sublime cry of "Allah o Akbar" [God is great], will bring down their iron fist on the brainless head of the infidel and Communist government.

'Mujahideen Muslims, remember that our weapons are the weapons of faith. These are the strongest and most effective weapons in the world. Even the most modern weapons will be unable to resist ours. That is why, if we resist Soviet imperialism's infidel government we will be victorious, and it will suffer a crushing defeat . . . The only path to happiness is faith in the jihad and martyrdom . . . '

While efforts such as these kept Afghan spirits buoyed, within months the six members of the Islamic Union for the Liberation of Afghanistan were working alone again, as they would for some time. Alliances were made and broken. The resistance faltered. Indeed it was not until 1985, under pressure from King Fahd of Saudi Arabia, that a broad coalition – the Islamic Unity of Afghan Mujahideen – was set up, comprising the four main Islamic and three moderate groups. Many Tehran-based religious groups, Afghan nationalists, tribal unions and anti-Soviet leftists were excluded and continued to operate alone, or within faltering coalitions.

Amid the petulance of aspiring Afghan leaders in Peshawar, Osama began to see more men like himself: Arabs and Muslims wishing to offer their services. Some, like Osama, were filled with religious fervour and were indignant at the Soviet intrusion onto Muslim soil. Others were thrill-seekers who sought the excitement of battle. The Afghans, still without leadership or common direction themselves, were hard pressed to harness the extra manpower available. As time went on, the number of non-Afghans simply hanging around Peshawar, waiting for something to happen, grew.

Ultimately this was to be Osama's path into jihad. Abdul Rasool

Sayyaf, erstwhile head of the Islamic Union for the Liberation of Afghanistan, pushed his ally to form a brigade of irregulars that could support the efforts of the Islamic Union. There were other potential leaders of this effort in Peshawar at the time and Sayyaf introduced Osama to Dr Sheikh Abdullah Yusuf Azzam, a man whom *Time* magazine called 'the reviver of jihad in the twentieth century' who was to become a towering influence on Osama.

Azzam had been born in the village of Ass-ba'ah Al-Hartiyeh, in Palestine in 1941 and had gone on to become one of the most eminent leaders of jihad until his assassination in 1989. After graduating he worked as a teacher in the village of Adder in south Jordan. Later he joined Sharia College in Damascus University where he obtained a BA in Sharia (Islamic Law) in 1966. After Israel captured the West Bank in 1967, Azzam migrated to Jordan. In the late 1960s he joined the jihad against the Israeli occupation of Palestine, but later went back to his studies and graduated with a Masters degree in Sharia Law from the University of Al-Azhar in Egypt. He returned to Egypt in 1971 after being awarded a scholarship that allowed him to obtain a PhD in Principles of Islamic Jurisprudence. While in Egypt, he met and befriended Sayyid Qutb, and evolved into a new breed of Muslim activist.

He returned to Palestine and jihad, but with the purist teachings of Qutb as his guide found the struggle to be politicised and far from the Islamic war he craved. Azzam was then recruited to teach at King Abdul Aziz University in Jeddah. It was here that the Islamic firebrand first met a student named Osama bin Laden. The two briefly crossed paths, and one afternoon Osama sat through an inspirational lecture by Azzam, who was famed for telling audiences: 'Jihad and the rifle alone. No negotiation. No meetings. No dialogue. Jihad and the rifle alone . . . '

Several years later the wilds of northern Pakistan were an unusual setting for a reunion. But one afternoon in February 1980, Abdul Rasool Sayyaf, Sheikh Abdullah Yusuf Azzam and an eager and rather serious 22-year-old Osama bin Laden met in the town of Banu to decide what they could do.

This meeting marked two beginnings. One was the birth of Mekhtab al-Khadamat (MAK), a support organisation for Arab volunteers that would evolve to become the foundations of Al-Qaeda. The second, and perhaps most important outcome, was that Osama finally found the loving father figure he had so long pined for.

The pair immediately bonded into a relationship that was part mentor/disciple, part father/son. The tough and hardened Azzam knew a golden goose when he saw one and was keen to take the young, naive Osama under his wing. For Osama, in Azzam he found the spiritual guide, father, teacher and perhaps even something of a homoerotic figure on which to focus.

Whatever each took from the relationship personally, in public the partnership crackled with energy. Azzam had been marginalised on arrival in Peshawar: an intellectual on the verges of the battlefield. He rejected this and wished to play a role, almost certainly in the hope of defeating the Soviets and establishing a nation modelled on his own principles of Islamic fundamentalism.

Osama was nothing if not organised. He transformed a backroom office in Peshawar to be the nerve centre of MAK, running the organisation like a business. The office buzzed with managers, accountants and other assorted staff members. Both the Pakistani and Afghan governments provided land and resources to back the effort. Osama opened a reception centre, training camps and begun purchasing arms for his men.

Using Osama's extensive funding and enthusiasm, MAK advertised all over the Arab world for young Muslims to come and fight in Afghanistan. Recruitment offices were opened in more than 50 countries, including a half dozen US cities, London, Paris, Cairo and many other major capitals. Most western governments looked the other way, keen to support efforts to oppose the Soviets. From Osama's own purse, MAK then paid the fares of the new recruits to travel to Afghanistan, and set up facilities to train them. From all over the world he sourced and hired experts on guerrilla warfare, sabotage and covert operations in order to train his men properly.

Almost every day, a busload of foreign recruits would make its way from Islamabad, rumbling into the mountains of Peshawar to be met at a reception point. Later the recruits were dispersed to isolated camps and would begin military training. Many MAK fighters later passed through the organisation's Masadat Al-Ansar, a support network of safe houses and rest homes in which men could enjoy rest and recreation between operations.

Within less than a year, MAK had several thousand volunteers in training in its private bootcamps. By its second anniversary, it was estimated that as many as 10,000 fighters had received training at bases in Pakistan and had gone on to gain combat experience in

Afghanistan. Only a fraction of these were Afghans. Nearly half of the fighting force came from Osama's native Saudi Arabia. Others came from Algeria (roughly 3,000) and from Egypt (2,000) while of the remaining thousands, the bulk came from Yemen, Pakistan, Sudan, Lebanon, Kuwait, Turkey, the United Arab Emirates and Tunisia. Osama was able to boast that each month the camps churned out 'not hundreds, but thousands'. Even westerners joined the fight – Muslims and non-Muslims – including Americans, British, French and Australians. These recruits were initially met with some skepticism, but most applied themselves with merit and were generally accepted, especially as a white European could get close to the Russians without raising suspicions.

Recognising at once that the Afghans were lacking in infrastructure, Osama also employed the support of his family. Millions of dollars worth of heavy construction plant was sent to Pakistan and remote Afghanistan to cut roads through the mountains, build tunnels and dig trenches. Later he designed and constructed defensive tunnels and ditches along the Pakistani border. Today, Al-Qaeda's public relations spin alleges that Osama himself was driving bulldozers and exposed himself regularly to strafing from Soviet helicopter gunships, but evidence of this is purely anecdotal. What is true is that his men blasted massive tunnels into the Zazi mountains of Bakhtiar province to house hospitals and arms dumps, then cut 'the mujahideen trail' across Afghanistan to within 15 miles of Kabul.

This equipment also had a humanitarian task. In areas which the Russians had attacked or even razed, Bin Laden civil machinery would rumble in to help construct and repair hospitals, schools and homes. He also put the equipment to work to help refugees. By the end of 1980, 1.4 million Afghans had fled to Pakistan alone; by the end of 1981, the number of Afghan refugees there had reached 2.3 million. Just as he would fight to liberate their homeland, Osama was generous in supporting the displaced. He spent millions of dollars in providing emergency aid such as tents, blankets, food and transport. Other funds were diverted into constructing proper temporary housing that would be home to many thousands during a freezing winter high in the mountains between Afghanistan and Pakistan, indeed for years to come.

All of this effort – real and imagined – helped establish Osama as a hero. Ironically, while he was winning a hearts and minds campaign, the Americans, who could easily have done the same, were pouring billions of dollars into arming the opposition, a strategy that would ultimately backfire with tragic consequences.

The fact that American and western governments would look the other way as MAK openly recruited in their countries gives a reasonable indication of their policy. US President Jimmy Carter gave all signs of adopting a diplomatic approach and also made sport a hostage to the crisis saying in early 1980: 'I have sent a message today to the US Olympic Committee spelling out my own position, that unless the Soviets withdraw their troops within a month from Afghanistan, the Olympic games will be moved from Moscow to an alternate site or multiple sites, or postponed, or cancelled.'

British prime minister Margaret Thatcher denounced the Soviet intervention, while all western governments froze or suspended their relations with Kabul, leaving only a few personnel in their respective embassies to collect intelligence information. Starting with a special session on January 15, 1980, every year the UN General Assembly passed a resolution demanding that foreign forces be unconditionally withdrawn from Afghanistan. In February 1980 the United Nations Human Rights Commission condemned the Soviet aggression against the Afghan people as a flagrant violation of international law and human rights.

In 1981 Carter was defeated in the presidential election by Ronald Reagan. Still several years away from his famed 'Evil Empire' speech of 1983, Reagan was far more vociferous in his approach to tackling the Soviet Union. He continued and built on Carter's policy of quiet support for the Afghan opposition. Indeed, while the international community pontificated in the United Nations, many western governments indirectly supported MAK and the Americans channelled ever more resources in its direction.

The war in Afghanistan was the stage for one of the last major stand-offs between the two superpowers. But while the Soviets fought their corner with their own flesh and blood, the Americans acted by proxy. In what was hailed at the time as one of its most successful covert operations, the Central Intelligence Agency launched a $500 million per year campaign to arm and train the impoverished and outgunned guerrillas to fight the Soviet Union. The most promising guerrilla leaders were sought out and 'sponsored' by the CIA.

Official sources are understandably vague on the question of whether Osama bin Laden was one of the CIA's 'chosen ones'. But as time has gone on it has become abundantly clear that Osama was not only one of this small group of US-sponsored freedom fighters, but also probably the biggest mistake in the history of the CIA.

Osama was himself an open book, already spitting out hatred toward America in a way that should, somewhere, have begun to set alarm bells ringing. Of course only later would he arrive on the world stage and begin giving interviews in which he widely expounded his view on the United States, but even in 1980, when first contacts were made with the Inter-Services Intelligence agency (ISI), a shadowy Pakistani equivalent of the CIA, he made no effort to hide his leanings. In one early interview he recalled: 'I always hated the Americans because they are against Muslims . . . We didn't want the US support in Afghanistan, but we just happened to be fighting the same enemy.'

As one influential writer, Michael Moran of MSNBC, wrote: 'Yes, the West needed Josef Stalin to defeat Hitler. Yes, there were times during the Cold War when supporting one villain (Cambodia's Lon Nol, for instance) would have been better than the alternative (Pol Pot). So yes, there are times when any nation must hold its nose and shake hands with the devil for the long-term good of the planet.

'But just as surely, there are times when the United States, faced with such moral dilemmas, should have resisted the temptation to act. Arming a multi-national coalition of Islamic extremists in Afghanistan during the 1980s – well after the destruction of the Marine barracks in Beirut or the hijacking of TWA Flight 847 – was one of those times.'

As early as 1980, Osama and his organisation had come to the attention of the ISI. General Akhtar, head of the ISI from 1979 to 1987, was technically second in command in Pakistan only to President Zia-ul-Haq, while the office he was heading was considered all-powerful in Pakistan and 'the most effective intelligence agency in the Third World'. The ISI was engaged in preparing reports on all Afghan resistance activities for the Americans and it did not take too long for Osama's name to come up. The Saudi and his foreign legions were ideal conduits for the CIA, being ultimately more one dimensional in their aims. The failed Islamic Union for the Liberation of Afghanistan had been a prime example of the factionalism of the Afghans, riddled with tribal loyalties. Osama's 'Arab zealots' were more predictable, the CIA believed.

According to media reports, between $500 million and $4.5 billion a year in cash, arms or military expertise was channelled to the Afghan resistance via the CIA over ten years. Careful throughout to distance himself personally from the US, Osama needed no extra funding, so made it known to the ISI that he preferred arms. After 1980, a variety of weaponry was shipped to him, including Stinger anti-aircraft missiles. In 1986, the CIA allegedly even helped Osama build an underground camp at Khost, where he was to train recruits from across the Islamic world in the revolutionary art of jihad.

All this investment on the part of the United States seemed, at the time, a cheap price for the US to pay: countering Soviet expansionism without endangering a single American life.

For the Soviets, almost from its outset, the campaign in Afghanistan was a disaster. The commander of the Soviet land forces in Afghanistan, General Valenkov, later a member of the Russian parliament, gave only few comprehensive interviews about his troubled years there. In one of these he commented: 'The United States played a really decisive role. We had decided to send our forces into Afghanistan; the Americans knew about our decision, which was very well known. However, the Americans kept silent. They did not show any stand, for fear that we might change our opinion. They wanted us to go there. But when we entered Afghanistan they did their utmost to fully support the Afghan opposition, materially, technologically and ideologically. They exploited the presence of Afghan refugees in Pakistan and Iran. They provided every material need to establish military camps, training centres, arsenals, and bases . . . '

Aside from the American reaction, the Soviets woefully underestimated that of the Afghans themselves. Afghans are a dynamic and excitable people. When left to their own devices they go quietly about their own pursuits. When provoked they may go to any extreme and, like most people, they are outraged when their values are denigrated. Attempting to control the high, remote mountain passes and vast arid plains of Afghanistan would prove a logistical nightmare.

★

This was the pattern of Osama's war over the early years of the conflict. MAK was pulling in thousands of recruits, and every new Soviet massacre or outrage highlighted in the western media politicised hundreds more who made their way, via MAK's offices dotted around Western capitals and the Middle East, to join the conflict.

Azzam, the mastermind, never saw a Russian during the initial period of the campaign. His few personal incursions into Afghanistan were to deliver rousing sermons to the mujahideen, although he remained well away from danger. Osama had his non-combat moments in the country, but mostly busied himself at the rear, organising MAK from a comfortable office in Peshawar, only rarely venturing into the field.

At other times Osama left the theatre of operations altogether, flying from Islamabad or Karachi on to other Middle Eastern states. Here he made the deals that resulted in weapons for MAK, met the many major donors to his organisation and, quietly, established direct contact with a variety of regional governments. This was a period when be began to lay a framework of the financial networks that he would require in the future. He called up many of Mohammed bin Laden's old business contacts seeking financial aid, and over time was referred to other rich donors willing to support the cause. Many of these men, millionaires all, would go on to become long-term supporters of Islamic fundamentalism, while others would find themselves victims of Osama through extortion.

From 1980 onwards, Osama's own government in Saudi Arabia was keen to establish a relationship with this increasingly well-known freedom fighter from the upper echelons of Saudi society. On his brief trips to Riyadh, Osama was fêted by the Al Sauds. At one point he was allegedly asked to turn his hand to organising a minor anti-communist insurgency into Yemen on their behalf. Using some groups of Arab-Afghans, supported by Saudi elite White Guards, the Yemeni campaign went on for some time but achieved no tangible results and was cancelled.

This favour extended by Osama drew him closer to King Fahd. At one face-to-face meeting in the early 1980s, the King offered Osama a $90 million contract for civil works on the Prophet's Mosque in Medina. He refused and asked for more direct aid for

MAK. Supported by Crown Prince Abdullah, who was also at this meeting, King Fahd pledged and subsequently gave massive financial support to the effort to free Afghanistan.

Jamal Ismail, who later became a correspondent for the Qatar-based Al Jazirah television channel, was studying in Peshawar at the time of the crisis and became immersed in the world of the mujahideen. He met and got to know Osama bin Laden during this period. 'I used to visit the Arab relief aid offices to report news to those interested at the time. I knew him first in 1984 when he established a services centre. It was called the Mujahideen Services Centre,' said Ismail. 'At the time, Bin Laden used to finance the biggest part of the MSC budget and some Arab preachers or mujahideen at the Afghan fronts. He was not a permanent resident in Peshawar or the Afghan territories. He used to come to these areas once every three or four months. Most of the time, he used to come to Peshawar to acquaint himself with the situation and to meet with the Afghan mujahideen leaders . . . Later, things developed for him . . .'

With its better organisation and leadership the so-called 'Arab-Afghans' produced by MAK became one of the most effective branches of the mujahideen, a colloquial term given to all branches of the Afghan resistance. Lightly equipped and ultra-mobile, the mujahideen could fight almost indefinitely and quickly had the Soviets on the defensive, particularly those well-armed and well-trained units sent into the field by Osama.

The Red Army contingent in Afghanistan grew in number to about 85,000 within weeks of the invasion. The ground forces were supported by Soviet warplanes from bases in Tajikistan, Uzbekistan and Turkmenistan. Army contingents were stationed in and around cities as well as along some main roads. A protective line was drawn around the city of Kabul. The Soviets acted on the view that since resistance to their invincible army was futile, it would be a matter only of weeks or perhaps months before the country settled.

With that in mind, the authorities instructed provincial governors to establish a dialogue with those who had taken up arms. They were to persuade the militants to lay down their arms and enjoy the benefits of a peaceful life. This approach only emboldened the mujahideen, who soon appeared close to provincial capitals, killing Communist Party members or driving them into the cities. The mujahideen even controlled some main roads in the sense that they searched transport vehicles for party members and government officers. The puppet government of Babrak Karmal gradually became confined to cities.

Popular opposition erupted in cities the length and breath of Afghanistan, including Kandahar, Herat, Mazar and Balkh, and this brought more Soviet army deaths. On February 22, 1980, the population of Kabul participated in the greatest uprising in its history and by the first week of March 1980 the main roads had become unsafe for traffic in spite of the military posts stationed along them. Accompanied by contingents of the army, transport buses and other vehicles had to travel in caravans.

The success of the mujahideen indicated their support by the locals, who either opposed the regime or refused to cooperate with it. Since Soviet soldiers could not differentiate the mujahideen from non-combatants, and since they could not engage the mujahideen in battles, the occupiers attempted to detach them from their own people. Intending to destroy the rebels' support among the civilian population, they then turned against civilians, destroying their villages, their crops and irrigation systems, and even massacring peasants. Indiscriminate destruction of property and human life, civilian as well as military, thus became a feature of Soviet military policy. Protected by an unmatchable air force, armoured units were able to carry out expeditions anywhere and drive the mujahideen to the inaccessible parts of the valleys, but it was too risky for the Soviets to remain there. Indeed, they could not even stay on the plains.

Thanks in no small part to 'the mujahideen trail', a route built by Osama to within 15 miles of Kabul, even the Afghan capital was not a refuge from the rebels for either the Soviets or their puppet government. Kabul was vulnerable from the east, west, and south. After nightfall the rebels easily entered the suburbs unnoticed from the hilly districts that surrounded the city. They kidnapped party men from their homes, destroyed security posts, or fought firefights with patrolling units. After the invasion, shots were heard almost every night. Sometimes the firing was intense, lasting for hours.

The shots heard on the night of October 8, 1980, in the suburban towns of Niaz Beg and Fazil Beg were part of a fully-fledged armed engagement between the opposing forces. Only when armoured units reached the area did the mujahideen leave. A week later shots were exchanged between the rebels and a military unit of the regime quartered close to Macroryan, Soviet-built blocks of apartments where Soviet advisers and top party and government officials lived.

The city's night security deteriorated still further. During the first week of July 1981, platoons of Osama's Arab-Afghans began to enter the city in large numbers, although the puppet government and its masters had taken new security measures. Losses were so high that Soviet forces were reluctant to patrol at night, even in tanks, because of armour-piercing rockets that Osama had obtained on the black market. The government security forces reportedly fired toward the sky, thus avoiding confrontation with the rebels. Gunfire was heard not only in the outskirts of Kabul but also in places such as Chindawal in the centre of the city, accompanied by the cry 'Long live Afghanistan!'

From the sidelines, Osama revelled in the success of the opposition and especially the exploits of his foreign irregulars. The men produced by his camps were single-minded and brave, considered the finest in the resistance and a credit to their 'commander' who was tireless in his search for better weapons and more supplies. He toured the Middle East on a fund-raising mission, dining with major donors, courting corporate support and in the process raising hundreds of millions of dollars to finance the campaign. At one point during the early years of the conflict, MAK was estimated to be raking in $25 million a month in donations.

Only occasionally did he relent from his tireless travelling. Then, when he could escape the deskwork in Peshawar to tour his own camps, deep in the Afghan mountains, he found the rush of adrenaline intoxicating. He knew the risks, but it was worth it. 'Those who risked their lives to earn the pleasure of God are real men. They managed to rid the Islamic nation of disgrace. We hold them in the highest esteem,' he said of those who became casualties in the fight. When groups of fighters returned to camp following action they found him eager to learn all the details of their operation. But it was rare for him to set foot in the direction of the Russian troops or areas of danger.

But if Osama was fighting Soviet oppression vicariously during the early 1980s, he was undergoing a personal evolution toward taking up arms and going into the field himself. Stories about him make much of a supposed turning point in his life when a camp in which he was staying was discovered and attacked by Soviet helicopter gunships. A shell is said to have fallen at his feet, but not exploded. If this did happen – and Osama claims that it did – it most likely occurred after he emerged as a fighter. Prior to his taking up arms he was never involved in a full-blown encounter with the Soviets. Never one to play down a good myth, however, the PR-conscious Osama still makes the most of the incident. What is apparent is that he tired of playing what he saw as a peripheral role. As time went on it was noticeable that his questioning of those returning from action became almost an interrogation. He was intrigued. The paymaster felt left out.

More than this, Osama shared with many others a deepening sense of frustration. The Soviets were largely pinned down in the cities now, apart from brief forays into the countryside using their superior hardware. The fighting had reached a standoff, the rebels picking off Soviets in the cities under the cover of darkness and the Soviets and dwindling government forces occasionally launching attacks into the rebels. While the world was surprised at the success of the mujahideen in the face of overwhelming Soviet manpower and technology, in Afghanistan and Pakistan a groundswell of opinion was building that while the Soviets remained on the defensive, more gains were possible.

Gradually, despite the relative successes of the rebels' commando-style operations, Osama and others within the opposition leadership began to feel that a more aggressive approach was needed. This desire was the catalyst to greater cooperation between the various Afghan factions, and to Osama coming to the conclusion that he would move into the front lines. He had formed, financed and armed arguably the most effective section of the mujahideen. Now it was time for him to see some real action.

CHAPTER EIGHT

Birth of an Icon

'Once I was only 30 yards from the Russians. They were trying to capture me. I was under bombardment but I was so peaceful in my heart that I fell asleep. This experience has been written about in Islam's earliest books. I saw a 120 mm mortar shell land in front of me, but it did not blow up. Four more bombs were dropped from a Russian plane on our headquarters but they did not explode. We beat the Soviet Union. The Russians fled.'

This is how a misty-eyed Osama recalled the closest he came to death during his decade-long fight for the freedom of Afghanistan. The story cannot be confirmed independently, but has been built into one of the many myths that surround him after he had taken up a Kalashnikov and gone into battle at the head of his band of fighters.

'He was a hero to us because he was always on the front line, always moving ahead of everybody else,' recalled Hamza Mohammed, a Palestinian volunteer in Afghanistan, quoted in *Time* magazine. 'He not only gave his money, but he also gave himself. He came down from his palace to live with the Afghan peasants and the Arab fighters. He cooked with them, ate with them, dug trenches with them. That was Bin Laden's way.'

Osama was nothing if not clever and carefully cultivated his image. Despite his largesse in supporting the effort, he knew full well that, while he was considered a fine man for showing such commitment, in western terms, he was also thought of as a lightweight – the millionaire on the fringes. He did not like this image and when he finally made the decision to take an active military role, it was with a great deal of forethought and planning.

After discussing the issue at length with his mentor, Azzam, he decided to avoid the heroic but dated image favoured by most mujahideen commanders, dashing around the countryside in jeeps barking orders. These men seldom saw any real action, but were always there when foreign television camera crews showed up. Osama detested such leaders, singularly seeking publicity to further their own political ambitions. He decided, somewhat cynically perhaps, upon a man-of-the-people approach. It has served him well to the present day. His men warmed to him quickly when he showed that he was willing to be one of them, getting dirty, hiding out in caves and taking on the most basic of duties.

With the rise in March 1985 of Mikhail Gorbachev, the scene was set for changes within the Soviet Union. In Afghanistan this change was marked by the replacement of Babrak Karmal in May 1986 by Mohammed Najibullah, first as general secretary of the PDPA and then as president of the Revolutionary Council. This change came after Gorbachev publicly described the Soviet war in Afghanistan as a 'bleeding wound', and floated a new Soviet policy that they would have troops withdrawn after a settlement had been worked out. According to a rumour circulated at the time, Gorbachev had given his military one year to suppress the resistance. If they failed, so the rumour went, he would then try to resolve the issue through diplomacy. Whatever the truth, for about a year after Gorbachev's rise the Soviets carried out the severest operations they had undertaken in Afghanistan.

Despite high hopes that Najibullah could bring stability and engineer a peaceful withdrawal by the Soviets, the situation in the country remained basically unchanged. During this period the Soviets followed first an 'enclave strategy' and later a 'scorched earth' policy. Under the former, the Soviets undertook less ambitious campaigns, restricting themselves to the defence of military bases, military installations, key cities, major roads, and communications, avoiding as far as possible countrywide campaigns. Only during the winter months were they consistently able to extend their defences, push their perimeter outwards, and capture mujahideen bases and arms in the hills surrounding Kabul. This was because the lightly-outfitted rebels could not sustain themselves through the cold Afghan winters and were forced to withdraw and wait for spring.

By 1985, though, this glaring chink in their armour was being tackled. Friendly governments, NGOs and private donors continued their financial and logistical support, but for the first time during the summer and autumn in 1985 the various mujahideen used some of their resources to prepare. Osama imported thousands of thick jackets, snow boots and ski tents. From Europe, his network got hold of 50,000 mini disposable gas stoves that would enable his men to heat drinks and cook food in the depths of a freezing and often snow-bound Afghan winter. This enabled them to remain in the field in large numbers, hiding out in remote caves by day and attacking by night.

Equally important, at last Osama's network began to find reliable, continuous sources of replacement arms and munitions. His men now utilised bazookas that would knock out a tank and heavy machine guns that could sustain a long barrage of fire. They were also supplied some relatively primitive SAM-7 missiles. Each man carried a Kalashnikov.

Now more involved on the ground in Afghanistan, Osama attached himself to a base named al-Ansar, 'the Lions' Den', by his fighters. He later took direct command over it. The Arab-Afghans of al-Ansar were among the toughest and most battle-hardened in Afghanistan. Among them were many who would work for Osama in later life and whose career paths were to intersect with their leader's. These included two sons of Sheikh Omar Abdel-Rahman, the blind cleric later convicted of the original World Trade Center bombings; Mahmud Abouhalima, who planned the World Trade Center attack and trained others to carry it out; and Ahmad Ajaj, who entered the USA on a false Pakistani passport, carrying bomb-making manuals and other material for the bombers.

Al-Ansar had been one of the first camps set up by Osama's MAK in 1980, deep in the mountains that overlooked the strategically important city of Jalalabad. Since then al-Ansar had entered mujahideen folklore, its Arab-Afghans overcoming the might of the Soviets time and again. A mixture mainly of Algerian, Egyptian, Pakistani and Turkish recruits, these men prided themselves on their reputation. Although probably unsure of the man who was their nominal leader, who had no experience in the field, they quickly warmed to him after he joined them in the spring of 1986.

April that year saw one of the key battles of the campaign to free Afghanistan. Informed of a major offensive against their Afghan allies, the men of the camp rushed southwest to the province of Paktia to join in the defence of a rebel base from a joint Soviet–Afghan government assault. The Red Army had occupied the base in Zhawara, near the city of Khost, but they retreated within hours under a heavy barrage of fire. This battle proved to be one of the turning points and transformed the mujahideen.

The assault cost the Soviets and their Afghan allies 13 helicopters and aircraft. More than a hundred soldiers of the regime were captured, and more than 1,500 either killed or wounded. Osama told the ABC television network later in an interview: 'We went through vicious battles with the Russians. It is enough to just say with Russians: they are known in the West for their brutality and viciousness. They used poisonous gas against us, and I was subjected to this. They used airplanes against our position, and we lost many fighters, but we were able to deter many commando attacks, unlike anything before.'

The better-equipped mujahideen now had a fighting chance and for the Red Army this meant only increased losses. Emboldened by this, the Arab-Afghans began to take on bigger, more daring missions. On September 25, 1986, an Arab-Afghan fighter named Abdul Ghaffar became the first man to successfully fire a Stinger missile when he brought down a helicopter landing at the Jalalabad airfield. It was another turning point of the campaign. From then on Stingers partly neutralised Soviet aerial offensives, one of their key strategic advantages.

The same year Osama's star shone still brighter when he and a few dozen Arab-Afghan defenders reportedly fought off a Soviet onslaught in a town called Jaji, not far from the Pakistan border. To Arabs, it was one of the first demonstrations that the Russians could actually be beaten. Later in 1986, he led an offensive against Soviet troops in the battle of Shaban. Vicious hand-to-hand fighting claimed heavy mujahideen casualties, but his men succeeded in pushing the Red Army out of the area. The nominal leader of the attack, Osama, was hailed as one of the brightest commanders in the field.

The first the Bin Laden family knew of Osama's self-promotion from backroom to front lines came during this time. Some time in late 1986, while on a brief campaign swing through the Gulf to raise funds for his MAK organisation, he arrived in Jeddah for two days. Uncles and brothers who hurried to his home to see him discovered their kinsman bruised and somewhat battered. Osama's feet were raw, his body was criss-crossed with scars, he had lost weight and looked drawn. He laughed off concerns for his safety, and after only a brief stay was off again on his travels.

In the campaign against the Red Army there were setbacks, however. But even these have been cleverly worked into a web of half-truths, exaggerations and plain lies that added to Osama's personal mystique. In one interview, he recalled an occasion in 1987 when the Russians finally caught up with their long-time adversaries, the men of al-Ansar. Discovering the whereabouts of an al-Ansar camp in the remote mountains, not far from Jalalabad, a full-scale assault was organised. 'The Afghan fighters who were there withdrew when the battle, the air attacks and the landing of paratroopers began. The Arab fighters, led by Abdullah Azzam and myself and a group that, as far as we knew, did not exceed 35 persons, held our ground for two weeks of fierce fighting . . . ' It is a wonderful story of success against all odds. However, like many tales of Osama, it is economical with facts to the point of pure fantasy. Abdullah Azzam, for example, while an inspirational figure, seldom set foot in Afghanistan and never reached a forward position.

Anecdotal evidence such as this helped boost the Bin Laden fairy tale, and a vast body of stories about his heroics under fire and his leadership continue to circulate. As Osama's genuine – if rather more pedestrian – accomplishments were embellished and added to those more fantastic accounts, a personality cult started to develop around him. He knew this and was happy to allow his supporters to expand on his legend. His few public utterances were designed to build his credibility and offer a false modesty. He said: 'I was never afraid of death. As Muslims, we believe that when we die, we go to heaven. Before a battle, God sends us tranquillity.'

Away from Osama's self-deluding myths, the Red Army was receiving an ever-greater drubbing. Utilising to the full their SAM-7 missiles, according to the estimates of Pakistan's ISI: 'During the summer of 1987 the mujahideen hit an average of 1.5 aircraft of varied description every day.' By the end of 1987 the military situation had deteriorated to the extent that even Afghanistan's puppet president Najibullah admitted that 80 per cent of the countryside and 40 per cent of towns were outside the control of his government.

Faced with mounting attacks by the mujahideen in 1987, Najibullah was ordered by his masters in Moscow to sue for peace. On January 15, 1987, while inaugurating the policy of 'national reconciliation', Najibullah invited political groups for a dialogue about the formation of a coalition government. He also invited leaders of the Islamic groups, who promised 'the continuation of armed jihad until the unconditional withdrawal of Soviet troops, the overthrow of the atheistic regime, and the establishment of an independent, free and Islamic Afghanistan'. For a year Najibullah tried everything within his power to prop up his government and keep the Soviets in Afghanistan, wooing and fighting the Islamists at the same time.

Throughout this period, the reputation of Osama and his men grew. The mujahideen as a whole was taking the war to the Soviets, who found their casualty rate rising at an unacceptable rate. Moscow, which had already indicated that it wanted out of the morass, had little patience

On February 10, 1988, Soviet diplomat Yuli Vorontsov informed Pakistani President Zia ul-Haq in Islamabad that 'Soviet troops would be withdrawn, with or without national reconciliation and with or without the Geneva settlement'. Peace talks had been going on in Geneva at intervals since 1982 under the supervision of the UN secretary general's personal envoy, Diego Cordovez. On April 14, 1988 a deal was signed by representatives of the governments of Pakistan and Afghanistan. Secretary of State George Shultz and the Soviet Union's foreign minister Edward Shevardnadze were present as the guarantors of the Geneva Accords. The Soviets undertook to withdraw their troops in nine months, completing the movement on February 15, 1989.

It was an extraordinary victory. Even after a decade, the mujahideen remained dozens of groupings of tens of thousands of men. Most carried little more than a Kalashnikov rifle backed up by a few bazookas, SAM-7 missiles and Stingers. Yet they had not only held off the Soviet armed forces, but forced them into retreat with heavy losses.

Between April 1988 and February 1989, the mujahideen

continued to jab at the Soviets. This was not just hitting an enemy in retreat, however. Moscow may have been happy to leave, but it was still doing everything it could to ensure the survival of the puppet regime it had installed a decade earlier. This plan was ill-founded, and Gorbachev knew it. Even before his troops had left Afghanistan, the Najibullah administration was crumbling.

The date April 14, 1988, the day the Geneva Accords were signed, was a watershed in Osama's life. At last an end was in sight. During the latter months of 1988 he continued his war with the same force that had established him as an icon of the struggle. He told family that he was delighted. After so long away from Jeddah, perhaps he even longed for his home and swapping the basic meals and dank tents of his frontline camps for the luxury of good food, a comfortable home and peaceful office. But there was still a job to be done during the intervening period, and the Arab-Afghans resolved to fight the Red Army until the last soldier was off Afghan soil. Osama also wished to aid the indigenous peoples to replace the puppet government with a representative body. Back in his safe office in northern Pakistan, Osama's mentor, Abdullah Azzam, was still preaching Islamic fundamentalism and hoped that a truly radical movement would take power.

While Osama was initially euphoric at the achievements of the mujahideen, all too quickly his happiness gave way to feelings of betrayal. The dream of the mujahideen was betrayed by the same swaggering commanders he had gone to such lengths to distance himself from. Even before the Soviets had left, before the battle to bring down the Najibullah government had even begun, they had started jostling for power. Worst of all, in Osama's eyes, large sections of the mujahideen now replaced the Soviets as oppressors of the Afghans.

As the withdrawal date approached, the Kabul regime rearranged its forces, setting the stage for events such as those that followed the evacuation of the government headquarters of the outlying province of Kunar. The mujahideen occupied it on October 11, 1988 and quickly showed signs of what could be expected. Thousands of fighters immediately made their way to Kunar. They looted and torched all buildings and properties that had been used by the government or Soviets. When there were no more of these targets to attack, the mujahideen turned on the local population, reasoning that by not taking up arms against the Red Army they were collaborators. Old men were murdered, women raped and children kidnapped, by the same men who had claimed to represent them and have fought for their freedom in the name of Islam. The inhabitants of the plain fled.

News of the Kunar disaster soon carried to Osama in his camp. If it was a disappointment, it was one that would only get worse as groups of mujahideen vented their anger on Afghan citizens and took retribution against them all across the country.

In late 1988, 74 officers and soldiers from government forces surrendered to the border authorities of Pakistan and requested protection. They were illegally handed over to a commander of the Hizb-e-Islami of Khalis, a section of the mujahideen. Later they were found dead on the Afghan side of the border having been bound and shot in the back of their heads.

Osama did his utmost to ensure that the Arab-Afgans were not involved in such outrages and for the most part it was the Afghan mujahideen who exacted revenge against their own people. But inevitably the bloodlust got into some of his men. In early January 1989, when the mujahideen overran the military post of Shewa, it was Arabs who slaughtered two officers who had surrendered and took sixteen women as war booty, while five other women were taken by members of two Islamic groups. Public perception of the mujahideen as saviours started to change as the jihad degenerated into a scrabble for spoils and revenge.

Gradually the government began to collapse as its Soviet allies pulled out. General Valenkov, commander of Russian ground troops in Afghanistan, recalled: 'We evacuated Afghanistan in circumstances that I vividly remember. There were lots of flowers. Similarly, the people were tearful. Of course, this was not the sentiment of all Afghans. Those who were hurt by the war or suffered a setback as a result of it had completely different sentiments. Nonetheless, most Afghans had fears about the repercussions of our withdrawal from the country. They even tried to obstruct this withdrawal. If we are to talk about Afghan leaders, they did not want this at all. I am talking about Najibullah and others.'

The departing Soviet troops left behind a huge arsenal of sophisticated weapons that fell into the hands of thousands of Islamic warrior factions. Such largesse would fuel civil strife for decades to come.

Unlike the Soviet Union, the United States, having achieved its goal of forcing the withdrawal of Soviet troops, gradually disengaged themselves, US intelligence services quietly claiming a moral victory. The error of this strategy would only become apparent years later. As former Secretary of State Madeleine Albright told CNN in more recent times: 'Basically the United States walked away from Afghanistan once the Soviets pulled out, leaving a vacuum. We have a tendency to kind of walk away before the job is done.'

No one had benefited more from US support than Osama and his network, yet he dismissed their input, saying: 'This is a US attempt to distort things. Praise be to God who made their plots backfire on them. Every Muslim who sees discrimination begins to hate the Americans, the Jews and Christians. This is part of our religion and faith. Since I became aware of things around me, I have been in a war . . . What they claim has never happened. Saying that they supported jihad or fighting, it became clear to us that this support was from the Arab states, particularly the Gulf states . . .

'The Americans are lying when they say that they cooperated with us in the past, and we challenge them to show any evidence of this. The truth of the matter is that they were a burden on us and on the mujahideen in Afghanistan. There was no agreement on this. We were doing our duty in support of Islam in Afghanistan, although this duty used to serve, against our desire, the US interests.'

Despite victory, the Afghanistan campaign ended with a bitter twist for Osama personally, who was manipulated and prodded into participating in the worst defeat suffered by the mujahideen. Within a fortnight of the Soviet withdrawal it appeared that the Soviet Union's puppet government had been bequeathed enough military hardware to survive in its heartlands, particularly in major cities such as Kabul, almost indefinitely. According to reports that have since emerged, the governments of Pakistan, Saudi Arabia and the United States pushed the leadership of the mujahideen to launch an all-out assault on Jalalabad, believing that taking this city would launch an ongoing battle that would lead to the fall of Kabul. Despite information that Jalalabad was very well-defended and that the garrison was well-armed, these three powers manipulated the mujahideen into agreeing to their plan. Osama was convinced and committed several battalions of his Arab-Afghans to the assault, which took place in March 1989.

The Afghan government had significant artillery in Jalalabad and, over a period of days, resisted the assault effectively. Thousands of mujahideen were killed, among them hundreds of Osama's men. It was a slaughter and he never forgave the foreign governments for their role in forcing the issue. Within days he had returned to Peshawar and poured his heart out to Azzam. Azzam was incensed and immediately began issuing statements drawing attention to the massacre and its roots, accusing Pakistan, Saudi Arabia and the United States of treachery. This was a mistake. The powers he publicly blamed for the Battle of Jalalabad were in no mood to hear themselves being linked to such a defeat. Within eight months Azzam was dead: his car blown up by a bomb as he was driving with his two sons to the mosque for Friday prayers in Peshawar.

Osama was distraught. The same day of the death of his mentor, Osama is known to have telephoned his mother. He was crying and virtually unintelligible. Between sobs he explained: 'They have killed him . . . Sheikh Abdullah . . . he's gone now . . . he has gone to God . . . '

Suspicion has often fallen upon Osama for the death of Azzam, with many writers hinting darkly that the two partners were preparing to move in different directions. But given his devotion to the man and his post-assassination reaction, this seems unlikely. Azzam was a father figure and mentor to him. Under his wing, Osama had found meaning and purpose. The removal of this calming influence pushed him, at the age of 32, into a period of uncertainty. Following the death of Azzam, Osama told a journalist: 'He motivated the nation from the farthest east to the farthest west. During that blessed jihad, the activities of Sheikh Abdullah Azzam, may God bless his soul, increased . . . The sheikh proceeded from the narrow, regional, and often city atmosphere that was familiar to Islamists . . . to the larger Islamic region and began to motivate the true Islamic world. We and the sheikh were in one boat . . . '

Without Azzam to steer that boat, Osama was soon in troubled water.

CHAPTER NINE

Blowback

'It was worth it.' This was a simple statement of fact made by Senator Orrin Hatch, a senior Republican on the Senate Intelligence Committee. Senator Hatch was commenting on the decision to fund and arm rebel opposition to the Soviet Union in Afghanistan. 'Those were very important, pivotal matters that played an important role in the downfall of the Soviet Union,' he said.

While the United States had a clear, well-defined policy aim during the conflict, little thought, or plainly not enough thought, had been given to the aftermath. The billions of dollars poured into supporting the mujahideen turned a disorganised army into a coherent fighting machine.

Certainly the CIA had its reasons for channelling much of this aid to the Arab-Afghans in preference to indigenous fighters. However with the strict Islamic fundamentalist creed and hostility to the West openly espoused by the leaders into whose hands these funds and sophisticated weaponry were being placed, the long-term implications might have been considered more carefully.

With the withdrawal of the Soviet armed forces during January and February 1991, Osama bin Laden's Arab-Afghans saw a reduction in activity. Osama led many small raids, picking off a few soldiers and adding to Moscow's agony by downing aircraft and destroying tanks. But for the most part the gradual departure of the Soviets was a reason for many fighters to think about returning to their respective homes. The battle for power that the Afghan mujahideen were now beginning to engage in was not a fight for their colleagues in the foreign legions. Their job, removing the non-Islamic scourge from Islamic soil, was largely over.

Gradually, over the first half of the year, Osama began the process of shipping his men home. Estimates at the time placed the total numbers, by this stage, at around 5,000 Saudi Arabians, 3,000 Yemenis, 2,000 Egyptians, 2,800 Algerians, 400 Tunisians, 370 Iraqis, 200 Libyans, and scores of Jordanians. Other countries well represented by their citizens were the United Arab Emirates, Sudan, Iraq, Lebanon and Syria. Estimates of the total number of Arab-Afghans trained during the struggle against the Red Army vary between 15,000 and 22,000. That a vast majority of these were recruited, transported, trained, armed and campaigned by Osama's organisation shows the sheer size of his achievement.

Across North Africa and into the Arabian Peninsula and the rest of the Middle East, thousands of battle-hardened Muslim zealots returned home. The impact of this was not immediate, but was as certain as if a ticking time bomb had been set under many regimes of the Arab world. Throughout the Middle East, US allies and foes alike would feel the effects of the CIA's generosity in Afghanistan. It is likely that there would have been Islamic eruptions whether there had been Arab veterans of the Afghan war or not. But what is undeniable is that these experienced warriors gave Islamic fundamentalism a powerful arm that they would not otherwise have had.

The trail of terror and instability appeared in Algeria. A bloody civil war hit the country after January 1992 following the removal of President Bendjedid, when the army denied power to the Islamic Salvation Front (FIS). The FIS regrouped into an armed wing, the Islamic Army Movement (GIA). Later hard-liners from the GIA joined various extremist groups. These groups launched attacks against regime targets, particularly police, security personnel and government officials. Assassinations and bombings were carried out. Since 1992, at least 70,000 people are believed to have died in Algerian violence.

One of the GIA's leaders was Tayeb al-Afghani, reportedly one of Osama's aides de camp in al-Ansar. After his capture in November 1992, the GIA was led by Sid Ahmed Mourad, alias Jaafar el-Afghani, another of Osama's lieutenants in the field. Fellow GIA leader Sherif Gousmi, known as Abu Abdallah Ahmed, is another who was recruited through a MAK office in Algiers to go to Afghanistan.

Kamar Kharban, a former Algerian army officer who became a

mujahideen commander in Afghanistan, boasts at having fought alongside Osama in the Battle of Jalalabad. Kharban is now an FIS leader and reportedly manages a gun-running network in the German cities of Aachen, Berlin, Hamburg and Munich.

Egypt is unarguably the greatest ally of the United States in the Arab world. Yet it is a country racked by problems with Islamic fundamentalists, a great many of whom are Osama's former cohorts. Indeed, today they receive funding and supply from their former boss. The most prominent of these groups is Egyptian Islamic Jihad, led by Mohammed Shawky Islambouli, brother of army Lieutenant Khalid Islambouli, who led the group that assassinated Egyptian president Anwar Sadat in October 1981. Mohammed Islambouli was sentenced to death in absentia by an Egyptian court in December 1992 for plotting to overthrow the government of present premier Hosni Mubarak. Egyptian Islamic Jihad claimed credit for Egypt's worst terrorist attack, the murder of 58 foreign tourists and wounding of 26 others in November 1997 in the Valley of the Kings near Luxor.

Other countries which have suffered in the aftermath of the Afghanistan conflict have been Tajikistan, Sudan, Eritrea, Yemen – where the fundamentalist al-Islah, or Islamic Reform Party, is active – and Palestine. One renowned Arab-Afghan is Mohammed Nazzal, a computer expert who studied in Pakistan and is now a leader of Hamas, the Palestinian fundamentalist faction which, in addition to fighting Israel, has been linked with attempts to topple the Jordanian government.

In Europe, the genocide of Muslims in Bosnia attracted Osama's former men. Around 300 Arab-Afghans organised into a unit known as the Guerrillas, and operated alongside the Bosnian 3rd Corps in Zenica.

In the Far East, terrorism is being spread by men trained and battle-tested in Afghanistan. Some are believed to be leading groups in the Muslim provinces of western China, while in the Philippines the extremist Muslim Abu Sayyaf faction – named after an Afghan mujahideen hero – is fighting for Muslim self-rule in the Mindanao region.

Bin Laden family members say that Osama, for his part, may have had no plans to remain permanently within the Islamic fundamentalist movement. In the wake of the assassination of

Azzam and the fiasco of the Battle of Jalalabad, all his communications with Jeddah indicated that he was tired of playing politics. But he was a perfectionist, and intended to tie up loose ends in his organisation before re-establishing himself in Jeddah.

Near the end of the struggle in Afghanistan, as men had started returning home, Osama spent time at a base he had purchased in northern Pakistan, about a mile from Peshawar. Bait al-Ansar (House of the Lions' Den) initially comprised a large stone house and a number of outbuildings, but had grown as extensions and new buildings were added over the course of the campaign. It had been the arrival point for many volunteers heading for training and ultimately the war zone. For others it had been an exit point; from there they were driven or flown to Islamabad or Karachi to connect with scheduled civilian flights home.

Well into the conflict, as the numbers of MAK men grew, so did the administrative demands on the group. In 1988, such were the numbers of fighters joining him and the demands upon his own time, that Osama fell behind in his previously meticulous documentation. It concerned him that he was not able to offer answers to families inquiring about their loved ones, many of whom had been fighting in Afghanistan for years, cut off from the outside world. Ever the technocrat, during that year Osama organised an administration department. This would be responsible for tracking the movements of fighters between Bait al-Ansar, training camps and forward attack groups over the border in Afghanistan. As it was handling sensitive information, he decreed that the department should not be based in any of the well-established MAK offices dotted around Pakistan, but in the well-defended Bait al-Ansar. He then renamed Bait al-Ansar with its more modern and better-known name, Al-Qaeda (the base).

The signing of the Geneva Accords on April 14, 1988, brought an end to ten years of a war of occupation in Afghanistan and quickly changed the entire atmosphere within the Arab-Afghan community. After years on the edge, surviving on their nerves, the foreign fighters found themselves adrift with an uncertain future. Although there were never the splits that shattered the Afghan portion of the mujahideen during this period, these men had a decision to make. Many of those who could opted to return to their homes, others to stay in Afghanistan.

The future was something that greatly concerned Osama and his partner Dr Abdullah Azzam during 1989. The firebrand Palestinian wished to retain a nucleus of their organisation in the north of Pakistan and friendly areas of Afghanistan, training the men who would lead his Islamic revolution. With Osama's money to support him, he saw himself as the leader of a Sunni Islamic revolution, somewhat akin to the Shiia-based Islamic revolution that has swept through Iran. Azzam believed that the people were ready to rise up in pursuit of an Islamic utopia. Osama agreed to underwrite Azzam's vision.

Everything changed with the death of Azzam in November 1989. Without Azzam's passion driving him on, Osama settled for a different dream.

The format of Al-Qaeda as a movement was not exactly planned, but evolved over time. With fighting in Afghanistan winding down, Arab-Afghan fighters were coming in from the mountains. Usually, their first stopping point in Pakistan was Al-Qaeda. The base was bathed in a mixed atmosphere of back-slapping euphoria and, not surprisingly, sadness. These were men who had trained and fought together, shared the pain of their comrades' deaths, prayed, eaten and slept together. Naturally there was a bond.

It was during this period that the ideas and aims of Al-Qaeda began to take shape in Osama's mind. His men might have been drained physically and emotionally, but all came out of the mountains believing just as fervently in the principles that had brought them there. Over meals of 'gritty bread, cheese and tea', Osama probed them. He was also networking. Many were handed the telephone numbers of his office in Jeddah, an office he himself had not seen for some years, and instructed to stay in touch. Others were informally promised financial support after spelling out their ideas for exporting Islamic struggle at home.

Years before, most men had left behind jobs and families to travel into the unknown of Afghanistan. Through MAK, Osama had paid a salary to their families. For this kindness and support, he had bought their loyalty. Now, sitting on the worn cushions of his majlis at Al-Qaeda, Osama heard clearly the dreams and aspirations of those who had fought so valiantly for Islamic fundamentalism. 'We deal with the Islamic world as a single state and cooperate with people on a basis of righteousness and piety as far as we can,' he said. 'We are a single nation with one religion.'

The quality time that Osama spent with his men – and the support he offered them – would also ensure that he had strong ties with men who would go on to be key allies as leaders of like-minded fundamentalist groups dotted around the Middle East. Many were returning to their own countries charged, more than ever before, with Islamic fundamentalism and a desire to topple their own western-influenced secular governments in favour of an Islamic regime. They could use the knowledge gained in the Afghan war to set up guerrilla and terror cells, to make bombs, plan armed raids and assassinate individual targets.

However, in many Arab countries, despite being hailed in many quarters as conquering heroes, these war veterans were not at all welcome, and governments kept a close eye on them. Saudi Arabia, for example, was reported to have been delighted to have thousands of potential troublemakers busy outside of its borders. Other states were more sympathetic and supportive of their citizens. In Sudan the government gave its former fighters jobs, helped them to set up training camps, and appointed some to government posts. Sudan also willingly took in many Arab-Afghans who were barred from returning to their own countries.

With continued support promised by Osama, others opted to return to Afghanistan. In the power vacuum caused by civil war in the country, many mujahideen training camps continued to operate, under Osama's sponsorship. These would become the practice grounds and homes to a new phenomenon: Islamic mercenaries. These fighters could be sent to fight wherever they were needed. Over future years Arab-Afghan veterans played a role in Islamic struggles in theatres of war as diverse as Somalia, Bosnia, Kosovo, and Chechnya.

They were also the nucleus of Al-Qaeda.

What is not altogether clear is what plans if any Osama had for himself at this point. Indications he gave to the family were that he was coming home, his job done, and that he intended to go back full time into the family business. This is what the family believes was always his plan.

Throughout his time fighting the Soviets in Afghanistan, he maintained intermittent contact with his kin in Jeddah. At times, up to a month would go by without him calling one of his brothers, his mother or his wife. But, strangely, even at the height of the conflict, he never forgot a birthday. During Eid, the Islamic festival comparable to Christmas, gifts from Osama would be delivered. At other times, whenever he was touring the Gulf states and Middle East raising funds and support, he loved nothing better than to arrive unexpectedly at home as a surprise.

There was also one visit home that took place amid tragedy. In 1988 the eldest of Mohammed bin Laden's sons, Salim, was killed in an accident while piloting an ultralight craft in Texas, aged just 36. It was Salim who had pulled Osama back from the brink of self-destruction and he had a special bond with his eldest brother. In little more than a year, he lost Salim and Dr Abdullah Azzam, the two individuals to whom he felt closest.

As the Red Army began to plan their withdrawal strategy, it appears Osama was doing the same. During the second half of 1988 and 1989, he began to make contact with his uncles and brothers more regularly. With more time on his hands, he discussed the family business at length. From these conversations, Osama offered every intention that he wished to wind up his activities with Al-Qaeda and return to the office he had occupied before the war.

There, amid the oak furnishings and potted plants of the Bin Laden Group's head office in Jeddah, he apparently wished to slot back in, dealing with clients and managing projects. No mention was made of financing a regional terror network. During early summer in 1989, Osama telephoned his mother to say he was coming home.

CHAPTER TEN

Homecoming of a Hero

Osama bin Laden flew into Jeddah quietly during the summer of 1989 aboard a private plane. He was not happy. The Red Army had finally pulled out of Afghanistan in the spring, but to his misery he had seen the country he now thought of as his second home descending into civil war. The mujahideen, of whom he had been so proud, were now fighting among themselves for scraps of power. Amid a breakdown in the rule of law, news of the murders of civilians, of rape and pillage, had now become commonplace. To a man who believed wholeheartedly in the cause and the country, it was a painful blow.

He had lingered in Afghanistan and Pakistan to wind up his organisation. He was tired after a decade on the move, latterly hiding in caves while Soviet helicopter gunships hovered nearby looking for any sign of life that would trigger an attack with high explosive ordnance. After that, he told his brother Bakr, a simple life looked very attractive.

But there was now one other consideration that had perhaps never occurred to Osama. He had become a fully-fledged celebrity.

During the second half of the 1980s, the Arabic media had picked up on this extraordinary figure and eulogised his efforts, building him into an enigma of sorts. It was a story that ran and ran. What was more, the well-educated and refined freedom fighter was adept at working the journalists he encountered. As his reputation grew, Osama had spoken at length with the media.

For one apparently so humble, his determined seduction of the press was extraordinary. His office in Jeddah handled press inquiries, channelling these to a member of his staff. The number of requests for interviews grew as his name became known. Few were turned down. His office also monitored the regional and international press. In his absence, packets of news clippings and videotapes of television appearances were shipped from Saudi Arabia to Afghanistan, via Pakistan, every week. Osama poured over these and revelled in the attention.

He was equally adept in public relations, turning on the charm when a media person was in the vicinity. After meeting Osama, Abdul Bari Atwan, editor in chief of the London-based *Al-Quds Al-Arabi* newspaper, wrote: 'I found him to be a man who is very modest in nature. He believes in every word he says. He does not lie. He does not exaggerate. He does not compliment anyone. He does not even try to hide anything. He expresses everything he feels. He is very enigmatic. His voice is calm and well mannered.

'I spent a whole day with him and I truly sensed his charm, his refined manners, and true modesty, not exaggerated or with fake modesty. He is a man who seeks the after-life and who truly feels that he has lived more than enough. You feel that there is sadness inside him – which he did not express – that he was not martyred when he was fighting the Soviets or the communists or the heathens. You feel like he is saying: "Why am I alive?"'

Osama's adept public relations won him a rapt audience. The Middle East had been starved of charismatic leaders since the days of Gamal Abdel-Nasser. Nasser was a pioneer of Arabic socialism and moral leader of the Arab world during one of the most critical periods in its history. After becoming Egyptian president in 1952 following a military coup, Nasser was praised throughout the Arab world for his nationalisation of the Suez Canal, his agrarian reform, and his socialist policies that lifted the vast majority of Egyptians out of poverty.

But more than this, Nasser achieved unprecedented popularity throughout the Arab world and was admired for his rousing support of Arab nationalism. In the wider Muslim world, he became something of a talisman. He supported liberation movements against all types of occupation in the developing countries and was a founding leader of the Non-Aligned Movement. Along with India's Nehru and Indonesia's Sukarno, Nasser became a major international power broker in the politics of the developing world.

Shortly after the Arabs' defeat by Israel in 1967, Nasser resigned, but hundreds of thousands of Egyptians marched in his support with similar protests held in capitals throughout the region and Nasser remained in place. When poor health claimed his life in 1970, shock waves were felt throughout the Arab world. In a stunning display of emotion, millions of Egyptians followed his funeral procession through the streets of Cairo and vast, unparalleled outpourings of grief were witnessed around the Middle East.

Since 1970, the ordinary people of the Arab world had been without a personality around whom they could rally. Many during the late 1980s were only too happy to latch on to Osama, the charismatic young Muslim who was both financing and leading the fight to oust the Soviet Union from Afghanistan. Ironically his story was one that also suited all the varied political shades of the region. In the Middle East's Islamic democracies and more extreme dictatorships he was portrayed as the pious Osama bin Laden, who had turned his back on the trappings of wealth to take up a noble cause. The oil-rich monarchies of the Gulf had a different angle. There he was held up as an example of how the Arab world's nouveau riche had not, after all, lost their religious beliefs.

Either way, Osama was Islam's rising star during the late 1980s. In offices and shops around the region, amid traditional Koranic inscriptions and the obligatory touched-up and sanitised photograph of one's leader, those well informed and politically aware now hung a photograph of Osama bin Laden.

Considering his new celebrity, Osama's plans to return to Jeddah and simply slip into his old life were probably one of his least accurate calculations over the last few decades. His plane taxied to a remote corner of Jeddah International Airport, where he was met by a few family members, and from there the freedom fighter returned to his family home, the palace where he had lived for most of his childhood.

He had asked one thing of his family: to be allowed to enter into the country without a fuss. To the best of their ability they tried, but in reality it was never going to happen. Word soon spread among the extended Bin Laden family that he was home. Uncles, cousins, nephews and all manner of relatives – and their friends – descended on the palace hoping to talk to him over coffee, a tradition of hospitality in Arabia. With dozens of staff working in the house eager to share the news with friends and relatives, it wasn't long before all of Jeddah knew that the hero of the Muslim world was home. Soon he was receiving family friends, then city fathers, then members of the local political establishment. Eventually even Prince Majid ibn Abdul Aziz Al Saud, influential brother of King Fahd and governor of nearby Mecca, paid an informal visit. Prince Majid was carrying a message from the monarch welcoming Osama home.

At one stage, servants were called upon to disperse loiterers hanging around the palace gates wishing to catch a glimpse of Osama. If he left home to visit one of Jeddah's many coffee shops, Osama would find himself mobbed by autograph hunters like a football star. Ordinary Muslims would approach the former mujahideen with cameras, asking for a photograph with their hero.

Osama lapped up such adulation and was noticeably keen to sit in coffee shops around the city. He loved the attention and showed boundless patience, signing autographs, posing for photographs and answering questions about his exploits. Shopping with his wife, he was delighted to enter some small stores on the streets of Jeddah and find that shopkeepers had hung up a newspaper photograph or even one of the few posters that were circulated at the time of Jeddah's most famous son. The former outcast had returned to find his face next to that of the king.

It was an extraordinary homecoming, considering the low esteem that his family had had for him before he found his faith and headed for Afghanistan. Those close to him at the time recall that Osama at first appeared somewhat taken aback by the depth of affection people now had for him. He shied away from suggestions that he take on a public role. Today there are even suggestions within the family that Prince Majid came with an offer of a government position. Understandably, King Fahd might have wished to keep this newly emerging figure close to him. Instead, Osama reiterated, he wished only to return to his humble office in the family business and pick up where he left off. And this is what happened.

During the summer of 1989, after just a few days of rest, he fell into a routine. After morning prayers, Osama would return home and eat a light breakfast washed down with sweet tea. Later he would drive himself to his office and would work solidly until mid-afternoon, his day punctuated only by midday prayers. He found a luxury apartment in Jeddah and he and wife, seeking some privacy, moved out the larger Bin Laden family complex. In his own words:

'I returned to road construction in Taif and Abha. I brought back the equipment I had used to build tunnels and roads for the mujahideen in Afghanistan.' For all intents and purposes, Osama bin Laden was home and getting on with his life, an ordinary citizen doing an ordinary job.

However, it quickly emerged that this was not the case. Unbeknown to his family, he was turning his office into something akin to the Oval Office of Middle Eastern Islamic fundamentalism. In between meetings with architects to discuss projects, Osama would work the telephones, supporting jihad around the region, which was now firmly in the hands of retired Arab-Afghans.

In the early days of Islam, the need to defend the believers and ensure the survival of the faith forced the Prophet Muhammad to elaborate on the concept of jihad or 'just war'. The aim of the religion, in its wars, battles and national uprisings against polytheism and materialism, has always been defence, not conquest, expansionism, or imperialism. The first revelations to the Prophet on jihad are enshrined in the Koran at Sura XXII: Hajj (verses 39 and 40), which says: 'Those upon whom war is made by unbelievers are granted permission to fight because they are being oppressed (verily God is most powerful to aid them) and have been expelled from their homes in defiance of right for the sole crime of saying "Our Lord is God."' In Sura II: Baqara (verse 190), the Koran says: 'Fight in the cause of God against those who attack you. But be careful to maintain the limit, since God does not love transgressors.'

In the case of the Soviet Union's invasion of Afghanistan, clearly the campaign to remove Moscow's forces was a jihad. However, the post-withdrawal activities of the many Arab-Afghan factions were outside of the boundaries set by the Koran and therefore un-Islamic by definition. Adherence to the letter of Islamic law seemed to have fallen by the wayside, while the interpretation of the Prophet's commands was progressively twisted to conveniently accommodate most behaviour. Islam was being corrupted by the men who had defended their religion so valiantly.

Osama's observations on jihad were scarcely more enlightening. 'Nowadays, jihad needs to be waged by the nation,' he said. 'The obligation to engage in jihad may be dropped if people suffer from disability. But we believe that those who participated in the jihad in Afghanistan bear the greatest responsibility in this regard, because they realised that with insignificant capabilities, with a small number of anti-tank mines, with a small number of Kalashnikov rifles, they managed to crush the greatest empire known to mankind. They crushed the greatest military machine.'

During this period in Saudi Arabia, his personal jihad was desk-bound. He stayed in almost daily contact with 'his men' around the region, talking over their plans, seeing where he could be of help. This was a period when the foundations of many of the modern Islamic terror groups were being laid, particularly in Egypt and Algeria where serious trouble was about to erupt.

All this was hidden, of course, behind a veneer of respectability. Osama appeared to be quietly going about family business, but it was a front, enabling him to shift large amounts of cash around the region to his allies. Money was channelled into the bank accounts of those wishing to buy arms and explosives to be used in a struggle at home; no thought was given to fatalities among fellow Muslims and their families. Large sums also headed to Al-Qaeda and the paramilitary training camps continuing to churn out trained fighters in remote Afghanistan.

It did not take long, however, for the authorities in Saudi Arabia to get wind of his activities. By 1990, the governments of Egypt, Algeria and Yemen are all believed to have made diplomatic representations to Riyadh after discovering that the Islamic opposition in their respective countries was growing and suddenly becoming better armed – and tracing the source of their new-found wealth to Saudi Arabia. Unsettling neighbouring states could not be tolerated, especially when the Saudi regime was keen to control its own internal opposition. The discovery of Osama's activities was a rude shock for the royal family, the Bin Ladens being so closely entwined with the House of Saud. King Fahd's brother, Minister of Interior Prince Naif, launched a low-key investigation. Osama was quietly monitored. The more the Saudi government learned the less they liked.

As early as this, in addition to his surreptitious banking activities, Osama had begun socialising in company that Naif and his organisation thought suspect. On the fringes of the religious conservative right, there had always been lingering doubt about the legitimacy of the Al Saud regime. Saad Al-Fagih, a prominent Saudi dissident living in exile in London and head of the Movement for Islamic Reform in Arabia, describes it as 'pathological rule of the royal family'.

The legitimacy of the Saudi royal family is based largely upon birthright and their standing as the guardians of the home of Islam. Some believed that the Al Saud family had lost this moral authority, not necessarily because of the wrongdoings of the king and senior members of the family, but through the often squalid behaviour of the princes. A Saudi dissident named Mohajir Al-Saeed, who studied at Ohio State University, wrote in a research paper that the government had 'corrupted those beliefs and turned with ever-increasing ferocity to the instruments of mass repression and surveillance. From the very beginning, this state has used foreign (and non-Islamic) powers to secure its external security (trading some degree or another of its sovereignty to first, the British, and more lately, the Americans, to protect it from the movements that swept across the Arab world since the end of the colonial era) . . .

'The Saudi regime has only been able to suppress dissent about its obvious failings by applying the most evil methods of state control. In day-to-day life within the country, hardship in living has increased to cover a much wider segment of populace. It is becoming clear to an enlarging circle of citizens that the failures of political will both domestically and internationally can only be lain at the door of the royal family. Despite several generations now of high GDP and GDP growth, fueled almost exclusively by the primary sector of the economy, that is, petroleum exports, Saudi Arabia is still a Third World country . . . A growing segment of Saudi society understands this, and realises that the government of Arabia has betrayed its Islamic principles, and has by nepotism of the House of Saud stolen the future of the country.'

Islamic conservatives were receptive to such thoughts. Osama's new contacts included several clerics and hard-line dissidents who had been identified by the government as troublemakers. Osama also began giving speeches to private organisations and sermons in some of the more controversial mosques in Jeddah, belittling the royal family and calling for change. As a celebrity, people wanted to hear what he had to say. Authorised tapes of his speeches sold a reported quarter of a million copies during this period, while there was a thriving black market in cheap bootleg tapes that must, at least, have ensured his circulation reached into the millions.

He also used his potent voice to warn of impending invasion by Iraq. At that time, King Fahd enjoyed a good relationship with Iraqi president Saddam Hussein and was at pains to keep him on side, both for the sake of Saudi Arabia and Kuwait.

As the Ministry of Interior looked harder at the hero of the Afghan campaign, it was like peeling an onion. They discovered underlying 'skins' that were incompatible with the state. It was inconceivable, however, that such a well-known figure would 'disappear' or be detained in one of Jeddah's notorious jails – a fate that allegedly befell many opponents of the state. Around this time representations were made to senior members of the Bin Laden family. Osama's uncle, Abdullah Awad bin Laden, was approached unofficially and made aware of his nephew's leanings. Osama's eldest brothers were also informed. Dark hints were made that such activities could endanger the long-standing commercial relationship between the government and the family business. This was to prove a shock to the clan. Osama's father had been closer to a succession of Saudi kings than most and the family prided itself on its loyalty. That any member of the clan, let alone its most famous son, could be involved in undermining the state was an abhorrence.

For a time, the situation was thought to have been brought under control. Osama was quietly relieved of his passport and told not to leave Jeddah without permission. But he continued his quiet support for groups abroad, albeit with a great deal more care. In appearance, it seemed that he had shelved his hostility for the Al Sauds. But then events took over.

On August 2, 1990, Saddam Hussein's forces invaded and occupied Kuwait, long considered by the Iraqi leadership to be a part of their country. This territorial claim had led to confrontations over the years, and ongoing hostility between these two Gulf Arab neighbours. After his attempted invasion of Iran had concluded with a return to the status quo at a cost of one millions lives, Saddam sought easier conquests against his weak southern neighbours. With rich deposits of oil straddling the ill-defined border, Iraq constantly claimed that Kuwaiti oil rigs were illegally tapping into Iraqi oil fields. Kuwait seemed an easy target.

The Iraqi invasion of Kuwait deeply shocked the people and governments of the Gulf. The Bin Ladens shared this reaction. By August 3, most women and children from the family had been packed off aboard a fleet of private jets to safer countries. Osama the freedom fighter was both shocked and excited. Although the country was in turmoil on August 2, he managed to make contact directly with the office of King Fahd with a breathtaking offer.

Within one week, Osama stated, he could assemble 10,000 mujahideen, under arms, either to defend the kingdom or go into Kuwait to seek to liberate the country by jihad.

The irony was perhaps lost on him in the heat of the moment. From criticising the Al Sauds, he was now willing to defend them and their kingdom, using the mujahideen, the world's most revolutionary-minded armed brigades, sworn to toppling every regime even remotely following alleged pro-western principles that Saudi Arabia's system stood for.

The same day he flew by private jet directly to Riyadh. The Saudi Arabian capital was in turmoil with tens of thousands of cars on the road, filled with citizens making their way to the airport, or intent on heading in any direction away from Kuwait and the Iraqi menace. Osama went straight to the office of King Fahd. The monarch was understandably busy, but he was ushered into the office of Prince Sultan, powerful full-brother of the king and minister of defence. Osama presented to the startled minister a handwritten ten-page memorandum outlining his plans for the defence of the kingdom. He promised to raise 4,000 trained Saudi-Afghans under arms within two days, followed by the arrival of 6,000 more men from around the Middle East, all of them trained fighters and veterans of the Afghan campaign.

The plan also laid out a detailed defence plan for Saudi Arabia. Osama was ready to use all the heavy equipment owned by his family's businesses, rush this close to the Kuwaiti border and begin construction of a line of proper defences.

Osama knew already that King Fahd was ready to reach out to the United States for support. But he promised Prince Sultan that an Arab-Afghan was more than a match for an Iraqi conscript and that his men could easily defeat Saddam's elite Republican Guard. He pleaded for the opportunity for a Muslim army to defend a Muslim country. Prince Sultan seemed convinced. He told Osama to return to Jeddah and make initial preparations for mobilisation, while he would show King Fahd the plan.

By nightfall, just one day into Iraq's invasion of Kuwait, Osama was flying into Jeddah. He went straight to his office in the company headquarters and began telephoning his network of fighters around Saudi Arabia and the Middle East. He informed some family members of the part the Bin Laden Group would be required to play in the defence of their country. Then he began contacting senior fighters in the kingdom. Within a matter of eight hours, Osama had his whole network on standby. The hero of the Afghanistan campaign was ready to assume what he saw as his rightful position as protector of Saudi Arabia.

Family members recall that for several days after making the offer Osama remained glued to his mobile telephone, expecting a reply from King Fahd. He called the monarch's office repeatedly, contacted several of King Fahd's aides to repeat the offer, sent several faxes and dispatched members of his office staff to the king's office with copies of his letters. Meanwhile, he worked day and night in his office marshalling his forces, mobilising them in preparation for action, confident that they would be the key to success in the war that lay ahead.

But then, on August 7, came the snub that has consumed and angered him until this day. On that day it was announced that United States troops would move into Saudi Arabia to protect Saudi oil reserves. The United Nations Security Council had already called for Iraq to withdraw from Kuwait, and subsequently enacted a trade embargo, but now the United States would begin preparing a global coalition that would aim to force Saddam Hussein to withdraw, or liberate Kuwait by force.

Along with US troops, an international coalition brought men from dozens of countries into the kingdom. Represented among Middle East, Islamic and Arab states were Afghanistan, Bahrain, Bangladesh, Egypt, Kuwait, Morocco, Oman, Pakistan, Qatar, Saudi Arabia, Senegal, Syria, Turkey and the United Arab Emirates. In addition to the United States, non-Arab, Islamic or Middle Eastern states participating included Australia, Belgium, Canada, Czechoslovakia, Denmark, France, Germany, Great Britain, Greece, Holland, Hungary, Honduras, Italy, New Zealand, Niger, Norway, Poland, Portugal, Senegal, South Korea and Spain. The effort was partly financed by countries that were unable to send troops. More than $53 billion was pledged and received. Saudi Arabia and Kuwait were the largest donors.

On November 29, the UN set a deadline of January 15, 1991, for a peaceful withdrawal of Iraqi troops from Kuwait. When Saddam refused to comply, Operation Desert Storm was launched on January 18, under the leadership of General Norman Schwarzkopf.

The US-led coalition began a massive air war to destroy Iraq's forces and military and civil infrastructure. Iraq called for terrorist attacks against the coalition and launched Scud missiles at Israel – in an unsuccessful attempt to widen the war and break up the coalition – and at Saudi Arabia. The main coalition forces invaded Kuwait and southern Iraq on February 24 and, over the next four days, encircled and defeated the Iraqis and liberated Kuwait. When President George Bush declared a ceasefire on February 28, most of the Iraqi forces in Kuwait had either surrendered or fled. Of Iraq's 545,000 troops in Kuwait, about 100,000 are believed to have lost their lives.

While the world rejoiced and Saudi Arabians celebrated, Osama nursed his wounded pride. The injury was if anything more painful than if he had been physically hurt. The offer to King Fahd had not actually been refused, simply because at no point did the king or any member of his government bother to contact the 'millionaire mujahideen' to even recognise that an offer had been made. Embittered, Osama turned completely against the regime that he had offered to help protect from the Iraqis, and against the Americans. If one incident in his life can be said to be a turning point that set Osama on his ultimate mission, it was this. The world had ignored his offer of help and instead turned to foreigners to liberate Kuwait. On home territory, the hero of Islam, vanquisher of the Soviet Union, had no role to play.

Even while Kuwait was still being pillaged by the Iraqis, Osama was campaigning to undermine Saudi Arabia's position. He restarted his mission to unsettle the religious right – a powerful lobby within the kingdom. After persuading one influential mullah to issue a *fatwa* (religious edict) for men to resist the arrival of western troops, it is believed that up to 4,000 volunteers were sent, at Osama's expense, to join Al-Qaeda in Afghanistan.

In an interview, Osama spelled out his views: 'Any government that sells its peoples' interests and betrays its people and takes actions that remove it from the Muslim nation will not succeed. We predict that the Riyadh leader and those with him that stood with the Jews and Christians, and forfeited Al-Haramien, the holy shrines, to Jews and Christians with American identities or other, will disintegrate. They have left the Muslim nation. We predict that like the Iran royal family, the Shah, they will disperse and disappear. After Allah gave them property on the most sacred land and gave them wealth that is unheard of before from oil, still they sinned and did not value Allah's gift. We predict destruction and dispersal . . .

in a great devastation against the Muslim nation, especially what happens to the Muslim people of Iraq.

'The Prophet said, "A woman entered hell because of a cat. She did not feed it and prevented it from finding food on its own." She is going to hell for starving a cat to death, but what say to those who agreed and gave reason for the hundreds of thousands of troops to blockade millions of Muslims in Iraq . . . '

This was, and is, Osama's potent cocktail of reasoning and hatred. In his view, armed infidels in Islam's holy land were a desecration, and this ended the Al Sauds' Islamic legitimacy. His fury grew still further when the Americans stayed on in the Gulf, and especially at bases in Saudi Arabia, after the war. 'You will leave when the bodies of American soldiers and civilians are sent [home] in wooden boxes and coffins. That is when you will leave,' he later told ABC's *Nightline*.

Within Saudi Arabia he now stepped up his activities, speaking at opposition rallies, making robust denunciations of the Al Sauds and government policy in the mosque and spreading disquiet. Now the Palestinian cause, an issue that had never interested him, suddenly became a useful tool for propaganda against the American menace. To one packed audience he stated: 'When we buy American goods we are accomplices in the murder of Palestinians. American companies make millions in the Arab world with which they pay taxes to their government. The United States uses that money to send $3 billion a year to Israel, which uses it to kill Palestinians.'

His provocative speeches and actions were always likely to bring repercussions on someone already being watched closely by the authorities. Rather than establish a dialogue, the authorities took a combative approach. Osama was harassed in the street. According to family members he was even roughed up by groups of 'youths'. One relative recalls Osama sporting a black eye and returning home covered in blood, such was the ferocity of one of the beatings. On another occasion, the government authorised the National Guard to raid and search his farm outside of Jeddah. This stirred Osama up even further. He protested to Crown Prince Abdullah, who is also head of the National Guard. Prince Abdullah apologised, saying he had not known of the plans, but it was unlikely that a raid on such a prominent citizen would have been sanctioned at anything other than the highest level. Pressure was also brought to bear financially.

Threats were made that valuable government contracts would be cancelled and that Osama's property would be seized.

Such physical and mental confrontation was a poor tactic on the part of the Saudi authorities. His record showed that Osama was a fighter and alienating him further was an ill-conceived idea. The tension between him and the Saudi government worsened. Confined to Jeddah, Osama was like a caged bear. Knowing that all his telephone lines were bugged and that he was being followed by state security, he was unable to speak freely with his network abroad.

In the spring of 1991, however, an opportunity presented itself for escape. This came when Prince Naif, the minister of interior, was sent abroad by King Fahd on official business. Osama believed that Prince Naif was personally handling his case. His absence opened a window of opportunity.

Osama visited his elder brother, Bakr, informing him that he had secured Bin Laden Construction a valuable road-building contract in Pakistan through his contacts. To finalise the deal, Osama had to visit Islamabad, for which he needed his passport.

Following the death of their father and the tragedy of Salim's fatal accident, much of the family's business portfolio had rested with Bakr. He was a safe and successful pair of hands and had guided the family through a transition without mishap. As a result Bakr was – and remains – highly respected. His many friends in government included King Fahd and Prince Ahmed, deputy minister of interior. Bakr also had a sparkling reputation as a philanthropist. He had consistently given to good causes in Saudi Arabia and throughout the Arab world, including sponsoring schools and orphanages in poor countries. He financed thousands of poor people to undertake Hajj and paid for specialist hospital treatment in the West for poor families in Jeddah. With his impeccable connections and scrupulous character, Bakr was able to retrieve his younger brother's travel documents. At some personal risk, Bakr vouched for his brother and Prince Ahmed was persuaded to hand over Osama's passport.

In the first week of April 1991, Osama's private plane touched down in Karachi. He had flown into certain exile. Later the same week he faxed Bakr a letter of apology for betraying his trust and telephoned some of his relatives to try to explain his actions.

Osama's former home, Pakistan, was now a dangerous place for a Saudi dissident on the run. The wily ISI was sure to hear quickly from the Saudi Arabian government that he was there and, in all likelihood, would not hesitate to arrest him and hand him over. Within a day, Osama had flown in a small aircraft to Peshawar, and later made the short hop to an Al-Qaeda base in the mountains of Afghanistan, not far from Jalalabad. It was another emotional homecoming. Trapped for so long in Jeddah amid suspicion and recriminations, he was now in his spiritual home. Several hundred Al-Qaeda fighters greeted him by shooting off volleys from their Kalashnikovs into the air.

But again he was disappointed. While his Al-Qaeda organisation was in fine health, Osama found Afghanistan in a worse position than when he had left. The country was gripped by civil war and society seemed to be breaking down. Within a month he had run out of patience with his former allies. Thinking himself capable of bringing the bloodletting to an end, Osama attempted to intervene. But at every turn he was rebuffed. In Kabul, the capital he had fought so long to free, he found gunmen on every street corner and civilians reduced to starving, wretched wrecks by the collapse of the country. The ten years of his life he had dedicated to freeing the Afghans had been to no avail.

Late in 1991, faced with reports that the ISI was out to capture him, and getting nowhere in his mediation efforts between mujahideen factions, he realised that revolution was going to need a proper base from which to grow. Only one country, Sudan, presented a real opportunity. At the end of the Soviet occupation several years ago, Sudan had not only welcomed home its Arab-Afghan fighters, but also those whose own countries had rejected them. Dr Hassan al-Turabi, the charismatic leader of the ruling National Islamic Front (NIF), was a true friend to the cause. He welcomed Osama bin Laden with open arms.

CHAPTER ELEVEN

Terrorism Inc.

Sudan is Africa's largest country, forms eight per cent of the African continent, and is roughly the size of Europe. The country borders Egypt and Libya to the north, Ethiopia to the east, Kenya, Uganda and Zaire to the south and the Central African Republic and Chad to the west. Strategically, Sudan controls the shipping routes leading from the Red Sea to the Gulf of Eilat and the Suez Canal. It became an independent state in 1956. While the majority of the population consider themselves part of the Arab world, the Christian and Animistic minority populations of the south see themselves as belonging to the black African states bordering Sudan.

Sudan's civil war – the longest-running internal conflict in the world today – has taken a horrifying human toll. By the end of the millennium, the war and war-related famines had claimed the lives of more than two million people and created about five million refugees within Sudan – the largest concentration of internally-displaced people in the world. The number of people from southern Sudan killed during this conflict is greater than all the victims in Bosnia, Kosovo, and Rwanda combined.

Sudanese spiritual leader Dr Hassan al-Turabi was educated at the Sorbonne in Paris and the University of London. He was considered capable of communicating with, and relating to, western-oriented audiences. People who know him describe him as charming and warm. Many believed that he would end civil strife in his home country and go on to become one of the most prominent and beloved leaders in Africa.

On June 30, 1989, a military coup had brought new leadership to Sudan under General Omar Hassan al-Bashir. The general was an Islamist and fell under al-Turabi's spell. After the events of the Gulf War – in which they believed, like Osama, that non-Islamic western troops should not have been utilised – Sudan slid into a dangerous extremism. By 1991 al-Turabi was head of the National Islamic Front in his own country, the Popular Arab Islamic Conference and was also a long-time member of the Muslim Brotherhood, an extremist Islamic group. He also pioneered a collective organisation for Sunni Islamic terrorist groups under the banner of Islamist International to coordinate work against the alleged 'Judeo-Christian' world order

In August 1989, within only six weeks of the coup that brought al-Bashir to power, al-Turabi attended an extraordinary meeting of the International Muslim Brotherhood in London. During this meeting he laid a ground-breaking offer on the table, one that opened Sudan's doors to any groups who wished to utilise the country as a base. In return for millions of dollars in payments to the ailing government, Sudan was ready to be an official conduit in the process of Islamic fundamentalism, a base from where groups could freely engage in terror campaigns against non-fundamentalist regimes. Later, in the wake of the Gulf War, al-Turabi went on to form the Islamic People's Conference, which encompassed the Popular International Organisation (PIO). The PIO was to be a sort of parliament for terrorism, a forum of 50 delegates, one representing each of the countries in which there was Islamic struggle.

Al-Turabi used his power singularly to become one of the most prominent supporters of terrorism worldwide, setting his country on a course that would see it providing military training, support or both to Hezbollah, Hamas, Palestinian Islamic Jihad, Egyptian Islamic Jihad and Algeria's Armed Islamic Group, to name but a few. Hundreds of activists from the Middle East and Africa reportedly received military training in Sudan in order to return to their countries, carry out attacks, and create anarchy with the intention of taking over their countries' institutions and setting up an Islamic regime.

Sudan was placed on America's list of state sponsors of terrorism in August 1993, but continued to press on with its activities. Soon the country was closely allied with Iran; the two states sharing technology and information as part of a strategic terror alliance.

Al-Turabi had been a keen friend to Osama bin Laden when, at the conclusion of the Afghanistan campaign, Osama was seeking a base for many of his Arab-Afghans. A couple of years later al-Turabi was only too willing to accommodate Osama, who was himself seeking a safe refuge and a base from which to operate.

In December 1991, Osama took off in a small plane from a bumpy airfield in Peshawar and flew to Khartoum, the capital of Sudan. As his aircraft taxied to a stop on the tarmac of Khartoum International Airport, he discovered a welcome committee courtesy of al-Turabi. Crowds of children waved small flags and sang revolutionary songs, a military band beat out the national anthem of Sudan and several government officials were there to greet someone who they clearly thought of as a VIP. All the trappings of a red carpet arrival had been laid on for a man who had previously all but defined the term 'low key'.

Osama was both embarrassed and honoured that the Sudanese would welcome a hero of Islamic fundamentalism in such a manner. But Sudan was to be the home that Osama had dreamed of. Al-Turabi made it clear that he could work unhindered and that the government and National Islamic Front would provide all cooperation to expedite his success. It was the beginning of a partnership that would last many years. Indeed, the 59-year-old patriarch of terrorists was possibly a surrogate father figure that Osama had been looking for following the assassination of Dr Abdullah Azzam several years earlier.

Within weeks, Osama had taken over a suite of offices in one of the few more modern buildings in Khartoum. He had one office for commercial work and another for Al-Qaeda, a plethora of secretaries and a growing general office staff. If the nature of the business going on within these offices were not exporting Islamic fundamentalism by violent means, this could have been an office anywhere in the world. Here, al-Turabi would often pass by to take Arabic coffee and share with Osama his vision of the Islamic world. The Saudi exile hung on every word and nodded throughout.

Joining the Al-Qaeda organisation in early 1992 was Wadih el-Hage, a US citizen who would later, in February 1999, go on trial in New York City accused of conspiracy and perjury in the East Africa embassy bombings case. El-Hage had been introduced to Osama by Azzam, his partner in Maktab al-Khidamat. He became involved in the campaign to oust the Soviets from Afghanistan and in 1992, having been offered a job in Osama's commercial office, moved with his family to Khartoum. His testimony in the later trial offers a rare first-hand account of life in that Khartoum office, while those of el-Hage's family were equally illuminating. One family member said in an interview: '[Osama] was a busy person and had hundreds of people working for him. You didn't get to see him unless he invited you.' Family members also said that el-Hage made frequent trips to Europe and elsewhere on business.

The Al-Qaeda office building was usually circled by a platoon of the Sudanese army. Osama's residence in the capital, palatial by Sudanese standards, was similarly guarded by 50 soldiers. Among a handful of other properties, he maintained a small farm on the banks of the Blue Nile where he delighted in taking western journalists to help dissuade them of his image as a master terrorist. In one interview, published in *Time* magazine in May 1996, writer Scott MacLeod stated: 'At the farm, he made a point of claiming that the Egyptians had cited it as a terrorist camp. All that could be seen were a few horses, cows and goats. "Take pictures of whatever you like," Bin Laden said with a smile.'

Away from the farm, Osama was quickly integrated into the al-Turabi circle. He was a mere 34 years old, but was about to crack one of the most important problems that the world of Islamic fundamentalism had to face.

On July 5, 1991, the Bank of Credit and Commerce International (BCCI) had collapsed. Investors large and small all over the world lost billions. Among them were just about every major Islamic terrorist organisation in the world: the BCCI had allegedly been a front for many of these organisations. This left Islamic fundamentalism with a headache and, worse, exposed. Without a system by which money could be shifted around the world invisibly, it would be relatively simple for terrorist funds to be traced. The cause would be bankrupted by having its accounts frozen, funds seized and assets impounded. Dealing with this crisis fell to al-Turabi. In desperation he turned to Osama. Over coffee in the Al-Qaeda office he dropped a bombshell. He had a task. The future of the entire struggle could come to rest on Osama's shoulders.

It was a call to arms that enthused Osama. Over several months, his office now became the 'World Bank' for terrorism as he and a small team of accountants and Islamic financial experts poured over a number of plans. Occasionally al-Turabi would drop in to remind his protégé that success needed to come soon, before the terrorist economy collapsed entirely and organisations were forced to lock up shop.

Several models were constructed and discarded during this process as too difficult to operate or maintain. Instead, Osama fell back upon his own experiences. During the Afghan conflict, he had handled almost all major financial transactions for MAK and, during fund-raising swings around the Middle East, had come to know who the sympathisers of the fundamentalist cause were. During the summer of 1991 he discreetly made contact with many of the wealthiest of these individuals, especially those with an international network of companies. Most were more than willing to support a scheme that would cost nothing while guaranteeing them favour with the leadership of the cause . . . just in case it took root and ousted the pro-western, capitalist system in their own countries.

Within months, Osama unveiled before an astonished al-Turabi what he called 'the Brotherhood Group'. This was a network of 134 Arab businessmen whose combined commercial empire extended around the globe and back many times. They maintained bank accounts in virtually every country and, collectively, routinely shifted billions of dollars around as part of their legitimate businesses. It was a perfect front. The Brotherhood Group came to be utilised by terror groups all around the world. Osama was the toast of his industry.

Osama's first commercial Sudanese venture was Al-Hijra for Construction and Development Ltd. Shrewdly, he chose to make senior officials in both the National Islamic Front and the Sudanese military partners in the company. It was a move that paid dividends many times over. These two organisations were effectively a government within the government and, as such, their leadership controlled all federal spending.

At this time, national focus was on plans to develop Port Sudan, well-placed on the coast of the Red Sea. Al-Hijra was contracted to built the new airport at Port Sudan and later a four-lane main artery to link Khartoum with Port Sudan. This was a massive project to build some 650 miles of paved road.

Elsewhere, Al-Hijra was quickly involved in projects in several areas to widen the Blue Nile. There was also work to be done on the country's railway system which is extensive, with about 3,000 miles of track linking most of the major towns and cities. Because of the civil war, however, the system was in a poor state of repair. Most of the system dates from Kitchener's offensive against the Mahdi in the 1890s, and is narrow-gauge, single-track line. Osama's firm worked on a key project to improve the line that connected Port Sudan in the east of the country and the city of Nyala in the west. There were also airport contracts for the cities of Kassala and El Obeid and road links in the west of the country. His military connections also secured him work on the 310-mile road that stretched between Khartoum and the cities of Shendi and Atbarah in the north.

With large jobs such as these, Al-Hijra for Construction and Development quickly eclipsed competitors that were both older and more established. Private works also came flooding in. He even secured the contract for the biggest civil engineering project in the entire country, the Rosaires Dam. Within a space of several months, the company had become a corporation with turnover and profits in the millions.

Elsewhere, Osama's commercial skills were helping him identify opportunities in other sectors. With the country's decision-makers safely in his pocket, raking in money from their shares in the construction business, Osama pressed ahead with his own independent interests. Two notables were the Wadi al-Aqiq and Ladin International Company: export–import firms. Within one month of their formation, Wadi al-Aqiq and Ladin International Company had a secured a bundle of contracts to provide imported foods to the Sudanese military; to handle coal imports into the country and for the supply of aircraft fuel, both for military flights and for Sudan's civil airports.

Osama was also handed opportunities in the under-developed mineral and oil sectors. Despite rich reserves – besides oil, Sudan has ample mica, marble, gypsum, iron ore, uranium, manganese, zinc and copper – this natural wealth remains barely exploited, contributing as little as four per cent to the gross national product. One of Osama's smaller enterprises was even involved in prospecting for gold in the Red Sea Hills.

Another of the firms in his portfolio was the Taba Investment Company Ltd. This was involved in currency trading, but also had a division called Themar al-Mubaraka Company that went heavily into agriculture. To support his efforts, the Sudanese government handed over one million acres of land, much of this in the west of the country.

Although around sixty-five per cent of Sudanese were believed to be directly employed in the industry, only about five per cent of Sudan's land area was used for farming A chronic lack of irrigation and poor general infrastructure meant that the full potential of the land was not being exploited. Using limited funds, Osama was quickly able to bring swathes of land into production, growing crops such as millet, sorghum, rice, cassava, wheat, peanuts, beans and bananas. One company-run farm at Al-Damazine was one of the largest operations in Sudan, producing sesame and peanuts. He also invested in cattle and owned many chicken farms.

Osama also placed $50 million into part-funding the creation of the Al-Shamal Islamic Bank in Khartoum, a joint effort with the NIF, which has since been heavily involved in the movement of terrorist funds in the Middle East.

According to some sources, Osama's business empire extended throughout the region and even to the West that he so despised, although he masked his ownership through holding companies and third parties. *Washington Post* staff writer Vernon Loeb, writing in 1998, said: '[Osama's] economic holdings include trading companies in Kenya, a ceramic manufacturing company in Yemen and a bank, construction company and investment firms in Sudan, where he and his associates secured a near monopoly on gum Arabic, the country's leading export and a staple of much fruit juice production in the United States.'

The success of his fledgling commercial empire was more important to Osama than most people, even his Sudanese hosts, knew. For while he had been able to escape Saudi Arabia, according to family members, only limited funds had gone with him. Transferring large amounts of cash abroad would have raised eyebrows at home, when he was attempting to talk his way around his brother and get his passport released. Osama is believed to have carried with him a bag containing nearly $1 million in cash withdrawn from current accounts in the days before his departure. Before his deception was discovered, he quickly dipped into accounts and moved money into banks out of Saudi Arabia's control. But these funds were being rapidly eaten up by Al-Qaeda, with its dozens of terrorist training camps in Afghanistan and pledges of financial support for Islamic resistance groups dotted around the Middle East.

When he reached Khartoum, Osama was a worried man. Time was running out. Every avenue open to him to draw more funds from Saudi Arabia was being blocked. The Saudi government, infuriated by his flight, was doing everything within its powers, inside and outside of banking regulations, to freeze or seize the money in his bank accounts. Typically, he had already taken precautions to counter such an eventuality. Over previous months and years, some of his money had been salted away in safety deposit boxes in Jeddah and around Pakistan. A few of his trusted associates had access and quickly emptied these, sending the contents abroad. He had also squirreled away funds in banks elsewhere in the world that he was now able to tap. These were not huge amounts whose movement would attract attention, but sums in the region of $1 million to $2 million. Testimony that would emerge later pointed to banks all over Europe, including Britain's high-street giant Barclays, as those he utilised.

Despite this preparation, Osama lost tens of millions. His 'fortune' has been estimated as high as $300 million, but the reality is that he was worth much less than this. It was not cash, but tied up as shares divided between the sons of Mohammed bin Laden upon his death. Access to millions was not a problem in Jeddah, but Osama had lost this in his flight from Saudi Arabia. Spending up to $5 million a month on his terror network, Osama had known he was in trouble. Al-Qaeda had not yet turned to criminal acts to finance itself – the drugs and protection rackets were still several years away – so aside from Osama's pocket a handful of donors was the only other source of finance. The opportunities that emerged in Sudan eventually bailed him out.

During 1991 and 1992, Osama went from being a terrorist on the run to a high-flying businessman. His factories and farms became places of employment for former mujahideen fighters. From all over the region, Arab-Afghans rejoined their former boss. According to one report, upwards of 300 were flown from Afghanistan to Sudan during May 1993 to take up positions within the new organisation. In a rare interview during 1996, granted to British broadsheet *The Independent*, writer Robert Fisk asked Osama directly about the jobs he was providing for the mujahideen and how many former fighters had joined him in Sudan. 'I don't want to say [how many],' he replied. 'But they are here now with me, they are working right here, building this road to Port Sudan. They like this work, and so do I. This is a great plan which we are achieving for the people here. It helps the Muslims and improves their lives.'

In 1992 Osama's twin interests, commerce and the Islamic struggle, were expanding quickly. First and foremost, Osama was attempting to boost Al-Qaeda's armoury. Evidence from the prosecution in the trial against Wadih el-Hage indicates that he had risen from secretary to a close aide to the Saudi dissident. United States investigators said that el-Hage was 'being investigated for his efforts to try to obtain chemical weapons for Osama bin Laden's organisation'. For the first time, Osama had the stability around him that would empower him to fulfil his greater vision for Al-Qaeda. He already enjoyed close relations with Egypt's Al Jihad and al-Gamaat al-Islamiyya, Iran's Hezbollah, Sudan's NIF, and jihad groups in Yemen, Saudi Arabia, and Somalia. Dozens of other like-minded fundamentalist groups were all clamouring to build bridges with Al-Qaeda.

Al-Qaeda's goal, he suggested, was to 'unite all Muslims and to establish a government which follows the rule of the Caliphs [successors of Muhammad]'. He believed that the only way to establish the Caliphate was by force. Al-Qaeda's goal, therefore, was to overthrow nearly all Muslim governments, which he viewed as corrupt; to drive western influence from those countries; and eventually to abolish state boundaries.

Osama envisioned Al-Qaeda as a multi-national support group, funding and orchestrating the activities of Islamic militants worldwide under its umbrella – which by definition was therefore his umbrella. His primary goal was the overthrow of what he viewed as the corrupt and heretical governments of Muslim states, and their replacement with leaders who would govern by the rule of Sharia or Islamic law.

Coupled with this was the belief that drove Osama on a strong anti-western and anti-American course. His use of this target was not unlike the approach of Adolf Hitler. The German leader focused his public anger upon the Jews and demonised them, using this group as scapegoats for all that was wrong with the world. Hitler successfully sold this to his people, and was then able to apply the worst program of genocide the world has ever known, while rallying his people to a common cause. Osama focused upon America as his demon. It was an obvious choice and easy to find support. The United States was – and is – deeply unpopular around the Muslim world for its support for Israel at the expense of the Palestinians. 'Our war is not against American or western people, it is against the corrupting influence of the West. What has the West given the world? A lust for power and a licence to loot and plunder the poorer countries,' he claimed in an interview with an Arab journalist.

To achieve these aims, Osama had a new vision of himself and Al-Qaeda. In his contacts with the likes of Hezbollah, Hamas and Islamic Jihad he had viewed their organisations with a critical eye. All were largely one-dimensional, poorly organised and unsustainable in the long term. They were organisations built by terrorists with the short-term aim of wreaking as much damage upon the enemy as quickly as possible. While he agreed with their aims, Osama thought them all entirely unprofessional and badly run, poor cousins to the group he envisioned. As with his commercial empire, Osama saw himself in a chief executive's role, managing the affairs of a global organisation. It was a bold and unprecedented concept, but one that served the world of commerce well. If it worked for Heinz, Pepsi or Nike, Osama believed, there was no conceivable reason why his Terrorism Inc. could not do likewise.

To achieve this, he set about drawing into his circle the men who would be his directors. Al-Qaeda was to have a board of management, below which the organisation would be split into several distinct departments. One was responsible for handling terrorist activities, another for handling religious matters and policy and a third would deal with administration: handling payment of salaries, maintaining accounts and other incidentals such as travel arrangements. Another smaller section handled corporate communications, including media relations.

This well-defined project was one that Osama had toyed with for some time, but it had hitherto lacked the sort of solid base presented by Sudan. During 1992, as his business empire boomed, paying for its sister organisation, Osama concentrated on Al-Qaeda, Terror Inc. He gradually formed his board, made up of trusted lieutenants from the old Afghan campaign plus some new blood on the scene and several highly regarded individuals from elsewhere in the region. One of those, headhunted for this role and who would steadily draw closer to Osama, was the influential head of Egyptian Islamic Jihad, Dr Ayman al-Zawahiri, who would go on to become a heavy influence upon Osama until his death in December 2001.

Around Al-Qaeda, the organisation brought more regional and international terror groups under its wing through the use of arms supply or financing. Osama was a keen supporter of all, but used a drip-feed method, supplying small amounts and limited supplies, in order to keep his allies subservient to the larger body.

The first real test of the new Al-Qaeda vision came at the end of 1992 when two projects emerged that needed Osama's attention. The first was the meltdown of Bosnia and unchecked genocide against the Muslims there. The second was a request for support from a group that was seeking to bloody the nose of the United States. Neither was a cause that Osama could resist.

Almost the first campaign that Osama involved Al-Qaeda in was Bosnia, where Slobodan Milosevic's Serbia had embarked upon the worst genocide in Europe since the Nazis in the Second World War. The West had seemingly abandoned the largely Muslim population of Bosnia.

Yugoslavia had taken shape around a Serbian core during a series of wars in the late nineteenth and early twentieth centuries, as the Ottoman Empire gradually lost control of its Balkan territories. In 1917, the Pact of Corfu proclaimed that all Yugoslavs (meaning southern Slavs) would unite under the Serbian royal house. At the end of the Second World War, the monarchy was abolished and Communist Party leader Marshal Tito took control. After he died in 1980, the fragility of the federation he ruled quickly became apparent.

Bosnia, with a landmass about the equivalent of the state of West Virginia, became an independent country as Yugoslavia disintegrated. Roughly four million people lived in Bosnia, and three ethnic groups predominated: Slavic Muslims (forming 44 per cent of the population), Serbs (31 per cent), and Croats (17 per cent).

In January 1992, nationalist Bosnian-Serb leaders proclaimed a Serbian entity within Bosnia. In a referendum shortly thereafter, over 63 per cent of Bosnians voting chose independence, meeting the criteria for recognition set forth by the US and the European Community several months earlier. The US, along with most of the international community, recognised the independence of Bosnia-Herzegovina in April 1992.

In the spring of 1992, after its offensive in Croatia had ground to a stalemate, Serbia launched a war against Bosnia under orders issued by Slobodan Milosevic, who wished to create a Greater Serbia. Serbian paramilitary forces, reinforced by the Serbian-dominated Yugoslav National Army with the fourth largest arsenal in Cold-War Europe, began a campaign of terror in eastern Bosnia. By early May the Yugoslav Army announced that it would withdraw from Bosnia-Herzegovina. In reality, however, some 80,000 men simply changed uniforms and, armed with tanks and aircraft left behind by the Yugoslavs, continued the war and the killing.

This reconfigured Bosnian-Serb force under General Ratko Mladic, aided by paramilitary groups, began seizing territory in northern and eastern Bosnia, expelled much of the non-Serbian population, and engaged in 'ethnic cleansing'. This campaign included mass killings of civilians, concentration camps, systematic rape, and the forced displacement of millions; creating the largest flow of refugees in Europe since the Second World War. This picture was supported by the State Department's 1992 annual report on human rights which stated that Serbian forces in Bosnia were conducting a campaign of 'cruelty, brutality, and killing' unmatched in Europe since Nazi times.

Evidence suggests that forward parties from several Islamic fundamentalist groups were already in Bosnia by late in 1992, as the Muslim community cried out for international support. Most Muslim states were bound by their membership of the international community, although some were involved in the covert supply of limited amounts of arms. Al-Qaeda was one of the first to respond and it is widely believed within the intelligence community that Osama personally visited Bosnia at least twice to ascertain what he could do to help.

Throughout this aggression the United Nations, the European Union and the United States were ineffectual in efforts to broker peace. Critically, they also allowed the perpetuation of an uneven field of battle. At the request of the Milosevic regime, in September 1991 the UN imposed an arms embargo on Yugoslavia in an attempt to contain the fighting.

Soon after his arrival in Sudan, Osama was contacted through illicit channels by leaders of the many Bosnian-Muslim militias that had sprung up. With the arms embargo in place, Muslims were unable to buy military hardware to defend themselves. It was a plea that Osama not only rallied to: he adopted the issue as a personal cause. Although his intentions were probably clouded by his desire to spread fundamentalism, in the absence of action in the part of the international community, preventing the slaughter of innocents is a cause that even a neutral observer can understand.

During 1992, Osama embarked upon a three-pronged offensive to support the embattled Bosnian Muslims. This began with his own men. He had hundreds, possibly thousands of fighters readied in Afghanistan. They were equipped with clothing suitable for a European theatre of war, mostly like their counterparts in the Bosnian-Muslim resistance, and Al-Qaeda began quietly flying men into Sarajevo airport. At the height of the conflict, analysts believe that anything up to 5,000 Arab-Afghans fought alongside their European brothers.

In his second initiative, Osama set up a number of charitable groups through which funds could be 'legitimately' transferred into Bosnia, both for Al-Qaeda battalions and also in order to support the Bosnian Muslims themselves. Finally, he quickly became one of the largest donors of arms and heavy artillery to the Bosnian Muslims. He purchased tens of millions of dollars of equipment through his contacts in the black market worldwide. Al-Qaeda arms dumps in Sudan and Afghanistan were requisitioned and millions of dollars of in-house supplies dispatched to the arming Muslim resistance. It was a massive logistical deployment and provided a clear illustration of the strength and organisation of Al-Qaeda almost a decade before the turn of the millennium.

Osama himself has seldom referred to his involvement in Bosnia and when he has it is only in passing, perhaps because it was not a jihad in the modern sense of the word. But his Arab-Afghans were nevertheless credited with playing a large role in the defence of the Muslim community in Bosnia.

Somalia, meanwhile, was in the grip of an unprecedented disaster. In January 1991, after a brutal 21-year reign, President Mohamed Siad Barre had been overthrown. If what Barre had inflicted upon his people was not bad enough, Somalia had then disintegrated into factionalism, largely based upon ethnically-divided groups. Armed gangs ran neighbourhoods, all civil services and government broke down. The power struggle carved a country of eight million people into a collection of fiefdoms run by warlords. More than 350,000 Somalis died during the resultant fighting and famine.

Gunmen from these fiefdoms hijacked emergency food deliveries sent by the outside world, further exacerbating the famine. Now one of the so-called Somali warlords, Barre deliberately politicised this humanitarian effort, claiming that the effort was being made in his support. This drew further attacks from the leader of the United Somali Congress (USC), General Mohammed Farrah Aidid who promised 'unprecedented bloodshed' should foreign forces land in 'his country'.

Eventually, however, images of starving civilians prompted the international community into action. The United States ordered more emergency supplies through Operation Provide Relief, although this was dangerous because relief flights were targets for anti-aircraft fire. Again the Somali warlords and their men stole this food as soon as it landed, which made the international community realise that food had to be delivered on the ground, with military support if necessary.

UN Security Council Resolution 794, passed on December 3, 1992, sanctioned an operation intended to simply prevent the warring factions from stealing the food and medicine deliveries. The troops were to act as a police force, ensuring the supplies reached the people who needed it. On December 9, 1992, US Marines went ashore in the Somali capital Mogadishu and quickly established an expeditionary infrastructure to facilitate security and the delivery of food to the starving Somalis. The Somali militia were all too keen to kill any American servicemen, so their landing was a very serious venture. Troops were cleared to 'shoot to kill' if their lives were threatened by hostile forces. These initial forces went on to secure the airport at Mogadishu and prepare it for the bulk arrival of the United Nations mandated forces. When they arrived, this force hurried to secure the food supplies and transportation routes. The landscape and the population were both devastated and starved. Foreign soldiers were horrified by what they saw.

Despite terrible conditions, the operation went well. Mogadishu was quickly secured and troops spread out into neighbouring towns. Engineers helped to rebuild the infrastructure as they went along in an attempt to make this awful situation a one-off, and equip the country to begin functioning by itself.

On December 11, Aidid signed a cease-fire with the other factions, and they agreed to pull their forces out of Mogadishu. This peace, however, was short-lived. After the initial success of Operation Restore Hope, the United Nations continued into UNOSOM II. This was intended as a 'without incidence' presence, allowing politicians to determine Somalia's future peacefully. This concept was perfect in theory, but it did not work in practice.

In no small part this is due to Aidid. Italian-trained, under Siad Barre he had served in the army, cabinet and as Somalia's ambassador to India. Barre named him intelligence chief, but later came to suspect Aidid of plotting against him and jailed him from 1969 to 1976. As Siad Barre's rule weakened, Aidid turned on his former boss and his fighters drove Barre from Mogadishu in January 1991. Shortly after, several groups emerged, all seeking to take the country. Aidid had been used to running things when the United States and United Nations started getting interested in Somalia. He was under no illusions that, should the international community be permitted to end the instability and return some semblance of normal life, the Somali warlords – himself included – would be marginalised.

During 1992 Aidid launched a round of international contacts with the leaders of the world's Islamic terrorist industry and gained immediate support from Iran and Sudan, the government of the latter seeking Osama and Al-Qaeda's involvement for a massive effort. The Islamic fundamentalist world was spoiling for a fight with the United States and Aidid was offering just that.

On several occasions Osama met Aidid. He found his behaviour repulsive: the General was profane, a heavy drinker, and despite coming from a relatively good background, was particularly uncivilised. What they had in common, however, was an enemy.

Well before the time of UN Security Council Resolution 794 in December 1992, Al-Qaeda had agreed to support General Aidid, who claimed that he wished to create a secular Islamic state. While this was doubtful, it nevertheless placed Osama in a position to fight the American threat, albeit vicariously. It was too good an opportunity to miss, as a former aide disclosed years later during trials connected with the embassy bombings in Africa. Jamal Ahmed al-Fadl, who had been close to Osama in his Khartoum office, quoted him as telling several dozen people at a meeting: 'The snake is America and we have to stop them. We have to cut off the head and stop them . . . [this is] what they are doing now in the Horn of Africa.'

In October and November 1992, Al-Qaeda worked as Osama had envisaged. After a brief 'board meeting' at which his decision to support General Aidid had been rubber-stamped, the organisation set itself in motion. Around Sudan a number of arms dumps were opened and an inventory of weapons selected. These were then shipped by road – a road built by Osama's Al-Hijra for Construction and Development – to Port Sudan. From there they travelled by boat – a vessel belonging to his import and export firm Wadi al-Aqiq – through the Red Sea and into the Indian Ocean, for delivery to General Aidid in a remote location along the Somali coast.

It was a swift and easy operation, just as Osama had imagined when he built the concept in his mind. It was terrorism run like an export business. Repeated shipments were made, not just to Somalia but to groups in Ethiopia, Kenya and Djibouti that had been set up by Iran or Sudan to support the effort. In remote parts of Somalia, Osama purchased large farms on which to build other facilities for the international coalition.

All around the Horn of Africa, men flowed in to new camps, preparing for the showdown with America. Among these were 3,000 Arab-Afghans, pulled out of camps in Afghanistan and transported from Pakistan to Yemen. Later, he airlifted these men to Somalia to participate in the resistance against US forces. Osama subsequently boasted that his commitment to transportation during this operation cost him $3 million.

Other funds were channelled to these new outposts of fundamentalism through Osama's existing network of commercial interests and via his Brotherhood Group, which proved remarkably effective. During the Somali campaign, the Brotherhood proved itself as the future of financing for the movement.

Al-Qaeda was also asked to hit the American military elsewhere as it hurriedly prepared for entry into Somalia. The United States was using the southern Yemeni port of Aden as a base for its build up in the region ahead of entering Somalia. Osama activated a group that had been under his umbrella for some time, Yemeni Islamic Jihad, which was made up of about 500 experienced Arab-Afghan fighters.

An ally from Afghanistan, Tariq al-Fadhli, was persuaded by

Osama to leave his semi-retirement in London to head the operation in Yemen. Within weeks, Yemeni Islamic Jihad had formed into a number of active, separate cells. More foreign expertise flowed into the country, reportedly including one of Islamic fundamentalism's 'stars', a Libyan bomb-maker considered the finest in his business. He began teaching Yemeni volunteers the basics of explosives in preparation for their effort.

What emerges, according to reports, is that a mass campaign was being planned by Al-Qaeda against American targets in Yemen. Fortunately it was exposed.

On December 29, two hotel bombs in Yemen killed two Austrian tourists and narrowly missed 100 American servicemen en route to Operation Restore Hope. The Aden Hotel and Golden Moor Hotel were both hit. Later the same day, moments from carrying out their mission, a strike team was discovered preparing to fire an RPG-7 rocket launcher at a giant C-5 Galaxy transport aircraft. Although no US targets were hit, these events rattled the American authorities. It was also a precursor for what was to come in Somalia.

With the success of the Al-Qaeda–run Yemeni mission, Aidid and his Islamic fundamentalist allies grew bold. Soon after UNOSOM II got into its stride in Somalia, terrorist groups began prodding defences with low-intensity attacks launched out of Aidid-held areas of Mogadishu. Then, on June 5, 1993, unknown gunmen ambushed Pakistani troops attached to the effort. The Pakistanis were not prepared and lost 24 soldiers.

That incident drove the United Nations troops to lose their neutrality in what was now no longer simply a peace-keeping mission. They began offensive operations in Somalia, with aerial strikes against Aidid's headquarters and arms depots between June 13 and 15. Patrols were sent along the outskirts of Mogadishu to hunt him out, but they were unsuccessful. During one raid, 50 Somali soldiers were killed, defending an assault on Aidid's house by US ground troops and Cobra gunships.

Attacks against UN troops intensified, leading US commanders to report to their political masters that Aidid needed to be either imprisoned, or killed, in order for the attacks to stop. The US sent in both the Rangers and Delta Force elite troops, but neither was successful, and a succession of botched raids saw United Nations-mandated peacekeepers attack hospitals and civilians by mistake.

A last-ditch attempt was made on October 3 to capture General

Aidid, but it too ended in tragedy. At around 3:30 p.m., six Blackhawk helicopters dropped 90 Rangers and Delta Force soldiers into the middle of General Aidid's neighbourhood, near the Olympic Hotel in Mogadishu. A group of his supporters was captured, and an escape convoy had pulled into place with another 52 Rangers aboard to provide covering fire.

The raid was seemingly a success when the first of two helicopters to crash went down. In the ensuing rescue operations, soldiers from both sides were slaughtered, as were civilians who poured into the streets to see what was going on. Later, when the bodies of two US soldiers were paraded around the city by rebel soldiers, television cameras were there to capture the scene and to underline to global audiences the callous and evil nature of the forces that the United Nations was dealing with.

While Osama and Al-Qaeda had no direct involvement in this incident, the eventual withdrawal of the United States and United Nations was, in no small part, directly due to their involvement in the fundamentalist coalition formed to 'defend' Somalia. Al-Qaeda had put more and better arms into the hands of Aidid and inserted thousands of men into the war zone, allowing his forces to produce the level of resistance that sapped the international community's ability and desire to help Somalia. Mass starvation had been overcome, and security was improved. But under international pressure, critical of its operations, the UN force was withdrawn. In mid-1994, the last US troops left Somalia, having failed in their task.

Later, Osama would comment: 'After Allah honoured us with victory in Afghanistan, and justice prevailed and the killing of those who slaughtered millions of Muslims in the Muslim republics, it cleared from Muslim minds the myth of superpowers. The youth ceased from seeing America as a superpower. After leaving Afghanistan they headed for Somalia and prepared for a long battle, thinking that the Americans were like the Russians.

'But they were surprised when the Americans entered with 300,000 troops, and collected more troops from the world – 5,000 from Pakistan, 5,000 from India, 5,000 from Bangladesh, 5,000 from Egypt, Senegal and others like Saudi Arabia. The youth were surprised at the low morale of the American soldiers and realised more than before that the America soldiers are paper tigers. After a few blows, they ran in defeat and America forgot about all the hoopla and media propaganda after leaving the Gulf War and destroying infrastructure – and destroying baby formula factories, all civilian factories, bridges and dams that help planting food – about being the world leader, and the leader of the new world order.

'After a few blows, they forgot about this title and left, dragging their corpses and their shameful defeat and stopped using such titles. And they learned in America that this name is larger then them. When this took place, I was in Sudan, and this great defeat pleased me very much, the way it pleases all Muslims.'

On the departure of the United Nations, warring Somali clan leaders had been unable to find common ground for agreement, and international relief organisations were forced to suspend operations because of widespread looting. As soon as the aid agencies began pulling out, law and order broke down again and the warlords resumed their fractional fighting.

In another interview Osama revealed his thoughts: 'The so-called superpowers vanished into thin air. We think that the United States is very much weaker than Russia. Based on the reports we received from our brothers who participated in jihad in Somalia, we learned that they saw the weakness, frailty, and cowardice of US troops. Only 80 US troops were killed. Nonetheless, they fled in the heart of darkness, frustrated, after they had caused great commotion about the new world order . . . '

American and UN troops were indeed harried out of Somalia – cause for celebration in Osama's Sudan headquarters – but with them went hope for the people of Somalia of a speedy end to the deadly civil war. As a direct result of his intervention and those of his allies in Iran and Sudan, hundreds of thousands more Muslim innocents died in the prolonged fighting. On this fact he has never commented.

The collapse of the South Tower of the World Trade Center after the terrorist attacks of September 11, 2001. (AP/WIDE WORLD PHOTOS)

Osama bin Laden (*center*) with his two top lieutenants in the Al-Qaeda network, Dr Ayman al-Zawahiri (*left*), a physician and founder of Egyptian Islamic Jihad who was his second in command, and Mohammad Atef (*right*), the chief military strategist, who is suspected of having helped plan the attacks on the World Trade Center and the Pentagon. (CORBIS/BETTMANN)

Osama bin Laden, a hero of the jihad against the Soviet occupation of Afghanistan, in Jeddah, Saudi Arabia, in 1988. (AGENCE FRANCE PRESSE)

Bin Laden in a photograph taken in April 1998, four months before the attacks on the American embassies in Kenya and Tanzania. The map in front of him is of Afghanistan. (AP/WIDE WORLD PHOTOS)

Sheikh Abdullah Yusuf Azzam, the "reviver of jihad in the twentieth century" (*Time*) and a towering influence on bin Laden, was both a mentor and a father figure throughout the Soviet-Afghan war.

Dr Hassan al-Turabi, Sudan's spiritual leader and a powerful supporter of terrorism worldwide, gave bin Laden safe haven after he fled Saudi Arabia in 1991 and harbored the Al-Qaeda network until 1996. He is thought to have been another surrogate father for bin Laden. (CORBIS/BETTMANN)

The February 26, 1993, truck bombing of the World Trade Center resulted in 6 deaths, 1,042 injuries, and damages of more than $500 million. Shown is the damaged underground parking garage.(ATF PHOTO)

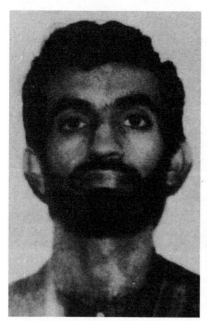

Ramzi Ahmed Yousef, mastermind of the World Trade Center bombing. (AP/WIDE WORLD PHOTOS)

Nidel Ayyad, the chemical engineer convicted in the World Trade Center bombing. (CORBIS/BETTMANN)

Sheikh Omar Abdel-Rahman, the influential Egyptian cleric convicted for his role in conspiring to blow up the World Trade Center and other New York City landmarks. (CORBIS/BETTMANN)

Wadih el-Hage, a US citizen who joined Al-Qaeda in early 1992 and worked closely with bin Laden in Khartoum, Sudan, admitted to being part of the 1998 embassy bombing conspiracy.

The American embassies in Kenya and Tanzania were bombed by Al-Qaeda on August 7, 1998. Shown here is a scene of horror from the bombing in Nairobi, Kenya. (CORBIS/BETTMANN)

Mullah Mohammed Omar, the reclusive leader of the Taliban, welcomed bin Laden to Afghanistan when he was forced to leave Sudan in 1996. (BBC NEWS)

Ahmed Ressam, a former member of the Armed Islamic Group in Algeria and veteran of an Al-Qaeda training camp in Afghanistan, was convicted of terrorism for plotting to bomb the Los Angeles International Airport during the millennium celebrations.

The USS *Cole* was attacked by suicide bombers while making a port call in Aden, Yemen, on October 12, 2000. Seventeen sailors died and 39 were wounded. (AP/WIDE WORLD PHOTOS)

The hijackers of American Airlines Flight 11, which was flown into the North Tower of the World Trade Center (*left to right, starting with top row*): Mohammed Atta, Abdulaziz Alomari, Satam M. A. Al Suqami, Wali M. Alshehri, and Waleed M. Alshehri.

The hijackers of United Airlines Flight 175, which was flown into the South Tower of the World Trade Center (*left to right, starting with the top row*): Ahmed Alghamdi, Fayez Rashid Ahmed Hassan Al Qadi Banihammad, Marwan Al-Shehhi, Hamza Alghamdi, and Mohand Alshehri.

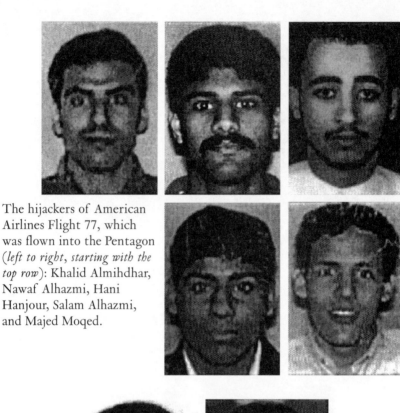

The hijackers of American Airlines Flight 77, which was flown into the Pentagon (*left to right, starting with the top row*): Khalid Almihdhar, Nawaf Alhazmi, Hani Hanjour, Salam Alhazmi, and Majed Moqed.

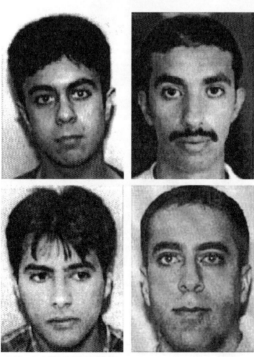

The hijackers of United Airlines Flight 93, which crashed in Stony Creek township, Pennsylvania (*left to right, starting with the top row*): Saeed Alghamdi, Ahmad Ibrahim A. Al Haznawi, Ahmed Alnami, and Ziad Samir Jarrah.

CHAPTER TWELVE

Establishing the Firm

By the time President Bill Clinton and his aides were discussing an exit strategy for United States troops in Somalia, Al-Qaeda had burst into life. For his contribution towards the much-touted victory in Somalia, Osama bin Laden was on his way to becoming one of Islamic fundamentalism's biggest powerbrokers. His personal vision, 'Terror Incorporated', now had a fully defined form; such were the demands of running this emerging global network of fear that its 'chairman' was being forced to draw away from his private commercial operations in Sudan.

Al-Qaeda was already the leading non-governmental terrorist organisation in the world; a giant dominating the 'industry' of Islamic fundamentalism. Osama clearly revelled in the role of the tycoon. His arrival at his office in central Khartoum in an armed convoy of four-wheel drive cars and jeeps, sirens blaring, was meant to impress. Unsmiling Al-Qaeda militiamen and Sudan Army soldiers wielding machine guns surrounded him, almost daring the residents of Khartoum to act suspiciously.

Osama was theatrically dismissive of the commotion around him on these trips, but family members recall him as always loving attention. A hair-raising ten-minute swing into Khartoum past staring onlookers at the side of the road would have perfectly suited his more childish fantasies and desire for attention.

But aside from his false modesty, the security around Osama was certainly required. What was going on in Khartoum cannot have escaped the CIA's attention even though its hands were officially tied. From Dr Hassan al-Turabi down, Sudan's government had cultivated a reputation as the home of Islamic fundamentalism, and terror groups operating from Sudan were spreading fear throughout the world. The Sudanese were involved with the Iranians, the Iraqis and Islamic elements that the Americans were engaging on every front. If the US intelligence community were for some reason unsure about the extent of Osama's ambitions, his praises were being shouted from the rooftops within his industry – an industry being watched carefully in Washington.

At least one attempt was made on Osama's life in Khartoum. Two gunmen, one riding a motorcycle, attempted to murder him while he was en-route to the office. Both were shot dead before they had a chance to get close enough. One militiaman was killed. Osama was unharmed but shaken. That same day he telephoned his mother to complain bitterly about the incident, apparently oblivious to the possible reasons. He blamed Saudi Arabia for the attempt, but there seems to have been little in the way of an investigation. The assassins themselves were dead and no foreign government has ever admitted involvement.

A day in the Al-Qaeda office was not that of any senior executive in a major corporation in the West. One fascinating glimpse inside Al-Qaeda was offered by one of the few defectors from the organisation ever to reach the western world. In February 2001, the trial of suspects later convicted for their involvement in the African embassy bombings heard evidence from Jamal Ahmed Al-Fadl, a Sudanese who joined Osama in 1990 and was with him from the beginning of his operation in Sudan. Later, after stealing money from Al-Qaeda, he had been apprehended by militiamen. He escaped and sought refuge in the United States, offering to testify against his former employers.

As he gave evidence, Al-Fadl explained to the jury that he had worked closely with Osama in Khartoum, and helped manage his payroll. That gave him access to files on each member of the group, which showed their salaries and aliases. Al-Fadl also described a global banking network, naming banks in Sudan, Malaysia, Britain, Hong Kong and Dubai where the group kept funds.

Al-Fadl also went on to describe labour disputes within Al-Qaeda. Osama had to grapple with complaints over the number of Egyptians among its leadership and the disparity in pay among the group's members. Employees received monthly checks of several hundred dollars. As the firm's accountant, he had also been asked by Osama to buy five farms around Sudan for the group to use as training camps. According to this testimony one farm had cost $250,000 and another $180,000. Al-Qaeda, he said, was sufficiently well organised that when Osama wished to travel or send his executives abroad, he would simply pick up a telephone and call internally to the Al-Qaeda travel office, which arranged plane tickets and visas.

Al-Fadl also detailed the operations of a military committee, which oversaw war training and weapons purchases; a finance committee; an Islamic committee that debated religious law; and a media committee which published the group's daily newspaper, *Nashrat al-Akhbar*.

Also working in Osama's office, according to this testimony, was Abu Muaz el-Masry, Al-Qaeda's in-house interpreter of dreams. 'If anyone had dream and believed that his dream could come true,' Al-Fadl said, 'he would go and tell him.' Abu Muaz, he added, had great experience with dreams: 'He's a scholar for that.'

During a normal day, Osama juggled the demands of a large and expansive operation from a plain, whitewashed office decorated with nothing more than framed Islamic posters, a plain green carpet and venetian blinds. After the attempt on his life, they were permanently closed for security reasons. A bookshelf dominating one end of the room was full of matching green leather-bound books dealing with Islamic topics. A plethora of unmatching floor cushions was piled haphazardly along a wall. This was his informal majlis. His chipboard desk was similarly unimpressive. One old-style dial telephone, a few papers and some Bic pens were scattered on its surface.

But if his office was unassuming, the visitors to Osama's lair were not. His patron in Sudan, al-Turabi, passed by on occasions. Another who got to know him over cups of sweet tea and Turkish coffee in his office was the president of Sudan, General Omar Hassan al-Bashir.

Sudan's great and good flocked to Osama's side. All passed several rings of iron-clad security and, just outside his office door, a handful of militiamen sat menacingly, armed with semi-automatic rifles. All visitors were eyed with suspicion and most were searched. After clearing this final hurdle, a secretary would usher the visitor into his master's office.

Osama has a powerful personal presence. With his height – six-foot-five – he towers over most men. Obviously shy, he takes time to warm towards a new person. His quiet speech and gentle mannerisms are similarly reserved. Nevertheless, those who know him say that, with age and having grasped some of the power he had sought for so long, he has developed a dignity and nobility that had been altogether missing in the straggling youth of previous days.

Despite his peaceful demeanour, visitors have said he projects something indefinably ominous in a room. Some have described this as intimidation by osmosis – the awareness that he is capable of terror beyond belief. To others, however, he is a charming, magnetic character. Perversely, while he rages against the infidels of the West, the few Europeans and Americans he meets are welcomed warmly and with courtesy.

On occasion, when confident of those around him, Osama opens up and is surprisingly lucid. If he were an Oxford scholar, he might have been in the Debating Club, as his argument and reasoning are well projected.

For all this, Osama is a listener at heart. He would offer refreshments, tea without milk or Turkish coffee, and invariably come from behind his desk to sit on some cushions next to his visitor, majlis style, preferring the informality that this offers.

Over the course of a morning, Osama would hold meetings and take telephone calls. Most days he would chair the Al-Qaeda high command, his board of directors that was responsible for all areas of the organisation's operations. This would be followed by individual meetings with assorted staff members, usually including accountants and the heads of his training and recruitment departments.

Although not a sheikh or prince, Osama liked to project himself as such; indeed a growing number of people were attaching this to his name. He did nothing to dissuade them.

Each day a steady stream of impoverished Sudanese beat a path to his door seeking help. For ordinary people, life in a Sudan wracked by civil war was not easy. The economy was in tatters, jobs were scarce and social programs non-existent. Foreign aid donors had long since turned their backs on Sudan as its government followed an extremist path, leaving the people without hope. The streets of Khartoum and other cities thronged with beggars. Al-Turabi's Islamic revolution would have been more welcome at street level had it brought bread or opportunities for his citizens to feed their families.

Most Sudanese knew Osama bin Laden's name and nothing else about this foreigner in their midst, but few were in any doubt about the charity of the man that sat in a sparse office in Khartoum overlooking the Blue Nile. By 1993, Osama began to hold court in his office for a short time each day, listening to the steady stream of Sudanese who asked for his help. The 'sheikh' dished out the equivalent of a couple of dollars to each, after first hearing their pleas in a satisfied silence.

As time went on, the gentleman businessman image he liked to project had more and more parallels with a mafia godfather or an oil sheikh in one of the Gulf states that he despised so much. At one time, he even boasted to family members of throwing coins from his car window while travelling through the impoverished areas of Khartoum – reminiscent of the behaviour of former kings of Saudi Arabia. Nevertheless, he was seduced by the respect that he was now being shown, and throughout his time in Khartoum, a day seldom passed without Osama handing out money to those who came begging.

The only time when the door of Osama's Khartoum office was closed was when the business end of Terror Incorporated was being discussed. Potential targets were mooted openly in a way that horrified some of his close associates. Even junior office staff were encouraged by Osama to offer an opinion, because Osama cared for the approval of ordinary Muslims. But when he and his board had made an executive decision to follow a particular course of action, the door was shut for planning to be done in private. For security reasons, meetings were often held at one of his farms outside Khartoum: international terrorism planned in the bizarre setting of a circle of cushions in the middle of a field – certainly away from any covert listening devices.

Like a corporation funding research and development, Al-Qaeda's terrorism wing had put out its feelers discreetly and made it known that 'useful concepts' would receive a favourable hearing for support. Many came through, were discussed by the military committee and discarded. Those that seemed interesting were passed on 'upstairs' for rumination among the board of directors and by Osama. Several quasi-independent operations were discovered and nurtured in this manner.

Osama enjoyed this part of his work. It made him feel like a philanthropist, perhaps like his father who gave millions to charity and was universally respected as a result. It also helped him keep his finger on the pulse of what was being done around the world to further the cause of Islamic fundamentalism.

Amid the flurry of activity it was inconceivable to Osama – as it must be to anyone – that he was not already being monitored closely by the foreign intelligence services. In Sudan it was common knowledge to the man in the street that Al-Hijra for Construction and Development Ltd was a front for Osama bin Laden, fundamentalist hero of the Afghanistan campaign. Most people also knew of his anti-American, anti-western rhetoric. He was in Sudan as a guest of the government and planning to export Islamic fundamentalism around the Middle East. Few doubted how he intended to do this. Most applauded him.

In September 1992, 26-year-old Palestinian Ahmad Mohammed Ajaj flew into New York's Kennedy Airport from Pakistan. He was arrested on a passport violation, having crudely super-glued a photograph of himself into a Swedish passport that was found to be stolen. In his luggage, Ajaj had many other fake passports, as well as Arabic manuals and video cassette tapes describing several methods of manufacturing explosives, including urea nitrate, nitroglycerine, lead azide, TNT and other powerful explosives.

Interviews and fingerprint examinations identified two other men who were later to become an integral part of the bombing of the World Trade Center the following year. The most important was Ramzi Ahmed Yousef, who had entered the United States on the same flight as Ajaj, but had been deported immediately. Yousef had been kicking around the Islamic fundamentalist world for some time after leaving the battlefields of Afghanistan with a big reputation, and was known to work within the Al-Qaeda network. His fingerprints were also found in the manuals on explosives located in Ajaj's checked luggage.

Amazingly, as Ajaj languished in jail for passport fraud, over a five-month period he spoke with Yousef on around 20 occasions. All prison telephone calls are taped, but Ajaj's were never studied because they were in Arabic. Ajaj was never identified as a potential terrorist because, as later emerged during testimony before a senate commission in June 2001, his Arabic terrorism journals were not fully translated into English for nine years. These lapses allowed Yousef to slip undetected back into America. He had a job to complete.

On February 26, 1993, an explosion in the World Trade Center parking garage resulted in six deaths, 1,042 injuries and damage of more than $500 million. The blast was caused by a bomb made of about 1,200 lbs of explosives, the main explosive charge consisting primarily of a home-made, fertiliser-based explosive, urea nitrate. The blast produced a crater, approximately 150 feet in diameter and five storeys deep. The device had been placed in the rear cargo portion of a Ford F350 Econoline van.

Initial inspection on February 27 was described as 'a scene of massive devastation, almost surreal'. According to one report it was 'like walking into a cave, with no lights other than flashlights flickering across the crater. There were small pockets of fire, electrical arcing from damaged wiring, and automobile alarms whistling, howling and honking . . . '

The explosion ruptured two of the main sewerage lines from both towers and the Vista Hotel and several water mains from the air-conditioning system. In all, more than two million gallons of water and sewerage had to be pumped out.

A vehicle frame fragment found on the site led to identification of the van used by the bombers. Federal Bureau of Investigation agents travelled to the Ryder rental agency in Jersey City, New Jersey, which had rented the vehicle and began an interview with the station manager. While the interview was under way, a man named Mohammed Salameh telephoned to ask for the return of his security deposit. A meeting was arranged with Salameh at the Ryder agency on March 4. When he arrived to pick up the $400 deposit, FBI agents were on hand to place him under surveillance.

The Jersey City address Salameh gave on the rental agreement was searched by investigators, who discovered tools, wires, circuitry, electromagnetic devices as well as explosives residue. This also led to Salameh's roommate, Ramzi Yousef. However, he had left the US for Pakistan the day after the bombing on board a Pakistan International Airlines flight.

Another man fingered through this search was Nidel Ayyad, a chemist working for the Allied Signal Corporation in New Jersey. Ayyad was connected to Salameh through telephone records and joint bank accounts. He was arrested and his personal computer was seized. Through further telephone records and receipts, a safe address that had been used as a bomb-making factory was located in Jersey City. A search revealed that acids and other chemicals had been used at that apartment to manufacture explosives. Traces of nitroglycerine and urea nitrate were found on the carpet and embedded in the ceiling.

Telephone records from Salameh and Ayyad showed that calls had been made to a self-storage centre not far from the bomb factory. An interview with its manager indicated that Salameh had rented storage space, and that four 'Arab-looking' individuals had been observed using a Ryder van several days before the bombing. During the search of the storage room rented by Salameh, chemicals and laboratory equipment were located. Among the items seized were 300 lbs of urea, 250 lbs of sulphuric acid, numerous one-gallon containers, some containing nitric acid and sodium cyanide. While examining a rubbish bin, a white crystalline substance was found. Chemical analysis identified this as urea nitrate.

On March 3, a typewritten note was received at the *New York Times*. The communiqué claimed responsibility for the bombing 'in the name of Allah'. Saliva samples from Salameh, Ayyad and a third man, Mahmud Abuhalima, were obtained and compared with the saliva on the envelope flap. A DNA-Q Alpha examination concluded that Ayyad had licked the envelope on the communiqué. Abuhalima, who was an integral part of the conspiracy, had fled the United States the day after the bombing. He was later arrested in Egypt and extradited to the United States.

The subsequent trial lasted six months. On March 4, 1994, exactly one year after Salameh's arrest, the jury found Salameh, Ajaj, Abuhalima and Ayyad guilty on all 38 charges. Abuhalima was identified during neighbourhood investigations at the bomb factory and storage centre through photos.

Also eventually tried and found guilty for his part in the plot was the blind cleric Sheikh Omar Abdel-Rahman. An Egyptian scholar, he was living in the US at the time of the attack and helped orchestrate the team involved. His connection to Al-Qaeda came via Egyptian Islamic Jihad and its leader, Dr Ayman al-Zawahiri. Sheikh Omar had been tried and acquitted in Egypt in connection with the assassination of Egyptian president Anwar Sadat, but was immersed in the cause and a known member of the group.

On February 7, 1995, FBI agents and State Department

diplomatic security officers apprehended Yousef, also known as Abdul Basit Mahmoud Abdul Karim, in Islamabad, Pakistan. He was charged, and later convicted of offences relating to his involvement in the World Trade Center bombing.

After his arrest in Pakistan, Yousef was flown back to the United States. He was blindfolded and handcuffed. Only once during the journey did any of his FBI handlers speak with him. On the final leg of his journey, by helicopter at night over New York, an FBI man reportedly pulled up his blindfold and motioned to the lights of the Twin Towers. 'Look down there. They are still standing,' he taunted the terrorist. Yousef fired back immediately: 'They would not be if I had enough money and explosives.'

In a subsequent interview with ABC, Osama eulogised Yousef. 'Ramzi Yousef, after the World Trade Center bombing, became a well-known Muslim personality, and all Muslims know him. Unfortunately, I did not know him before the incident. I remember him as a Muslim who defended Islam from American aggression. He took this action to let Americans know that their government assaults Muslims to insure Israeli interests . . . America will see many youths who will follow Ramzi Yousef.' What Osama was less than keen to give away was that Yousef was a senior field operative for Al-Qaeda.

During the gap between the 1993 bombing and his 1995 arrest, Yousef went into overdrive and came close to hitting several major targets for Al-Qaeda and Islamic fundamentalism, emerging in early 1994 in the Philippines managing an active terror cell. The Manila cell began orchestrating plans for a series of simultaneous US aircraft hijackings from airports all over Asia, involving up to a dozen aircraft. These aircraft were to be brought down in the ocean, killing possibly thousands of passengers. The theme of simultaneous hijacks was one that Osama would return to later in his campaign, but at the time it was a plan so audacious that Al-Qaeda believed there was little chance that it would be stumbled upon.

Training began at Al-Qaeda camps in Sudan or Afghanistan, while Yousef and Wali Khan Amin Shah, who had been searching for a cause since the end of the war against the Soviets, set about establishing a network of safe houses around major Asian air transportation hubs, gathering intelligence and putting together a team.

The plot was taking shape when the pair also got wind of a

staggering new opportunity. President Clinton was planning a tour of Asian countries. Yousef, now established as Osama's golden boy, easily sold the idea of assassinating Clinton in Manila and was given a green light to pursue the plan at whatever cost. Through his contacts with fundamentalist groups in Iran, Sudan and elsewhere, Osama began requesting reliable sharpshooters to be seconded to Al-Qaeda for training. Osama wanted to create a multiple cell unit in Manila that would plan several attempts on Clinton's life in the Philippines, in the hope that if one or more were discovered, an attack could still go ahead. The plan was only scrapped when Clinton was forced to alter his travel plans. But these preparations were not wasted as a second Yousef concept, a plot to murder Pope John Paul II, was also pursued. Methods of attack discussed included bombs, a missile attack on the papal motorcade and a sniper attack using mercury-tipped bullets.

Two projects – the multiple hijacking and papal assassination – were progressing when the plotters brought everything to an end through their own incompetence. On January 7, 1995, Abdul Hakim Murad, a member of Al-Qaeda's lead cell in Manila who was also wanted in the United States in connection with the World Trade Center bombing, was working on an explosive device when he broke a basic rule of bomb-making. He washed his hands, mixing the water with chemical residue in the kitchen sink. This set off a minor blast and started a fire. Firefighters were called to an emergency at a rented apartment in the Malate district of Manila, just 200 yards from the Vatican's embassy, a week before the arrival of Pope John Paul II. Worried firemen reported their suspicions to the authorities and, later the same day, a raid on the apartment uncovered a Pandora's box of terrorism.

Police were shocked by what they found: besides a smoking mixture of explosives in a sink, there were street maps and garments similar to those worn by the Pope's entourage, suggesting a plan to get close to the pontiff before shooting him. Also found were computer disks containing detailed plans to blow up US airliners. This involved leaving bombs on flights taking off from Tokyo, Seoul, Taipei, Hong Kong, Bangkok and Singapore that would explode over the Indian Ocean.

More astonishingly, Yousef had also implicated himself by leaving abundant evidence around the apartment linking himself and his co-conspirators with the bombing of a Philippine Airlines

Flight 434 on December 11, 1994, from Cebu to Narita which had served as a test run. A small incendiary device had gone off, killing one passenger.

One of the most surprising revelations in the wake of the 2001 World Trade Center bombing was a claim from the Philippines that the 1995 apartment raid also produced evidence of another of Osama's grand designs. At the time of the raid, officers recovered a laptop computer. On this were discovered brief development notes for a 'Project Bojinka'.

Project Bojinka (land explosions) was a code name originally linked with the plot to plant bombs aboard 16 US airlines simultaneously, downing them in the Indian Ocean. No one at the time questioned this, despite Bojinka meaning land explosions, which has little association with downing civil airliners over the ocean. Tragically an alternative interpretation of what was contained in that laptop only emerged later.

Interviewed after September 11, 2001, by Singapore's *Straits Times*, Chief Superintendent Avelino Razon, then head of Manila Police and the officer who had led the raid on Yousef's apartment, claimed that Project Bojinka had a far greater aim. 'This could have been part of an overall plot,' said Razon. 'During the course of the investigation, we found out through a laptop computer confiscated from Murad that they were also going to implement a terrorist plot called Project Bojinka.'

Murad was immediately arrested and was all too ready to detail the operations of the terrorist cell in Manila, its counterparts in other Asian states and the cell's central projects. The ringleaders, Yousef and Shah, had broken the cardinal rule of terrorist cell commanders and shared comprehensive information on plans with someone lower on the command chain. More than this, he had all but handed over sensitive, inside information of some of Al-Qaeda's future projects, too. According to reports, Murad informed a joint US and Philippine police investigation that, among others, Project Bojinka aimed to hit targets such as the FBI headquarters and CIA headquarters in Langley, Virginia, with a civil airliner.

Several years later ABC's John Miller questioned Osama bin Laden about Shah, who was by then in jail. The Afghan's extraordinary ineptitude in that Manila apartment in January 1995 was a huge breach of Al Qaeda security. Osama gave no indication of any bitterness when he said: 'Wali Khan is a Muslim youth. In

Afghanistan, he was nicknamed "The Lion". He is one of the best youths. We were good friends. We fought together in the same trench against the Russians until Allah sent them away in humiliating defeat. You mentioned that he works for me. We do not have anyone who works for someone else. We all work for Allah and await his reward.

'And regarding your mention of his attempt to assassinate President Clinton, it is not surprising. I did not know about it, but it is not surprising. As I said, every action solicits a similar reaction. What does Clinton expect from those whom he killed and assaulted their children and mothers? This is not a surprising matter.'

Yousef and Shah had provided the authorities with an important coup. In shattering the Manila cell, the authorities seem to have stumbled upon the embryonic stages of planning for a hit directly on the United States using civilian airliners. Osama was far too clever too let any man, least of all a field operative with the limited intellect of Yousef, know the full extent of his scheme. But even losing minor details to the FBI was a blow that needed careful consideration. That a lowly foot soldier such as Murad could give his interrogators information that the FBI and CIA headquarters were being targeted shows concrete proof that Osama was actively planning a civilian airliner strike upon the United States more than half a decade before September 11, 2001. The plan he called 'al basal' (the onion) was a long way from completion, even in terms of planning. Al-Qaeda would have to be much more careful.

Predictably, there was a surge in troubles that year, all over the world, and most had deep roots in Al-Qaeda. From its bases dotted around Sudan and Afghanistan, Al-Qaeda had dispatched hundreds of men to Bosnia, where Slobodan Milosevic had launched his infamous ethnic cleansing campaign. In Algeria, the Armed Islamic Group (AIG) embarked this year upon a new tactic – the massacre of large groups of civilians. The AIG's leadership was heavily influenced by Arab-Afghans, its fighters were mostly trained in Sudani camps and funding and arms were both supplied by Al-Qaeda.

CHAPTER THIRTEEN

Full Circle

Extraordinarily, given the growing evidence that his hand was on the 1993 World Trade Center bombing, Osama was able to travel openly to Britain in 1994. Less than 18 months after the bombing in New York, with the Saudi Arabian authorities seeking his arrest, Osama flew into Heathrow Airport. He stayed for about three months.

His aim in making the trip that spring was, on the surface, to set up an information service for Al-Qaeda under the guise of being an Islamic charitable mission. While it was undoubtedly useful for Al-Qaeda to have a propaganda machine in London – and with its renowned political freedoms London was certainly the place to be – it is unlikely that he would risk capture when an accomplice could have taken on such a low-grade responsibility.

Britain remained a key centre of operations for Islamists of all creeds; a centre from where it was easy to operate with only minimal supervision by the authorities. Despite a close relationship between London and Riyadh, with its liberal visa regulations the British capital was the focal point for exiled Saudi dissidents, and Osama was therefore in good company. Many of those who were *persona non grata* in their homeland were fundamentalists and natural supporters of his. He used his time to network and build alliances.

London was to be a staging post for Al-Qaeda's expansion into Europe on several fronts. The city was Europe's financial capital, and Osama's allies would do his banking there. Funds would be drip fed into London via a number of commercial and charitable fronts and – untraceable amid the tens of billions that flowed in and out of the financial markets each day – laundered through a spider's web of accounts and bogus companies, ready to be dispatched anywhere in the world.

During his visit, Osama purchased a house on, or near, Harrow Road in the Wembley area of London. He paid cash, and used an intermediary as the named owner. After he left Britain the house was used by many of his contacts and also as a base where the organisation he formed in London, the Advisory and Reformation Committee, could meet discreetly. The house was equipped with a bank of fax machines, computers, photocopiers and printing equipment.

Reliable allies in London, such as fellow Saudi dissident Sheikh Omar Bakri, would later use the facilities offered by the Advisory and Reformation Committee to spread fundamentalist dogma. Essentially, this humble residential address in the suburbs of the British capital was the office of Islamic fundamentalism's spin doctors for the western world. Courtesy of all the normal, mundane channels of communication, the Advisory and Reformation Committee could spread the militant view of any event that occurred worldwide to thousands of its supporters and media organisations.

More than 20 years had passed since Osama's first and only previous visit to Britain and what is known is that he had developed and retained a liking for the country. At the time of his 1994 visit, while technically under suspicion for non-conformist activities in his homeland, he had not been exposed for any radical acts and had only been whispered about as the paymaster of the World Trade Center bombings, over one year earlier. Although there was resentment toward him for his unbending attitude toward the Al Sauds, and the devious way he had tricked his brother to escape Saudi Arabia, contacts remained with a number of family members.

Because of this, during this period, away from the phone tapping and observation he knew he was subject to in Khartoum, Osama was able to taste – probably for the last time – the simple pleasures of an anonymous and free man.

Osama had played soccer as a boy, kicking the ball around with his brothers, and he enjoyed the sport. In London during the early months of 1994 he was able to attend his first competitive soccer game at Arsenal's Highbury Road stadium. The thick-bearded Islamic fundamentalist must have been a strange sight in the stands, but nevertheless, if he felt out of place, he didn't seem to worry about it. On March 15, just one week after the Saudi Arabian government had withdrawn his citizenship, he was one of 34,678 spectators for the follow-up match that saw a single goal separate Arsenal from Torino of Italy, and send the Gunners into the semi-finals of the European Cup Winners' Cup competition.

The atmosphere that evening captivated Osama, who later told friends of the excitement he encountered. He commented that the passion of soccer fans was like nothing he had ever seen. He was back in the stands one month later – just prior to leaving the country – to see Arsenal dispatch the French team of Paris St Germain to reach the final of the competition. On his return to Sudan, Osama brought gifts for all his sons, including a replica Arsenal shirt for 15-year-old Abdullah, his eldest, and trinkets from the souvenir shop at Highbury for the others.

While he would never return to his hedonistic Beirut ways, Osama used the opportunity of being in London to reacquaint himself with the culture of the West. Undoubtedly he understood the storm that would surround him if the cells he had already planted into the West and Saudi Arabia were successful, and as the fundamentalist organisations he had brought under the Al-Qaeda umbrella began to expand their operations. He was rapidly becoming a target.

He had been provided with a BMW car and a driver by a wealthy supporter and, alongside trips into the financial districts on official business and visiting supporters elsewhere in the south-east of England, he used this freedom to the full. He is known to have explored at length the British Natural History Museum and British Museum, especially its Egyptian exhibit. Several of London's museums had Islamic exhibits which he also visited.

Osama was given to sending postcards. This paper trail shows that he toured the Tower of London and the Imperial War Museum. He also left the south of England on at least one occasion and was one of the million people every year who visit Edinburgh Castle in the Scottish capital. He lapped up these simple moments of anonymous tourism, moments that enrich the lives of ordinary people, and showed no signs of wanting to leave.

However, his departure was sudden. The Saudi Arabian government was keen to have him arrested and made representations to Britain. Hearing news of inquiries into his whereabouts, Osama immediately made for the airport and returned to his base in Sudan.

Osama also knew he was being monitored in Khartoum. It was more instinct than anything else, but was certainly supported by the knowledge that, having been linked directly to a plot to kill the leader of the free world, President Bill Clinton, and the leader of the Roman Catholic world, Pope John Paul II, he must have captured someone's attention. He quietly had his office swept for bugs, then his car, then his home in the outskirts of Khartoum, then his farm. Security at all had been breached; all contained listening devices. One bug was even discovered hidden behind the resevoir in the 'executive toilet' in his office in downtown Khartoum.

An international terrorist never really knows the identities of his enemies, but given that Osama had already been implicated as a supplier of arms to General Mohammed Farrah Aidid in Somalia, and then the financier of a plot to assassinate Clinton among other anti-US activities, there was not much guesswork involved.

In the spring of 1995, Osama's routine changed dramatically. He still held court in his simple office on McNimr Street in Khartoum, met local politicians, dished out money to the poor and took meetings for Al-Hijra for Construction and Development Ltd, Wadi al-Aqiq and Taba Investment Company Ltd, the main elements in his business empire. But those listening to his conversations will have felt a change.

Knowing that his enemies were monitoring his every word, Osama now used his Al-Qaeda office to bait them. He would speak at length with aides about plots that did not exist, hinting darkly that his men were preparing an imminent attack upon unnamed targets in the United States. He alluded to assassination attempts on President Clinton and his family, on Britain's prime minister John Major and a host of other world leaders. After a few weeks of non-events, Osama's audience would have realised that they were the victims of a dark joke. In quieter moments, away from listening devices, he could be found laughing heartily at the security alerts he must have sparked around the world. Eventually, tiring of this game, he ordered all buildings swept for listening devices and thereafter checked on an almost daily basis.

While posturing in the direction of an unseen listener was fun, Osama's deceit also extended to his own comrades. Some within Al-Qaeda knew of the existence of a project aimed at targeting mainland America with civil airliners, but the chief executive was careful that even his closest lieutenants did not know too much. Perhaps no one aside from Osama himself knew exactly how far he was planning to go, and how many men he was willing to sacrifice, to reach his ultimate objective.

In 1995 he was still several years from issuing his infamous Declaration of War against the Unites States, but plans were already in hand for his pièce de résistance, Project Bojinka. In the meantime, however, Osama waged a low-grade war upon the US and her allies, occasionally showing his hand with more ambitious attacks. But in the final analysis, after September 11, 2001, even the likes of the embassy bombings seem part of an elaborate smoke screen to deflect the attentions of the FBI and CIA from his ultimate objective.

To achieve this, Osama embarked on a massive program to acquire and ship the most modern arms he could to his bases in Sudan and Afghanistan. During the 2001 trial of the men subsequently convicted of bombing the American embassies in Kenya and Tanzania, one key witness offered an interesting insight into this drive.

Egyptian-born flight instructor Essam al Ridi worked for some time as Osama's pilot. Giving testimony in New York he admitted that he had helped Al-Qaeda buy a decommissioned military jet for $200,000 in order to ship anti-aircraft missiles from Pakistan to Sudan. Al Ridi told the jury that one of the defendants in that same trial, Wadih el-Hage, had acted as Osama's representative in the 1993 deal, explaining that the plane would be used to transport the shoulder-fired American Stinger missiles to Al-Qaeda bases.

Al Ridi was given a specification — including that the aircraft should have a flight range of at least 2,000 miles — and a budget of $250,000. He found a suitable T-39 in Tucson, Arizona. After refurbishing the aircraft, he flew it to Khartoum. In the Sudanese capital, Al Ridi claimed to have handed over the keys to Osama during a celebratory dinner.

With commitments to groups around the region growing, Osama's T-39 became a beast of burden, flying all over the Middle East and Africa ferrying shipments of arms and men. Other aircraft were purchased and joined a growing fleet.

Osama's roots went deep in Sudan. When his citizenship had been revoked by the Saudi government in April 1994, he had been given a Sudanese diplomatic passport under an alias. But more than this, Osama had settled well and his plans were evolving quietly, away from the glare of unwanted publicity. He was working towards something on the lines of Project Bojinka, and setting in motion the 'events' that would be his smoke screen to hide this. But while these plans were moving sweetly, other events again brought him into the spotlight, for once one that he wished to avoid.

Back in his homeland of Saudi Arabia, the government had attempted to forget about their errant citizen following his April 1991 flight into exile, making only quiet attempts to locate and arrest him. Briefly they had asked Pakistan's ISI agency to arrest him while Osama initially remained in Afghanistan. But following his settling in Sudan the Al Sauds had been happy to wash their hands of him. Family members recall that the Saudi Arabian security services asked for notification of any direct contact with Osama, but this seemed to mark the extent of their interest.

But as Al-Qaeda had begun to function fully, supplying training and arms to a variety of groups, the Saudis discovered that Osama was a problem that would not go away. During 1993 and 1994, high-level diplomatic channels between the kingdom and many of her Middle Eastern neighbours were filled with references to Al-Qaeda. One such contact reflects the emerging seriousness of the situation. Early in 1994, during the course of one of their regular telephone conversations, Egyptian president Hosni Mubarak brought up the matter with King Fahd. What was Fahd going to do, he asked, about the Saudi dissident who was inciting Egyptian Islamic Jihad, al-Gamaat al-Islamiyya, and other fundamentalist groups? Mubarak went on to explain that his Ministry of the Interior was briefing him that Al-Qaeda was training men from both those groups in Sudan, preparing for the overthrow of the Egyptian government.

This call, from one of the Arab world's most powerful leaders, was the final straw for King Fahd. He had already heard representations from Yemen and other Arab governments, claiming that Osama was out to destabilise them. The question was, what could he do? With few practical options open to him, King Fahd opted for a symbolic route, saying to the rest of the world: 'He's no longer one of ours'. In April 1994, his Saudi citizenship was revoked for 'irresponsible behaviour', and he was informed that he was no longer welcome in his land of birth because he had 'committed acts that adversely affected the brotherly relations of the kingdom of Saudi Arabia and other countries'. Surprisingly, this was a decision that both astounded and angered Osama. When he finally returned from his extended trip to Britain, more emphasis was now placed upon what could be done to topple the House of Saud.

His first salvo in this personal battle was to issue a statement condemning the decision and retorting that he did not require Saudi Arabian nationality to identify himself. Weeks later, his second move was the formation of a group of activists named the Advice and Reform Committee (ARC). The ARC was defined, according to its own press releases, communiqués and agenda, as a political group that aimed to be an effective opposition inside and outside of the one-party system in Saudi Arabia. The ARC published around 17 statements, most of which contained meandering criticisms of the government and plenty of religious rhetoric. However a peaceful approach never appealed to Osama and he quickly lost interest in ARC, allowing it to lapse.

Instead, he plotted armed revolt and issued dark statements. When the opportunity presented itself, through a press interview or television appearance, he repeated his mantra of accusations against the House of Saud, conveniently forgetting that in 1991 he had offered to defend the kingdom from Iraq with his Arab-Afghan fighters.

An interview with Osama in the November 1996 edition of . *Nida'ul Islam* magazine focused heavily upon his distaste for the Al Sauds and offers an apt portrayal of his bitterness. He was asked for his evaluation of the Al Saud regime's policy towards the Muslim world. He replied that it was 'tied to the British outlook . . . then it became attached to the American outlook after America gained prominence as a major power in the world after the Second World War. It is well known that the policies of these two countries bear the greatest enmity towards the Islamic world.

'The regime does not cease to cry publicly over matters affecting Muslims without making any serious effort to serve the interests of the Muslim community apart from small efforts in order to confuse people and throw dust into their eyes . . . The people's sympathies are with the working scholars who have been imprisoned . . . which led the people to support the general rectification movement led by the scholars . . . This movement is increasing in power and in supporters day after day at the expense of the regime. The sympathy with these missions at the civil and military levels are great, as also the sympathies of the Muslim world with the struggle against the Americans . . . '

At a time when the Saudi Arabian government was prodding the hornet's nest in Khartoum, they were helping to alienate people at home. In September 1994, Sheikh Salman bin Fahd al-Udah, a charismatic and well-known figure within Islamic circles in the kingdom, was imprisoned. He was a powerful voice, and one that had been raised against the royal family. But arresting him was a mistake. Sheikh Salman's incarceration invigorated the grassroots movement against the regime.

Never one to miss an opportunity, Osama was ready for such a blunder on the part of the Al Sauds. His organisation had been quietly recruiting among the disaffected youth of the country. Several thousand 'retired' Arab-Afghans were living quietly in the kingdom, and they had acted as agents, contacting suitable candidates from movements such as Sheikh Salman's. By 1994 it was estimated that between 15,000 and 20,000 young men had left the country in previous years to take part in Al-Qaeda training programs at camps in Afghanistan, Sudan, Iran and Yemen. Osama had laid the foundations of the armed resistance movement in Saudi Arabia, seemingly without the government getting wind of the underground army that now patiently bided its time.

The beginning of this battle came on November 13, 1994, in the Saudi capital Riyadh. Just before lunch a car bomb exploded in a parking lot in front of a three-storey building that contained a popular snack bar. It was always packed with Americans attached to the Military Cooperation Program, a joint effort between US forces and the Saudi National Guard.

The blast killed six people, five of them American. Around 200 lbs of Semtex produced a force that removed the front of the building and shattered windows for a one-mile radius. Subsequent investigation showed the operation to have been so well executed that it was impossible to trace to any organisation or individual.

A terrorist act in the centre of the Saudi capital was scarcely believable. *Al-Yawn*, one of Saudi Arabia's leading Arabic broadsheet newspapers, commented: 'This was a desperate attempt to destabilise the security of Saudi Arabia.' But there was more – and worse – to follow for the kingdom later.

★

Intelligence shows that Al-Qaeda was active on other fronts too. Indeed, the strength of the organisation as it stood during the mid-1990s is astonishing. Osama's global outlook is no better illustrated than in the case of the once little-known Caucasus state of Chechnya.

The Chechens are an indigenous people of the North Caucasus. They speak a distinct language, non-Slavic, non-Turkic, non-Persian. Chechens have traditionally been fiercely independent and democratic mountaineers. The Russian poet Lermontov wrote of them in 1832: 'Their god is freedom, their law is war.' From the seventeenth to the mid-nineteenth century, the Chechens were converted to the Sunni branch of Islam, the branch followed by Osama, and their religion plays an important role in Chechen society. The Russians conquered the region in 1859 after decades of resistance and more than 800,000 Chechens were deported to Central Asia by Stalin in 1944 for alleged collaboration with the Germans.

Chechnya itself is approximately 6,000 square miles, a little larger than the state of Connecticut. Its key resources are the rich oilfields surrounding the city of Grozny that have been exploited since 1893. Although petroleum production is declining, Grozny has remained a major centre of refining and petrochemical production, a hub for rail and road transport, as well as for important oil and gas pipelines.

Under the Russian Constitution, the Chechen Republic is part of the Russian Federation. However, in 1990 a secession movement began to gain force, and in November 1991, following the seizure of power by General Dzhokhar Dudayev, the region declared its independence. After a brief, unsuccessful attempt to quell the rebellion, Moscow entered into negotiations over the republic's future, and in 1992 Chechnya became an autonomous republic. Later the same year, fighting broke out between forces loyal to Dudayev and anti-separatist opposition forces, backed by Russia.

It was at this point that Dudayev moved on contacts already established with Osama and Al-Qaeda. With Russian troops set to flood into the region, Dudayev sent an emissary to Khartoum appealing for urgent support. Osama needed no encouragement. He had made his own reputation fighting the Soviet Union, and the chance to take them on again was too good an opportunity to miss.

Dudayev, a fellow Sunni Muslim, was rewarded with a pledge of money and supply of arms.

For a while Al-Qaeda's involvement in Chechnya seems to have amounted only to this. But civil war developed in August 1994 and that December Russian forces entered Chechnya and bombed the capital. By March 1995 an estimated 40,000 civilians had been killed and 250,000 were refugees. By June 1995, the Russians had overrun most of the republic's urban centres, forcing the Chechen rebels to resort to guerrilla tactics. Al-Qaeda's Arab-Afghans were in their element.

Though most of Dudayev's men had military backgrounds, they lacked the experience of waging a drawn out guerrilla conflict. Al-Qaeda fighters supplied this experience in abundance. Up to 2,000 fought alongside their Chechen counterparts and were responsible for some of the rebels' major successes.

From 1994, the Al-Qaeda network began ferrying men from its bases in Afghanistan through neighbouring Turkmenistan, across the Caspian Sea, landing in Daghestan and then travelling overland into Chechnya. The return journey was taken by many of Dudayev's men who would be trained in guerrilla warfare tactics at Al-Qaeda bases in Afghanistan.

A peace agreement was signed in July 1995. But fighting broke out again that December as rebels attempted to disrupt local elections. Dudayev was killed in a Russian rocket attack in April 1996. In January 1997, Russian officials announced that all Interior Ministry troops had left the rebel region.

Osama believes that he and his Arab-Afghans have now won two victories over the Russians. Yet the problem rumbles on even today. It is believed that Al-Qaeda continues to maintain a strong presence there.

On other fronts, too, there was activity. Another car bomb in Riyadh in the spring of 1995 was the first major anti-American action in the kingdom. Osama never claimed responsibility, but the Saudi government quickly uncovered definitive evidence linking the incident to Al-Qaeda. Later, Saudi Arabian television showed videotaped confessions of four Arab-Afghans involved in the bombing. Another attack in November of the same year targeted a US liaison office connected to the elite Saudi National Guard. On this occasion a car bomb killed five Americans and two Indians.

Subsequently, the State Department received further threats and in January 1996 announced: 'The US Embassy has received new and disturbing reports that additional attacks may be planned against institutions identified with the United States and its interests in Saudi Arabia.' Such was the nervousness of the State Department that they successfully lobbied for a postponement of Secretary of State Warren Christopher's planned visit to Riyadh to meet with Crown Prince Abdullah. When the two did meet, later in 1996, Abdullah assured Christopher that the two countries would not abandon their close ties.

By November 1995, evidence showed clearly that Al-Qaeda's range was broadening. As the network became stronger, Osama was asserting himself in a variety of different theatres of operation; Chechnya offers a prime example of just how powerful he believed himself to be. Along with many governments around the Middle East, the United States was linking more and more terrorist activity in the region with Al-Qaeda. The body of evidence and information was overwhelming, even by this point.

When Christopher met Abdullah in Riyadh, inevitably Osama bin Laden's name cropped up. As a result, over the early months of 1996 concerted diplomatic pressure was brought to bear on the Sudanese authorities from all sides. Al-Qaeda's hosts had been on the USA's list of state sponsors of terrorism since August 1993. Following a thorough intelligence review, Sudan's government was found 'to be providing sanctuary, safe passage, military training, financial support and office space in Khartoum to officials of international terrorist and radical Islamic groups . . . '

Only recently, however, has evidence emerged of botched negotiations at the highest level that might have led to the arrest of Osama as early as 1996. According to a report produced by CNN, 'US officials confirmed that in 1996, when Bin Laden was living in Sudan, the government in Khartoum offered to turn him over to Saudi Arabia for trial. A three-way negotiation went on, with the CIA representing the United States, but the Saudis decided to decline to accept Bin Laden, and he was allowed to go to Afghanistan instead.'

This failure represents an extraordinary lapse of judgement on the part of both the Saudi Arabian and American governments. While the Al Saud family would have faced additional problems at home with Osama in captivity and, presumably, being tried for his crimes in the kingdom, it would have been a small price to pay to remove him from the Islamic fundamentalist equation. Both Saudi Arabia and the United States would pay dearly for the failure of these talks.

Quite aside from this, the tide of events had begun to turn against Al-Qaeda in Sudan. Much of this was due to the shockwaves from an ill-conceived yet high-level plot hatched by one of the organisations sheltering under its umbrella of finance and arms supply, Egyptian Islamic Jihad. The Egyptian group had had links to Osama since his days in Afghanistan and, at the conclusion of the conflict there, Al-Qaeda had been committed to support efforts by the many Arab-Afghans who joined Egyptian Islamic Jihad to depose President Mubarak and install an Islamic fundamentalist administration.

Osama had grown close to Dr Ayman al-Zawahiri, leader of the group who went on to become his number two in Al-Qaeda. Al-Zawahiri had thrown his efforts into jihad and played a key role in the Somalian campaign. This had propelled him further into the centre of the Islamic fundamentalist world. By the middle of 1995 he was running an office in Geneva from where Osama and the main states sponsoring terrorism, Iran and Sudan, hoped to launch the jihad directly into the USA.

There had been several attempts against Mubarak before, most notably during a visit to Italy. Not one had progressed past planning. In 1995 a state visit to Addis Ababa, the capital of Ethiopia, presented another opportunity; Mubarak would be less well guarded than at home. Al-Zawahiri was put in charge of the operation by Sudanese powerbroker Dr Hassan al-Turabi and Osama. Over several months, the best bomb-makers, sharpshooters, military planners and strategists were drawn together in a remote base in Sudan to perfect their plan. The normally desk-bound Osama even left the comfort of Khartoum to oversee the preparations he was funding, while al-Zawahiri slipped into Ethiopia under cover to study the situation personally. Weeks before Mubarak was due to arrive, ten operatives were flown into Ethiopia in one of Osama's private aircraft to finalise their preparations.

On June 26, 1995, however, the entire project fell apart. Gunmen armed with AK-47 rifles and vehicles armed with rocket launchers rumbled into place – and attacked the wrong car. They had thought that Mubarak would be travelling in an Ethiopian official car, but he had brought his specially made Mercedes, which was armour plated to resist rocket fire, and was travelling in this. A back-up plan, to detonate a bomb under his car, was foiled when Mubarak's driver threw protocol to the wind, pulled his car into a 180-degree turn and sped back towards the airport.

Ethiopian security forces rounded up several of the militiamen with ease. Three others escaped over the border into Sudan. During a subsequent investigation, the Ethiopian government became convinced of Sudan's official complicity when it was discovered that the weapons used had been flown into Ethiopia via the Sudanese state airline. What was more, the label on the airfreight container that contained the weapons listed the sender as the Sudanese Intelligence Bureau in Khartoum!

Still giving orders from behind the scenes in his country, Dr Hassan al-Turabi prevented President Omar al-Bashir from making any moves to surrender the gunmen. Sudan provided safe haven to the three suspects and refused to extradite them to Ethiopia. This would prove a mistake by al-Turabi, and signal the beginning of the end for Osama in Sudan. Unaware of the international movement growing against his country, in a rare interview al-Turabi was quoted as saying: 'People all over Africa and all over the Arab world, I mean they just love the Sudan.'

The United Nations did not, and imposed diplomatic sanctions on Sudan in 1996 for its failure to turn over the fugitives and for general Sudanese support of international terrorism. For the same reasons, the US implemented both diplomatic and economic sanctions on Sudan. Also in 1996, the United States evacuated its Khartoum embassy and expelled a Sudanese diplomat suspected of supplying inside information about the United Nations to the group of terrorists convicted of plotting a 1993 bombing of the UN and other New York landmarks.

Within months of the Ethiopian fiasco, Osama's world had begun to unravel.

These economic sanctions added to an already terrible scenario in Sudan – a civil war that President al-Bashir and Dr al-Turabi had done nothing to end. This bitter struggle pitted the Sudanese government, dominated by Muslim Arabs from the northern part of the country, against opposition forces comprising predominantly black Christians and Animists from the southern part of the country. The war and resultant famines had claimed the lives of more than two million people and some five million had been forced to leave their homes, a disaster of a scale never seen before.

For President al-Bashir and Dr al-Turabi, it was a remote fight in which they showed remarkably little interest. But in the face of new, harsh sanctions, the country faced imminent collapse. In a bid to save their own skins, the pair sought to remove the most visible signs of their sponsorship of terrorism, so that they could make a case for sanctions to be eased or dropped altogether.

From his office overlooking the Blue Nile, Osama had watched in horror as his erstwhile allies had brought themselves to the brink of collapse. While president and henchman had floundered in the face of mounting international pressure, in almost parental fashion he prepared Al-Qaeda for the worst, a forced move. Ever the long-range strategist, however, Osama had started to plan for this eventuality long before.

The world first became aware of a group named the Taliban a year earlier when they were appointed by the Pakistani government to protect a convoy attempting to open up a trade route between Pakistan and Central Asia. The group, made up of Afghans trained in religious schools in Pakistan along with former Islamic fighters or mujahideen, proved effective bodyguards, driving off other mujahideen groups who attempted to attack and loot the convoy.

The Taliban had been formed by Mullah Mohammed Omar, a one-eyed puritanical cleric who was himself described as 'one of the most improbable characters in Afghanistan's tortured history'. A prominent fighter in the struggle to eject the Soviets from his homeland, he had become disgusted with his former friends in the mujahideen. According to one report produced after a rare interview during his early days in power, one outrage that provoked Omar's wrath was a deadly tank battle in Kandahar between two militia commanders who fancied the same handsome boy. While this account may be apocryphal, either way he emerged as a leader whose vision attracted many people similarly disenchanted. He recruited students from Koranic schools and this resulted in the Taliban being referred to in its early days as a student movement.

As the group grew in numbers and reputation, it spread quickly across much of Afghanistan. The Taliban's popularity with many Afghans initially surprised the country's warring mujahideen factions. They took the city of Kandahar in November 1994, beginning a remarkable advance that led to their capture of the capital, Kabul, in September 1996.

Osama bin Laden joins the Taliban story prior to the battle for Kabul. Whether he made contact with Mullah Omar, or vice versa, is unknown. But it is known that prior to his departure from Afghanistan several years earlier, Osama had also become disenchanted with his former comrades and their brutal ways. He welcomed the emergence of a force that could unite the country and, sometime during late 1995, began supplying funds directly to Mullah Omar.

The man later dubbed 'Commander of the Faithful' by his followers credited Osama with bankrolling the bloody battle that effectively brought him to power, the Battle of Kabul. Success in Kabul was the making of the Taliban. From this point onwards they were able to overwhelm the opposition, squeezing them progressively tighter into a pocket in the north of the country. Mullah Omar never forgot his friends, and Osama had proven as good a friend as the Commander of the Faithful would ever need. It was the beginning of a special relationship.

After the Battle of Kabul, ordinary Afghans welcomed the arrival of a new, stable force in Afghanistan. Tired of the lawlessness, they welcomed promises of stamping out corruption and restoring peace even if it came at a price. The Taliban resolved to create the world's purest Islamic state, banning 'un-Islamic' entertainment such as television, music and cinema. Other even more extreme edicts would follow, some that would prove restrictive to the point of evil towards women. But by the time that all this became clear to the population of Afghanistan, the Taliban had become the strongest political and military force in the country and were unstoppable.

In March 1996, Osama was in his office in Khartoum when the visit he had expected so long occurred. Blaring sirens in the street below heralded the arrival of a large convoy of cars. A few minutes later his sponsor, the influential Dr al-Turabi entered the room. Over small cups of Turkish coffee, the Sudanese powerbroker informed his guest that Sudan could not continue to host Al-Qaeda. There was just too much pressure on him, from the United Nations, the United States and Saudi Arabia. It was time to move on.

Al-Turabi had made millions of dollars from his business interests with Osama. The two were friends. After the assassination of Dr Abdullah Azzam in 1989, he had become a new father figure to Osama. In 1996 al-Turabi was 64, while Osama was 39. He was the perfect age for such an attachment, but a questionable role model. Relatives of Osama recall that during brief contacts with them from Sudan, even after months without talking to his family, he gushed incessantly over al-Turabi's talents and humanity. This led some to wonder if he was besotted, perhaps even indulging in a second homoerotic infatuation with his new mentor.

Al-Turabi promised Osama that Al-Qaeda would not be simply shut down, but be given a short time to organise a cohesive move elsewhere. As much as possible, the business empire that Osama had built would remain unhindered, in order that Al-Qaeda's cash flow would not be impeded.

Despite the loss of a base that Osama had grown fond of and made millions of dollars from, a smooth transition was already assured thanks to his networking with Mullah Omar. What was more, while his Sudanese hosts had clearly, for some time, been heading in a direction that would force them to abandon their overt sponsorship of radical Islamic groups to survive, Osama was secretly being courted by another nation interested in 'the business'.

Even before Al-Qaeda had completed the process of moving its assets to Afghanistan, its campaign against Saudi Arabia had begun. But this had been nothing more than a beginning. On June 25, 1996, US Air Force security police Staff Sergeant Alfredo Guerrero was patrolling the roof of Building 131 at the Khobar Towers housing complex in Dhahran, Saudi Arabia. Around 10 p.m. something caught his attention. A fuel truck, followed by a car, was moving through a car park on the outside of the fence surrounding the complex. Both vehicles stopped, and the truck turned and backed into some hedges along the fence adjacent to the eight-storey barracks where Guerrero stood. Two men got out of the truck and into the car, which sped quickly away.

What had brought Guerrero to Saudi Arabia was the same as his thousands of military colleagues living at Khobar Towers. Their mission was Operation Southern Watch, which began in 1992 following the Gulf War when the 4404th Fighter Wing (Provisional) moved into Khobar Towers to enforce a 'no-fly' zone in southern Iraq. During the years following the Gulf War, these daily air patrols exposed the planes of the US and its allies to Iraqi air defences without losing an aircraft. In containing Saddam Hussein, the Americans were protecting Saudi Arabia itself from one of the world's worst despots. But as the men and women who made up Operation Southern Watch were about to find out, Hussein was less of a threat than Islamic fundamentalism. It would be a painful reminder of the risks Americans in uniform take every day around the world.

Spotting the odd behaviour of the men, Guerrero immediately radioed a security desk and, with two other guards, urgently began pounding on residents' doors, ordering them to evacuate. Seven minutes later, by the time he and the other guards had worked their way through the top three floors, an explosion tore through the barracks. The bomb stripped away an entire wall of a high-rise building. In the attack and its immediate aftermath 19 US airmen were killed and more than 500 were injured.

Early that year, US embassy officials in Saudi Arabia had issued an unusually strong warning of potential terrorist attacks against US personnel in the kingdom. Threats such as this were taken very seriously following the 1983 attack on a US barracks in Beirut that had killed 241 Marines. But for a variety of reasons, Khobar Towers was exposed.

In April 1996, despite several incidents that indicated Khobar Towers could be under surveillance by terrorists, command officials declined to elevate the threat level because they felt it would be difficult to justify a request for additional security police. Because of the temporary nature of the mission, the command lacked resources that would be found in a permanent wing; for instance, the command had an ad hoc intelligence structure, and there was only one Arabic interpreter assigned to the entire 3,000-member unit.

Nearly five years later, in 2001, terrorism charges were brought against 13 members of the pro-Iran Saudi Hezbollah, or 'Party of God'. Another unidentified person linked to the Lebanese Hezbollah was also charged in the attack. An indictment alleged that the suspects were directed by Iranian government officials. In 46 charges, the indictment alleges that all 14 men were members of the Islamic militant group Hezbollah, which federal officials said received support and inspiration from individuals within the Iranian government. No Iranian officials were named in the indictment.

'The indictment explains that elements of the Iranian government inspired, supported and supervised members of Saudi Hezbollah,' said Attorney General John Ashcroft. 'In particular, the indictment alleges that the defendants reported their surveillance activities to Iranian officials and were supported and directed in those activities by Iranian officials.' An unspecified number were in custody. Ashcroft said the planning in this bombing began in 1993 with 'extensive surveillance to find American targets in Saudi Arabia. After amassing large amounts of plastic explosives, the terrorists, assisted by an as yet unidentified member of Lebanese Hezbollah, . . . converted a tanker truck into a huge bomb.'

If the authorities were correct in their assessment, Khobar Towers represented a new and sinister threat facing the world, not just because of its size or ferocity, but due to the fact that it was the outcome of an extraordinary new alliance that had brought together the 'cream' of Islamic fundamentalism.

What was more, Osama had sold his soul to even darker forces than the Sudanese for a place at the head table.

CHAPTER FOURTEEN

International Merger and Expansion

Islam shares structural similarities with the other great monotheistic religions. All believers hold the Koran sacred, but may differ on some interpretations. The principal division is between the majority Sunni and minority Shiia traditions. The minority group regards the Prophet's son-in-law, Ali, and his descendants as divinely authorised to rule the Muslim community. The majority group believed that the caliph should be appointed through the consensus of the community.

While Sunni and Shiia Muslims consider themselves two parts of a whole, they are constantly aware of their differences – not unlike the relationship between the Catholic, Protestant and Orthodox sects of the Christian faith. Although they usually work in tandem, in some situations adherents are wary of each other. This split has been evident at the top levels in the world of Islamic fundamentalism.

Osama bin Laden was born a Sunni, the sect that dominates Saudi Arabia, the same as the government in Sudan, his hosts during the early 1990s. But the world's leading exporter and sponsor of Islamic fundamentalism was the conservative Shiia state of Iran that arose after the downfall of the Shah and the Iranian revolution in 1979. During Ayatollah Khomeini's rule, from 1981 until his death in 1989, sponsorship of terror became one effective way to export religious fervour aboard.

In some ways, the Shah hastened his own demise by encouraging the rising expectations of his people during the 1960s and 1970s. The Shah's land reforms and a thriving economy brought rapid growth but also widened the gap between the elite and the masses. Modernisation was blamed for widespread misery. Increased revenues following oil price increases meant simply more arms and industrialisation rather than tangible well-being for the common man.

Ayatollah Ruhollah Khomeini represented much of the discontent of the religious sector of Iran. Exiled in 1963 for speaking out against the Shah's rule, by the late 1970s Khomeini was based in France. He gained tremendous popularity with the masses, and became the symbol of the opposition.

Waves of opposition had begun building after 1975, due to the formation of the Rastakhiz, the legal political party in Iran, and the banning of opposition political parties. In mid-1977 religious leaders began demonstrating against the modernisation brought on by the Shah. That November, several people were killed when police broke up demonstrations. Violence on both sides escalated; those who had been moderate in demands for reform became more radical.

In the autumn of 1978, strikes against the oil industry, the post office, government factories, and banks demolished the economy. This pattern continued throughout most of 1978 culminating in the December 10 march against the government of the Shah, in which eight million Iranians protested. This massive demonstration was the turning point. The Shah left Tehran on January 16, 1979, for an 'extended vacation'. The opposition leader, Ayatollah Khomeini, returned to Iran in triumph on February 1. His agenda was a stable government that could cope with the problems of reconstruction. He wanted to eradicate the evil roots of the old system, which he described as satanic. On April 1, 1979, after a landslide victory in a national referendum, Khomeini declared an Islamic republic. This republic consisted of a new constitution reflecting Khomeini's ideals of Islamic government. He was named Iran's political and religious leader for life.

From this point, Iran's relationship with the US went downhill. The US had always supported the Shah, as a foil to Gulf Arab leaders who controlled much of the world's oil supplies. On November 4, 1979, 500 extremist students seized the US embassy in Tehran. They took hostage 66 citizens at the embassy and the foreign ministry. The takeover, seemingly sanctioned by Khomeini, continued for the next 444 days, and American–Iranian relations sank to an all-time low. A botched US raid to free the hostages was one of the key events that led to the defeat of President Jimmy Carter in the 1979 election and the elevation of Ronald Reagan, whose conservative stance towards the Iranian regime aggravated the situation.

Supporters held food riots in Tunisia, and others staged six car bombings in Kuwait. Khomeini sponsored Islamic Jihad, whose suicide bombings killed 241 US and 58 French troops in Beirut. Despite being roundly condemned as terrorists, at home they were seen rather as patriotic heroes.

Ayatollah Khomeini died in May of 1989. His elected successor was Ali Hashemi Rafsanjani who came to power two months later. By the middle of the 1990s, Iran had evolved Khomeini's policy of encouraging Islamic fundamentalist principles abroad into a government policy of support for Shiia terrorist groups. According to US intelligence reports that surfaced in 1996, Iran's terrorist infrastructure extended to a network of 11 training camps. The largest of these sites was said to be the Imam Ali camp east of Tehran. Others were located northeast of Tehran in Qazvin; in Qom, south of Tehran; and in Hamadan, south-west of Tehran. All were described as being designed to look like small villages, with houses, shops and mosques. The camps were closed to the general public, but had allegedly been discovered through satellite observation and intelligence gathered by the National Security Agency.

Two groups – the Organisation of Islamic Revolution and Hezbollah – were said to have received bomb training at the Imam Ali camp. US intelligence sources said that most of Iran's terrorist attacks were planned from Imam Ali. Classified US documents allegedly indicated that the camps taught students how to assemble bombs and carry out assassinations. Up to 5,000 men and women were believed to have been trained at these camps. Trainees are said to have come from Algeria, Egypt, Iran, Jordan, Lebanon, Libya, Palestine, Saudi Arabia, Sudan, Syria, and Turkey. According to the documents, President Rafsanjani set up the camps several years earlier, using instructors drawn from Iran's Revolutionary Guard and intelligence service. All plans for terrorist acts were said to be approved in advance by Iran's Supreme Council.

In April 1995, President Clinton imposed a total US trade embargo on Iran. On June 7, 1996, Iran's spiritual leader Ayatollah Ali Khameini delivered a Friday sermon that more or less followed his usual patterns, attacking America, disparaging western values and talking up the Islamic Revolution. But tucked in there was a new phrase for Ayatollah Khameini. He stated that Hezbollah must operate on 'all continents and all countries . . . '

To a majority of the thousands that listened to the weekly mantra of rhetoric and hatred, it was a comment that passed without inspection. Only someone with prior knowledge of what was going on behind the scenes in government would have understood the implications of his message.

Rafsanjani had established under his control a Supreme Council for Intelligence Affairs, interpreted elsewhere as a Supreme Council for Terrorism. The council was responsible for the funding and management of the state's budget and infrastructure for the 'promotion' of Islamic fundamentalism. By June of 1996, this organisation had laid the foundations for a new broad-based terror group, Hezbollah International, and this was what Ayatollah Khameini was alluding to.

By this time, representatives of the Shiia-dominated Supreme Council for Intelligence Affairs had made contact with the leaders of the top Sunni terror groups. Dr Mahdi Chamran Savehie, who had been installed as head of External Intelligence, travelled to Afghanistan to see the head of Al-Qaeda.

Osama had received a warm welcome in his old stomping ground of Afghanistan when he had flown from Khartoum in Sudan into a private airfield near Jalalabad on May 10, 1996. Days later he had taken a helicopter some 225 miles south-west to the city of Kandahar to greet the man who was his new sponsor. Mullah Mohammed Omar welcomed Osama like a son, despite not being noticeably older than his guest. It was understandable behaviour, however. When it came to Osama bin Laden, Mullah Omar had a great deal for which to be thankful. Al-Qaeda had bankrolled much of the Taliban's campaign to take over Afghanistan. Osama had sent aircraft filled with arms at a time when the Taliban needed them most, enabling them to successfully take the capital, Kabul – a victory that all but cemented their grip on power. In one of his few contacts with his family during this period, Osama told them proudly that Mullah Omar had thrown his arms around him, focused his one good eye on him, and said: 'By Allah's name, this is your home now, as it is mine.'

By the time of his arrival in Afghanistan, Osama had already met on a number of occasions in Khartoum with Dr Savehie. The Iranian approach had surprised him, but was nevertheless welcomed. Osama had never been one to feel encumbered by religious dogma, his pragmatic corporate approach to the business of building a far-reaching terror organisation being an example of his new thinking.

This was important for the Iranians. Al-Qaeda was the undoubted leading force in Sunni Islamic fundamentalism. An all-embracing governing body could hardly be created without the support of this presence. Although a Sunni, Osama was quite open to Dr Savehie's suggestions. After several meetings, Osama had agreed on the principles and structure of Hezbollah International. Finally, he agreed to send a personal representative to a summit meeting of major Islamic fundamentalist groups scheduled to be held in Tehran in June 1996, while encouraging many of those organisations affiliated with Al-Qaeda to join in this event in the Iranian capital.

During the early morning of June 21, 1996, Mohammed Ali Ahmed, Osama's personal representative, flew aboard a private plane from Jalalabad to a private airfield outside of Tehran. He was met at the plane by Dr Savehie, who brought with him a personal message of welcome from President Rafsanjani. The two drove to an anonymous government building on the outskirts of Tehran that had been selected to host this extraordinary meeting.

Later that day, Dr Savehie convened a conference attended by the biggest names in the Islamic fundamentalist underground. Among those present were Mustafa Al Liddawi of Hamas, George Habbash of the Popular Front for the Liberation of Palestine, Ahmed Sala of Egyptian Islamic Jihad, Abdullah Ocalan of the Kurdish People's Party and Ramadan Shallah of Palestinian Islamic Jihad.

Amid these leading figures were dozens of others from many smaller organisations. The Iranians had also granted observer status to a variety of lesser-known groups, invited guest speakers on specialist topics and prepared briefing papers detailing new technologies and techniques. Except for the topic, that June conference could have been a conference of any industry anywhere in the world.

Even among this company, Osama was a respected figure. He had sent his lieutenant with full authority to speak on behalf of Al-Qaeda. Ali Ahmed played a key role, helping shepherd what was after all a group of terrorists – men more familiar with weapons, murder and mayhem than with corporate nuances – into a cohesive organisation in which they could genuinely agree to operate. It was an extraordinary plan.

Among other resolutions were decisions to standardise training, unify financial reporting, and a semi-unified command in order to avoid replication of work – all the aims of a mainstream industry-based organisation. Finally, on June 23, the last day of the meeting, one unanimous vote created a Committee of Three as the supreme council of Hezbollah International. This would be the organisation's steering body and work in tandem with the Iranian command, Dr Savehie reporting directly to President Rafsanjani and his Supreme Council for Intelligence Affairs.

Voted on to the Committee of Three were Osama bin Laden, Imad Mughniyah, the representative of Lebanese Islamic Jihad, and Ahmed Salah of Egyptian Islamic Jihad. It was a balance of power with which all sides of the religious divide were comfortable. Two of the committee were Sunni, while the committee was very much under the control of the Iranian Shiia. In many ways, it was a perfect arrangement for all the protagonists. The official formation of Hezbollah International would begin a new era for Islamic fundamentalism.

Just two days later, on June 25, 1996, Hezbollah International arrived officially with the bombing of Building 131 at the Khobar Towers housing complex in Dhahran, Saudi Arabia. Osama commented during a later interview: 'We roused the people . . . to eject this enemy from the holy land . . . They have raised the head of the Muslim nation high, and washed away some of the dishonour we had to bear by the Saudi government's collaboration with the American government in the land of Allah. We look at these young men as great heroes and martyrs . . . We pray to Allah to accept them and bless their parents with patience.'

In another interview, with *Nida'ul Islam* magazine, he added: 'There were important effects to the two explosions in Riyadh . . . Most important among these is the people's awareness of the significance of the American occupation of the country of the two sacred mosques, and that the original decrees of the regime are a reflection of the wishes of the American occupiers. So the people became aware that their main problems were caused by the American occupiers and their puppets in the Saudi regime . . .

'These missions also paved the way for the raising of the voices of opposition against the American occupation from within the ruling family and the armed forces; in fact we can say that the remaining Gulf countries have been affected to the same degree, and that the voices of opposition to the American occupation have begun to be heard at the level of the ruling families and the governments of the . . . Gulf countries.'

One interviewer for a US-based television network asked him: 'You have been painted in America as a terrorist leader. To your followers you are a hero. How do you see yourself?'

He replied: 'As I said before, we do not worry about what America says. We look at ourselves and our brethren as worshippers of Allah who created us to worship him and follow his books and prophets. I am one of Allah's worshippers. I worship Allah, which includes carrying out the jihad to raise Allah's word and evict the Americans from all Muslim land.'

In a separate press statement he dubbed the attack as 'praiseworthy terrorism' and claimed for himself, for the first time, the attacks in Somalia declaring that 'we used to hunt them down in Mogadishu'.

Osama was pleased with the Khobar Towers operation. But this was to signal a sad change in his life. An act of terrorism so massive and so destructive in his native Saudi Arabia was always likely to draw a response. The Saudi government had already withdrawn his citizenship and cancelled his passport. There was nothing else that King Fahd and his government could do, other than perhaps rue their fateful decision not to grab him when the Sudanese administration had offered to hand him over in chains. This was one of several lucky narrow escapes, some of which Osama only discovered himself during the media frenzy that followed September 11, 2001.

Despite the exploits of their increasingly infamous relative, the family had always attempted to reach out to him. Some hoped that he could be redeemed in the same manner he had before, during Hajj, when he rejected his errant ways in favour of his religion. For that reason, some of the family, including several brothers, had attempted to retain contact. His uncle Abdullah had even made the trek to visit Osama in the hope that he could be persuaded to return to the fold.

The legitimate Binladin business empire had several suppliers in Sudan. Occasionally during Osama's Khartoum years, one of his brothers, or an uncle or cousin, had reason to visit the African state. Whenever this happened, Osama would welcome his relative with genuine warmth and hospitality. He would talk openly and argue forcefully for his standpoint and his cause. He would not hear of tempering his behaviour, and even less of returning to the kingdom

191

and apologising to King Fahd. But as evidence mounted of Al-Qaeda's activities during the first half of the 1990s, fewer of Osama's closest relatives persevered.

This fleeting contact was far from a one-way street. As if crying out for a voice from the past, when life was more normal, he was in the habit of reaching out to his family, by telephone, from Sudan or Afghanistan. It was often a reflective Osama who called on these occasions. Unlike the stiff fundamentalist they had encountered face to face in Khartoum, he was more relaxed, often talking over old childhood memories, sharing anecdotes about his father.

One close family member recalls being woken in the early morning hours in Jeddah. It was Osama on the line. He wanted to talk about his mother, enquire about the family business and swap gossip about family friends. The recipient of the call recalls clearly the half hour he spent in small talk, and gained the overriding impression that Osama was pining for home.

But the bombing of Khobar Towers all but ended this occasional contact. It widened the chasm between the family and Osama. Aside from their own disgust in finding his hand in such a deed, the bombing contradicted the frequently-stated family position. The Binladin clan repeatedly made clear its overwhelming support for the legitimacy of Al Saud rule in Saudi Arabia and their abhorrence of terrorism in any form. After Khobar Towers, an already strained relationship collapsed. Osama was shunned. Since then, although he has occasionally reached out through a crackly satellite telephone link, it has been rare for Osama to find a relative who would speak to him. On the limited occasions when he did get hold of someone to talk to, he received a strained and cold reception. The damage he had done could never be repaired.

On July 17, 1996, about 8:45 p.m., Trans World Airlines Flight 800, a Boeing 747-100, had climbed to approximately 13,800 feet after take-off from Kennedy International Airport when air traffic control lost radar contact. There were no reports of the flight crew reporting any problems. Witnesses along the coast of Long Island reported seeing a fireball light up the darkening sky. The flaming wreckage then plummeted into the water about nine and a half miles south of the Suffolk shore. Radar showed that the plane, or part of it, continued to 'fly' for up to 30 seconds following the explosion. On board the TWA jet were 212 passengers and 17 crew.

The aircraft was destroyed and there were no survivors.

Only three weeks had passed since the destruction of Khobar Towers. America was jumpy. Inevitably, initial reaction focused on a terrorist act. However, a top Clinton administration official quickly announced that no warnings had been received from any group, and there was no evidence of an attack from a terrorist bomb. Within hours, James Kallstrom of the FBI's New York office announced that the agency was taking over the investigation under the aegis of its joint terrorism task force with the New York Police Department. A massive search for pieces of wreckage was mounted.

But as days stretched into weeks, then months, and then years, no evidence was ever discovered to link the tragedy to terror. When sophisticated equipment detected explosive residue on the plane's wreckage, it seemed a promising lead. That was until the discovery that the plane had been used in the months prior to the crash to train bomb-sniffing dogs. Nothing indicated the sort of damage associated with a bomb.

Early in 1997, one CNN report concluded: 'Six months into the most costly plane crash investigation ever, there are still more questions than answers about the deadly mid-air explosion of TWA Flight 800.' Six months into the probe a small fleet of scallop boats continued to search the area where the 200-ton plane went down. By this stage some 95 per cent of the TWA 747 had been retrieved from the Atlantic and painstakingly pieced together in a hangar. Six hundred FBI agents worked on the case, conducting more than 4,500 interviews with witnesses. Even the bodies of the passengers were probed for clues. Despite this, there remains no clear explanation as to what happened that fateful night. What is known is that the centre fuel tank exploded. But the same CNN report stated that 'off the record, criminal investigators were convinced a crime was committed. All they need is the proof . . . '

Despite this assertion, between August 22 and 23, 2000, the National Transportation Safety Board (NTSB) met in Washington DC to consider its final report on the crash of TWA Flight 800. The NTSB refused to let any of the 736 official eyewitnesses, several of them experienced military observers, testify at the hearing. According to the NTSB, the tragedy was caused by a spark in the plane's centre fuel tank. Boeing has acknowledged there are times during a normal flight when a nearly empty fuel tank can be full of vapours heating to volatility. Safety features are designed to keep any source of heat or electricity from igniting this explosive brew.

However, this theory has been shot down by many respected members of the community. Among them was Commander William S. Donaldson III, US Navy (Ret), an expert with 24 years of experience in virtually all phases of naval aviation. Commander Donaldson, who died in August 2001, commented: 'What happens after a disaster like the TWA crash is that the parties submit their conclusions independently. One of the parties that has the best credentials in investigating crashes is the International Aerospace Workers (IAW). These people build and maintain the airplanes. They know what the parts look like every day because they work with them hands-on. They specifically stated that the cause of the crash was not an event started in the centre wing tank but a high-pressure event that started on the left side of the aircraft. They concluded that the subsequent centre wing tank explosion, which they agree occurred, was a product of that initial event caused by something that preceded it.'

In the years since the crash of TWA Flight 800, investigators have found no evidence to suggest that the tragedy was linked to subversive activities emanating from the Middle East. Indeed, the US government, the FBI and bodies of enquiry, have all but discounted the terror theory in the absence of evidence to support it. However, there remain sources who have continued to press this theory. Stringing together unrelated and unspecific statements in the right-leaning Arabic media, vague threats from one terror group, and making comparisons with the disaster and other attacks (PanAm Flight 103) their work tells a different story.

One of the building blocks of the terror theory was a newspaper editorial. This appeared on July 16 – a day before the TWA Flight 800 disaster – in *Al-Quds Al-Arabi*, an Arabic newspaper published in London and sympathetic to fundamentalism. It stated: 'What happened in Cairo, Riyadh and Khobar is only the beginning . . . ' But the smoking gun, as far as terror theorists go, is a statement issued by the Jihad Wing (Arabian Peninsula) of the Islamic Change Movement. The Islamic Change Movement can be linked to Al-Qaeda, and representatives were in Iran in June that year for the creation of Hezbollah International. In a flurry of threatening statements around this time, the Islamic Change Movement attacked, among others, the House of Saud and the United States. One boasted that 'the Islamic Change Movement had proven that it has long arms by targeting the pilots' complex in Khobar.' On July 17, another statement promised that 'the mujahideen will give their strongest reply to the threats of the foolish US president. Many people will be surprised by the size of our reply, the date and time of which will be determined by the Islamic Change Movement. The invaders will leave either dead or alive, but their time is at dawn. Is not the dawn near?'

From this, say conspiracy theorists, one can decipher the clear intention that an attack was imminent and a plot already under way. Only hours after the statement was issued, TWA Flight 800 went down.

A day later, the Jihad Wing (Arabian Peninsula) of the Islamic Change Movement issued a communiqué claiming responsibility for TWA Flight 800. On July 20, its representatives at a management meeting of Hezbollah International in Tehran were reportedly lauded for their success

But while the Islamic Change Movement was happy to claim the tragedy as their doing, the problem remains that there is – officially at least – no evidence to support their claims. Those who drew parallels to PanAm Flight 103, which was downed over Lockerbie in December 1988, conveniently forget one aspect. The remnants of PanAm Flight 103 were pitted with evidence that not only showed clearly that a bomb was the cause of the tragedy, but offered enough residual proof to convict a Libyan man for his involvement. An explosive device of any kind must, as part of the destructive process, leave evidence. A Boeing 747 cannot be destroyed by a cataclysmic event without there being some indication of the cause. In the case of TWA Flight 800, minute forensics studies have indicated nothing of the sort. Unless . . .

Numerous private investigators, who take issue with the National Transportation Safety Board findings but were not allowed to testify at the August 2000 meeting, believe that TWA 800 was destroyed by a missile. According to some reports, as many as 60 people on the ground and in the air, including two fighter pilots less than one mile from Flight 800 and who were watching it from their aircraft, said they saw a guided missile come from below and hit Flight 800. The source of the missile is the subject of speculation.

In his investigative book, *The Downing of TWA Flight 800*, James Sanders writes: 'As the evening of July 17, 1996, began, Eastenders on Long Island's south fork had no idea that only a few miles away a joint naval task force was assembling for a critical test of a top secret weapons system. In towns like Westhampton, Mastic Beach, and along the Shinnecock Bay Inlet, as midweek parties began, as recreational boaters set out into the warm night, they could not have foreseen the light show that would soon light up the skies. At 2000 hours, July 17, 1996, a world away from the town of Southampton's resort beaches, military zone W-105, thousands of square miles of ocean located south and southeast of Long Island, was activated by the United States Navy. Within minutes, from different locations around the sector, military activity increased as the various units participating in the operation deployed their aircraft and surface vessels.'

If it was friendly fire, it would not be the first – or last – time that a civilian airliner was downed mistakenly by the military in recent years. On September 1, 1983, the Soviet air force attacked and destroyed Korean Airlines Flight 007, which had strayed into Soviet airspace during a flight from Alaska to Japan. A US Navy warship in the Arabian Gulf mistook an Iranian civilian jetliner for an F-14 fighter plane and shot it down with a heat-seeking missile. But why then cover it up?

Unlike these and other aircraft disasters, the causes of which have been definitively proven, the uncertainty of the FBI, NTSB and other investigators has encouraged a plethora of conspiracy theories to spring up.

Dr Thomas Stalcup is another highly-respected voice affiliated to the Flight 800 Independent Researchers Organisation. He said: 'I was watching a CNN broadcast on November 18, 1997, the date of the FBI press conference where the CIA's animated version of what happened was shown. It seemed to me that they were trying to prove what didn't happen rather than what did happen. Words stating "not a missile" were underlined and shown multiple times; there was dramatic music; it was more like propaganda than news. This disturbed me, and I felt something was wrong – especially when the CIA's "cartoon" claimed that part of the plane climbed 3,000 feet after the break-up.

'Also, there was a claim made during the FBI press conference that no one saw two objects in the sky. But I remembered reading that witnesses had said exactly the opposite, that one object hit the other . . . [National Aeronautics and Space Administration (NASA)] found nitrates, which is evidence of externally caused explosions, on a piece of wreckage labeled CW504 . . . CW504 was a piece of the centre wing tank near the point where we believe the missile hit . . . '

Commander Donaldson added: 'The FBI would bring parts in after they were retrieved from the water, lay them on the hangar floor, and run bomb-sniffing dogs over them. When the dogs detected something, they'd take the piece into another room for advanced detection with a chemical sniffer that is the best in the world. They had at least a dozen hits on chemicals known as PETN and RDX on pieces of wreckage, and these are the substances found in a missile warhead. PETN is a booster high explosive, and RDX is the main charge . . . There's an inward bulge on the bottom of the centre wing tank that the NTSB won't talk about. It's never been explained. If there's an explosion inside a tank, there's not going to be any inward bulge; it will be outward.'

Commander Donaldson also contended that computers showed that if a Stinger-type missile had hit that aircraft in the wing, it would have gone through the wing, and would have travelled between a half mile and a mile-and-a-half away from the aircraft. 'The radar clearly shows that two big pieces of metal went ripping out 3,200 feet in seven seconds. That could only be from a missile or an anti-aircraft shell. It went half a nautical mile in seven seconds and then, as you watch the next couple of radar sweeps, you see those parts falling into the water into a distinct debris field all their own.'

So what did happen at 8:45 p.m. on July 17, 1996, some nine-and-a-half miles off the east coast of the United States? The FBI and NTSB say categorically that there is no evidence of a bomb on board the Boeing 747. And the US Navy says that they did not do it. Yet the Jihad Wing (Arabian Peninsula) of the Islamic Change Movement claims credit.

According to a body of evidence, however, NASA found nitrates, which is evidence of externally-caused explosions, and others state clearly that radar evidence suggests another body involved in the tragedy. Some 60 people – a roll call headed by two fighter pilots less than one mile from Flight 800 – claim to have seen a guided missile come up from below and hit Flight 800.

What few seem to have considered is that Al-Qaeda has possessed surface-to-air missile systems since the early 1980s. While fighting the Soviets in Afghanistan, Pakistani intelligence – on behalf of the

CIA – supplied Osama's Maktab al-Khidamat (MAK) with SAM-7 missiles, commonly known as Strella missiles. Despite their ageing technology, the reliable SAM-7s and more recent models remain standard equipment for organisations as diverse as UNITA in Angola, Hezbollah in Lebanon and the Irish Republican Army in Britain. The Strella is only effective at altitudes of 8,000 to 11,500 feet, and the TWA Flight 800 was at around 13,800 feet when it blew up.

Altogether more serious as a weapon, however, were the portable Stinger missile systems. These were also supplied to MAK during the 1980s, while Osama purchased more modern versions for Al-Qaeda in 1993 on the black market in Pakistan. The Stinger, a full-dimensional guided-missile system, is designed for short-range air defence against low-altitude airborne targets such as fixed-wing aircraft, helicopters, unmanned aerial vehicles and cruise missiles at an operational ceiling of about 10,000 feet. Fired from the shoulder, it is a 'fire-and-forget' weapon employing a passive infrared seeker and proportional navigation system.

Giving testimony in a New York trial during 2001, one pilot associated with Osama admitted purchasing a T-39 aircraft in Tucson, Arizona, on behalf of the millionaire. An aide, Wadih el-Hage, told him that the plane would be used to transport Stingers to Sudan.

Could a Stinger have had the range to hit a Boeing 747 at a height of 13,800 feet? Could it be possible that terrorists had managed to slip a small shoulder-fired guided missile system into the United States, or off its coast? And that, under cover of darkness, they had used a Stinger to bring down a civil aircraft? It would be an extraordinary and improbable theory without the events of September 11, 2001, to give context to the capabilities of modern Islamic fundamentalist terrorists – and perhaps worthy of a US government cover-up, considering the panic the news of such an attack could cause among the American public.

Osama has never publicly commented, or been asked directly, about this. But Jihad Wing (Arabian Peninsula) of the Islamic Change Movement has openly admitted that it is responsible for blasting TWA flight 800 out of the sky, and this organisation has been closely allied to Al-Qaeda for some time.

CHAPTER FIFTEEN

Diversification of the Core Business

'All gratitude to Allah, our relationship with our brother mujahideen in Afghanistan is a deep and broad relationship where blood and sweat have mixed as have the links over long years of struggle against the Soviets. It is not a passing relationship, nor one based on personal interests. They are committed to support the religion approved by Allah, and that country remains as the Muslims have known it, a strong fort for Islam, and its people are amongst the most protective of the religion approved by Allah, and the keenest to fulfil His laws and to establish an Islamic state . . .'

In many ways, Osama bin Laden's return to Afghanistan in May 1996 was a return home. He had been rejected by the Saudi Arabian government and stripped of his citizenship, but as he did not recognise the authority of the Al Saud dynasty, that invalidated the status of Saudi Arabia in Osama's eyes. Instead, he had come to think of Afghanistan as his home.

Talking about his adopted country during an interview for *Nida'ul Islam* magazine in October 1996, he was full of praise for the Islamic renaissance that his hosts were initiating around Afghanistan. 'That passing phase of infighting [the civil war] has saddened us as it has saddened all Muslims. However, we wish to illustrate that the picture of events as painted by the international press is grossly distorted.

'This infighting is much smaller and less fierce than Muslims on the outside may imagine. Most of the country is living a normal peaceful life, apart from some petty crimes here and there as some elements attempt to create corruption under cover of the disputes amongst some of the groups. We are hoping that Afghanistan would regain very soon – God willing – its Islamic position which would befit its history of jihad.'

There was a great deal for Osama to do in 1996 in order to transplant Al-Qaeda from Sudan to Afghanistan. His sponsor in the African state, Dr Hassan al-Turabi, had been generous considering that he had secretly been attempting to hand Osama over to international justice. Not only had al-Turabi given a period of several months for Al-Qaeda to transfer its base operations smoothly, he was keen that Osama maintain his business empire in Sudan, albeit taking a back seat. This was hardly altruism; al-Turabi was a partner in many of them and making a small fortune in profits each year.

Osama had always relied upon managers for his legitimate businesses so that he could concentrate upon his main interests. On that basis, leaving behind his African corporations in their capable hands was not a stretch. By this time, his Sudanese empire was valued at hundreds of millions of dollars, with a bundle of government contracts and favourable terms pushing turnover ever higher. By 1996, his commercial empire had extended to include companies in most African states and many Middle Eastern countries.

With Al-Qaeda comfortably funded by his commercial empire – as well as from extortion and protection rackets against wealthy Gulf Arabs – Osama now turned his attention to his new home. After nearly two decades of war, the country was mired in debt and suffering from economic meltdown, its people surviving to an increasing degree on foreign aid.

By 1996, Afghanistan had only one notable export: drugs. It is an industry to which Osama has referred in private. In an attempt to justify his personal involvement in the evil trade he told one relative: 'The West is exporting to us its corrosive culture. We are exporting something back that corrodes their society. Their society is as wicked as their culture.' Al-Qaeda has been as involved in the taxation, protection and encouragement of the industry as has the administration of Mullah Mohammed Omar.

Opium is obtained by collecting and drying the milky juice in the unripe seed pods of the opium poppy, *Papaver Somniferum*. Its chief active principle is the alkaloid morphine, a narcotic. Other constituents are the alkaloids codeine, papaverine and noscapine (narcotine). Heroin is synthesized from morphine. Morphine, heroin and codeine are addictive.

The medicinal properties of opium have been known from the earliest times, and it was used as a narcotic in Sumerian and European cultures at least as early as 4000 BC. The drug was introduced into India and its use spread to China. Early in the nineteenth century, against Chinese prohibitions, British merchants began smuggling opium into China in order to balance their purchases of tea for export to Britain, an act that set the stage for the Opium Wars.

The consumption of 'intoxicants', including opiates, is contrary to Islamic doctrine and therefore, by extension, cultivation of the opium poppy, the manufacture of morphine and heroin and trafficking in these drugs is in violation of Sharia law. It seems an open-and-shut case. But just as the Koran deplores murder or the instigation of violent acts, even the most ardent Islamic fundamentalist can forget bits of the life code he follows so closely when it suits him.

Taliban leader Mullah Mohammed Omar banned television and imposed puritanical restrictions on women, among other initiatives, but cleverly turned a blind eye to drug production. He argues, like his protégé Osama bin Laden, that the drugs Afghanistan is flooding onto the world market affect only the West. This makes it all right.

But this too is a fallacy; no culture or creed is immune to heroin addiction. Mullah Omar's neighbours have been flooded with heroin produced under his patronage. From a population of 135 million, Pakistan had a reported four million addicts, while Iran has 1.2 million. Drug use has also been a major contributor to the spread of AIDS and HIV around the Middle East.

After Soviet support for the Kabul regime and US arms shipments to the rebels ended in January 1992, Afghanistan's role as a major heroin supplier increased sharply. This was anticipated in late 1991 by the United Nations anti-drug commission, which reported that the Afghan guerrillas, anticipating a cut in US covert support, were already planting a greatly expanded opium crop as an alternative source of finance.

Large regions of Afghanistan are fertile and kept that way mainly by need and ingenuity. At the foot of mountain valleys across the region, irrigation channels and tunnels, some of ancient origin, have been dug to tap the groundwater resources. Called *qanats*, these tunnels are cleaned regularly of silt and sand, so that water may be lifted or pumped, or flow out to irrigated crops. Even in largely arid areas, valley farmers have a reliable source of water for their crops, of which opium is a clear favourite as it earns them three times as much money as food crops.

In Mullah Omar's Afghanistan, the key months for agriculture are the poppy growing season that begins in October/November and ends by May/June. Farmers spend May and June in their fields tending to ripe opium bulbs with special knives and scraping off the gum which oozes out. The raw opium, plus morphine, is then sold to local traders and smuggled over a labyrinth of trails into neighbouring Pakistan, Turkmenistan, Tajikistan, Uzbekistan and Iran by camel, donkey, truck and on foot; dried and refined into heroin in laboratories along the way.

Although opiates from Afghanistan are consumed in these neighbouring countries and in India, the primary destination for approximately 80 per cent of the crop is Europe, followed by North America. Ten kilos of opium yields one kilo of morphine, which can be processed into one kilo of heroin. The wholesale price of heroin in the United Kingdom can reach $25,000 a kilo and $100–$160 per gram on the street. It led British prime minister Tony Blair to say in 2001: 'The arms that the Taliban are buying today are paid for with the lives of young British people buying their drugs on British streets. That is another part of their regime that we should seek to destroy.'

The centres of Afghanistan's poppy production are in the eastern province of Nangarhar, which is located between Pakistan's North-west Frontier province and Kabul, and produces about 20 per cent of Afghanistan's opium, and Southern Helmand province, which produces around 50 per cent of the poppy crop. Poppy production in Helmand province is estimated to have increased by 800 per cent since 1993. Helmand borders Kandahar province, Kandahar being the Taliban's power base and Mullah Omar's home city. Kandahar province is the central home of the traditional smuggling routes to Pakistan.

It is one thing to ignore this trade and another to profit directly from it. In the absence of any other assets, the Taliban administration is funded to a large extent by taxes upon the opium trade at all stages. This process begins with agricultural tax. The Taliban admit to having imposed a ten per cent tax, the same on crops of poppy as they impose on other agricultural crops. This tax can be paid in cash or kind.

Numerous reports also indicate that both Taliban and Northern Alliance officials receive payments from drug traffickers to facilitate the shipment of heroin and morphine through Afghanistan. The practice of collecting a road tax at checkpoints on the value of goods being transported is also widespread and a major income generator for government funds. This tax is applied to drugs, just as it is for any other goods being shipped.

In addition to widespread bribery, this is the accepted way in which the Afghanistan of the Taliban movement operates. Despite Mullah Omar periodically offering token edicts banning the trade, nothing of any consequence has materialised. His last ban on the trade, issued in July 2000, lasted one growing season and all signs are that production resumed quickly.

Afghanistan's opium crop of 3,656 metric tons accounted for 72 per cent of the world's illicit opium in 2000. Poppy cultivation overall for Afghanistan has climbed from 103,000 acres in 1998 to roughly 160,000 acres in 2000. Taliban-controlled Helmand province alone accounted for 39 per cent of the world's illicit opium. An annual report produced by the CIA in 1999 stated that Afghanistan was 'the world's largest illicit opium producer, surpassing Burma, a major source of hashish; increasing number of heroin-processing laboratories [were] being set up in the country; major political factions in the country profit[ed] from drug trade'.

But if the traffickers have made the biggest profits, even the growers have done well out of opium, which is precisely why foreign efforts so far to wean them off poppy cultivation and to persuade them to grow other crops have had such limited success. In more recent times, UN International Drug Control Program (UNDCP) initiatives made slow progress, while a US funded non-governmental organisation (NGO) program achieved many of its alternative development goals. 'In Afghanistan it is a matter of helping the Taliban do something they want to do anyway as strict Muslims,' said Pino Arlacchi, director of the UNDCP. 'The key is to mobilise resources from the international community to provide farmers with the irrigation, seed, fertiliser and machinery they need to raise alternative crops.'

Within months of Osama's settling in Afghanistan, Mullah Omar repaid the debt he owed his ally and now close friend with a gift.

Large areas of Nangarhar province were put under his de facto control. The drug revenues generated within these were his, as were monies collected from the many Al-Qaeda tax-roadblocks that sprang up alongside existing government stops. In return for gratuities, Al-Qaeda's militiamen would also offer 'protection' to farmers, although in reality the only danger to them was having their crops burnt by Al-Qaeda forces should they decline to pay these taxes. In return for a further consideration, Al-Qaeda would also ignore the operations of drugs refining laboratories operating within areas under their control.

Drug money quickly became a significant revenue stream for Al-Qaeda, and the organisation went on to encourage as many farmers to take up drug cultivation as possible. Cases have been reported where Al-Qaeda militiamen have deliberately burnt some farmer's food crops as a punishment for not growing poppies instead.

Privately and professionally, arrival in Afghanistan brought another a watershed in the life of Osama bin Laden. Being forced out of Sudan had shown him that he was, perhaps, more vulnerable than he had previously thought. He had treated threats to his personal security lightly, laughing off the discovery of listening devices in his offices in Khartoum, his homes and even in his car. But the international community had eventually forced Sudan's hand, and then the Khobar Towers bombing had upped the stakes considerably. Osama knew beyond doubt now that people would be out to get him.

This scared him. Changes in his personality and behaviour were noticed. The Osama in Afghanistan would never hold open court like a sheikh in his office, as he had in Khartoum. He would never again take high profile rides through a city amid a motorcade of blaring sirens.

For his own safety, in order to ensure that he was around to lead Al-Qaeda, Osama reverted to a role he was no longer used to – that of the anonymous businessman. The high life he had so clearly cherished was over.

Suspecting that his former allies, the CIA, would be keen to murder him, Osama went low profile. Fewer people knew his whereabouts; he travelled with fewer guards and revealed his travel plans only to a small cadre of trusted aides.

The early months in Afghanistan were about planning. Al-Qaeda could never again be the large, centralised organisation it once was.

Osama understood that his structure in Khartoum – corporate offices, several major training camps – invited attack and destruction of all he had worked for. His was now an underground organisation. Not that this was unfamiliar, especially in Afghanistan, although it must have seemed a backward step.

Osama came to be based in and around Jalalabad with an entourage of about 50, including wives, children, servants and hand-picked guards from his militias. It was rare, even then, for Osama to sleep in the same place for more than two consecutive nights. He maintained several remote villas in the Jalalabad area, where his extended family stayed permanently, while he circulated between these buildings and a few primitive camps in the mountains. In one telephone call home to his mother, Osama was full of optimism, claiming that he was delighted to be back to his roots, the familiar territory of the mountains. She, meanwhile, demanded that her grandchildren should be released from such a life and returned to the safety of Jeddah.

Jalalabad was not in an ideal situation, as he must have known, being so close to the Pakistani border from where infiltrations could easily be planned and executed. Later when reports filtered through his network of people asking pertinent questions on his whereabouts in Peshawar, he unwisely ignored them.

Two attempts were made to assassinate him early in 1997. The first was a small incendiary device, planted close to a route into Jalalabad city that he often took. Again he dismissed the threat, and this almost cost him his life. Used to being the hunter, rather than the hunted, Osama continued to make one major tactical blunder: he followed a regular routine. While he took advice regarding sleeping arrangements and moved constantly, he was still a creature of habit. One of his pleasures was to visit a former colleague, an Afghan commander who had served alongside Osama and his Arab-Afghans on occasions during the struggle against the Soviets. The Afghan had eased back into a 'normal' life after the Soviet pullout and had not taken any part in the bloodletting among mujahideen that had followed. But after witnessing the calamity that had descended upon Afghanistan, he had happily joined the Taliban as they swept through the country. Years later, he now held a senior position within the security services in Jalalabad.

Osama was in the habit of visiting this old friend several times each week to drink sweet tea and chat. On the morning of March 19,

1997, he had just left the building and driven away when a massive explosion all but flattened the Jalalabad Police Station. More than 50 people died and 150 were injured. The bomb was clearly intended to include Osama as one of its victims. Within weeks Osama and his family had moved to the district around Kandahar where Mullah Omar resided – an area considered a Taliban stronghold and far less open to infiltration.

Between these moves and his own personal threats, Osama set about building a new Al-Qaeda. With him in Afghanistan were his closest aides, the directors of Terrorism Incorporated. Most important to him was Dr Ayman al-Zawahiri, a qualified pediatrician and head of the Egyptian Islamic Jihad, most notably implicated in the 1981 assassination of Egyptian President Anwar Sadat. As well as being mentor to the 'chairman' and one of those at the top of the Al-Qaeda organisation, al-Zawahiri headed its religious department.

Like Osama, al-Zawahiri came from an unusually privileged background in an environment dominated by rebellious men drawn from working-class backgrounds. His great-uncle was the first secretary general of the Arab League and his grandfather was Grand Imam at Al-Azhar University. It may be that al-Zawahiri felt a stronger need than most to establish his credibility as a revolutionary, or he may suffer from personality complications because of his alleged pedophilic tendencies; he embraced a path of violence with enthusiasm and a noted bloodlust.

Others prominent in the Al-Qaeda hierarchy were Mohammed Atef, a former Egyptian policeman who was indicted for his key role in the 1998 attacks on American embassies in Kenya and Tanzania and, as Al-Qaeda's chief military strategist, is suspected of having participated in the planning of the September 11 attacks; Abu Zubaydah, a Saudi-born Palestinian who heads recruitment for Al-Qaeda and manages several training camps; and a little-known Sheikh Said, who is reputedly head of financial affairs. With key members of his board of directors around him, Osama was able to throw himself into reforming Al-Qaeda for its new surroundings. Instead of a handful of large camps, he opted to create a network of smaller, more portable and specialist bases.

Within weeks of his own arrival in May 1996, Osama was overseeing the arrival of plane-loads of his men from Sudan. Many were already fighting in Bosnia, while others continued to slip quietly into the Russian province of Chechnya. Up to 2,000 continued to serve in Somalia and training camps were quietly maintained in Sudan. According to some reports, only 200 Al-Qaeda fighters travelled to Afghanistan initially. These were mostly terrorism specialists and teachers, needed to train the many new recruits now filtering into Afghanistan. Around a dozen bases were established before the end of 1996 and a further dozen opened the following year to meet demand, so great were the numbers of volunteers arriving for indoctrination and training.

The move from Sudan had been a time of uncertainty for Al-Qaeda. But Osama's early preparations and the commitment of the men around him had allowed a seamless transition. Instead of suffering, Al-Qaeda was growing. On a wider field there was now international support to encourage Osama. In addition to the soft landing provided by Mullah Omar, this was highlighted by his new affiliation to Hezbollah International. The successful alignment of Shiia and Sunni groups had added impetus, while connecting Al-Qaeda to Iranian expertise. This was a further coup and helped upgrade the organisation and its capabilities.

So many terrorist acts had been brought to fruition in 1996 that Osama was emboldened. Even before the attempt on his life in February 1997, he knew that the United States would like to see him dead. So, with his confidence high, he judged that this was time to put his conflict with the US on an official footing.

On August 26, 1996, he issued his first *bayan*, or 'statement', a 12-page document in Arabic titled 'The Declaration of War' by Osama bin Mohammed bin Laden. In it he issued a final warning for all American troops to leave the Land of the Two Holy Places: 'Muslims burn with anger at America. For its own good, America should leave . . .' If they did not, he warned, military action would be taken against them by the same young men who, 'with the help of Allah, defeated the largest infidel superpower in the world in Afghanistan'.

While it was not unusual for groups to release long-winded tirades against the United States and the West, this was different. It was almost two months to the day after the Khobar Towers bombing. Osama was a hero in the Islamic fundamentalist world; in some parts of the Middle East, ordinary Muslim communities took to him as a Robin Hood type figure, simply searching for hope in a life they believed dominated by US-sponsored oppression – the Palestinian issue being a prime example.

Opinions about Osama polarised. Love him or hate him, by 1996, people knew exactly who Osama bin Laden was, and when he spoke they were forced to listen and study his comments. This was why his Declaration of War received possibly the widest consideration of any document since British prime minister Neville Chamberlain's famed treaty of 1938 with Adolf Hitler, following which he declared he had gained 'peace in our time'.

If it was unprecedented for a terrorist to enjoy so much credibility, Osama's exploits should by now have defined him as a cut above the rest and therefore a threat that should be nipped in the bud at all costs, not just with a low-tech and poorly executed bombing campaign in Jalalabad that missed him altogether. In a subsequent series of carefully orchestrated interviews with western and Arabic media representatives, Osama placed a spin upon his 'Declaration of War'. To *Nida'ul Islam* magazine he spoke of a 'fierce Judeo-Christian campaign against the Muslim world . . .

'The Muslims must prepare at all possible levels to repel the enemy, in military, economic, missionary and all other areas. It is crucial for us to be patient and to cooperate in righteousness and piety and to raise awareness to the fact that the highest priority, after faith, is to repel the enemy that corrupts the religion and the world. Nothing deserves a higher priority . . . And we ask Allah to give this community the guidance to exalt the people who obey Him and humiliate those who disobey Him.'

The message was clear: Al-Qaeda was going on the offensive.

CHAPTER SIXTEEN

Smoke Screen

Even discounting the possibility that Osama bin Laden and his Al-Qaeda network were involved directly in the tragedy of TWA flight 800 on July 17, 1996 – despite Jihad Wing (Arabian Peninsula) of the Islamic Change Movement claiming responsibility – by the end of 1996, the only major terrorist act in which he had been involved was the Khobar Towers bombing, an attack against an American military target. He remained something of a snob in Islamic fundamentalist terms. Many of the groups allied to him, such as Egyptian Islamic Jihad, were indiscriminate murderers and almost exclusively attacked unprotected civilian targets.

If Osama knows the legend of Robin Hood, he would undoubtedly like the comparison between himself and the English rebel who stole from the rich, to give to the poor. While Osama targeted the rich in the form of America and the West, Al-Qaeda had a well-funded department that took care of the welfare of the Taliban in Afghanistan through bribes. The similarities were plain to see.

Claiming to represent ordinary Muslims and Arabs, he drew a line at killing them, unlike most of his allies who found almost anyone expendable. As for Osama, his noble designs also extended to non-Muslims. According to family sources, when he was pressed by his mother and other family members to give up his errant ways, he defended himself by claiming that he only ever attacked legitimate military targets. 'We have never killed a child and never will,' was his mantra. On another occasion he stated: 'How can I be doing wrong, when all I seek to do is drive these people out of our lands

[Saudi Arabia]? We use military means against their military.'

This line in the sand seems to have been important to him. He believed that this defined him as someone above those around him whose bloodlust against non-Muslims – and Muslims who were considered collaborators with the infidels or who simply got in the way – was almost legendary. One of those was a man considered something of a mentor or guide to the weaker personality of Osama.

Born in 1951, Ayman al-Zawahiri, erstwhile head of Egyptian Islamic Jihad, became a pediatrician after a long and successful education. He knew intimately the workings of the human anatomy. He had saved lives of children. Yet he had turned his back on this work. He was driven by a thirst for blood that seemed unquenchable, stronger even than that of the Mujahideen in Afghanistan. Civilians of any religion were legitimate targets to him.

Al-Zawahiri's post-Afghanistan career began with Egyptian Islamic Jihad. This group was responsible for the 1981 assassination of Egypt's president Anwar Sadat and the attempt to murder his successor, Hosni Mubarak, that immediately led to Osama being forced to switch his base from Sudan to Afghanistan. Al-Zawahiri's spiritual mentor was the blind cleric Sheikh Omar Abdel-Rahman, who is serving a life sentence in a US prison for his involvement in the attack on the World Trade Center in 1993.

But al-Zawahiri nursed another secret that had nothing to do with jihad. His reason for abandoning a comfortable upper middle-class existence in Egypt in 1984 was not just a desire to liberate Afghanistan. He had been accused by several parents of molesting children under his care. A police investigation had begun into his activities, probing allegations that the pediatrician had used his status to have boys and girls left in his care, leading to a series of alleged sexual assaults.

When it seemed probable that charges were to be pressed, al-Zawahiri's family used its considerable influence to suppress the investigation. Although never formally charged, the persistent cloud that surrounded him in his home country followed him when based later in Sudan, Switzerland and Afghanistan. This is something that has never been backed up by individual pieces of evidence and legal record, but throughout his adult life he has been under suspicion of being a pedophile.

The depth of Osama's need for a father figure and a spiritual guide can be measured by the fact that he brought such a man into his inner sanctum. Worrisome too – especially for those relatives in Jeddah who consider Osama's children victims, who should be allowed a normal life – al-Zawahiri was welcomed into the family home as an 'uncle', such was the closeness of their relationship.

By the mid-1990s, Osama had known al-Zawahiri for as long as a decade, having met the Egyptian during the Afghan campaign. During the Khartoum years they had got to know each other well, working on a variety of projects such as the Somalia campaign and the failed attempt on Mubarak's life, as a result of which both men had gained stature in the eyes of international Islamic fundamentalists.

By the time of Osama's exile to Afghanistan, al-Zawahiri began to exert a heavy influence on him. He had a key role in determining the direction in which Al-Qaeda would develop and its strategies. Al-Zawahiri also had a say in shaping Osama's Declaration of War, and in the months following its issue, pressed hard for Al-Qaeda to change its stance regarding the murder of civilians, particularly Americans.

This struggle shows itself clearly in Osama's media interviews when he refers openly to the issue in conflicting terms. In one interview with an Arabic publication he stated: 'American policy does not admit to differentiating between civilians, military, and child, human or animal. Examples I mentioned before are Nagasaki and Hiroshima where they tried to eliminate a whole people. When it comes to Muslims, there is testimony from westerners and Christians who testified to the death of hundreds of thousands of our children in Iraq. And there is Qana, Sabra and Shattila, Dir Yasin and Bosnia.

'The crusaders continued their slaughter of our mothers, sisters and children. America every time makes a decision to support them and prevent weapons from reaching the Muslims, and allow Serbian butchers to slaughter Muslims. You do not have a religion that prevents you from carrying out these actions and therefore you do not have the right to object to like treatment. Every action solicits a reaction. It is a punishment that fits the crime. At the same time, our primary target is military and those in its employment.

'Our religion forbids us to kill innocents – children, women who are not combatants. Women soldiers who place themselves in the battle trenches receive the same treatment as fighting men . . . '

Here, he clearly defined targets that he considered out of bounds. But this ideological debate ended with al-Zawahiri's approach dominating. The best early evidence of this fact was the November 1997 massacre of tourists in Luxor, Egypt, carried out by elements linked to al-Gamaat al-Islamiyya, an Egyptian group long associated with Al-Qaeda. Four Egyptians and fifty-eight tourists – thirty-five of them Swiss – were killed in the attack by Muslim militants. Switzerland's federal police chief, Urs Von Daeniken, made it public in 1999 that Egypt suspects the Luxor massacre was ordered by an Egyptian named Mustafa Hamza, a military leader of al-Gamaat al-Islamiyya, and carried out with funding from Al-Qaeda.

While it is certainly true that a change in policy occurred, Osama attempted to bring the people of the Middle East with him. The anger he expressed was tangible. He accused the United States of 'crimes' against civilians that need a full grasp of modern Middle Eastern history to understand.

Many Americans will wonder about Qana and Sabra and Chattila, questioning what these incidents have to do with the United States. Most may not have heard of them. However, what took place at these locations has a great deal to do with the anger that the people of the Middle East feel toward the United States. While only a tiny minority of Muslims could ever condone the extreme actions of Al-Qaeda against the United States – indeed, their religion does not allow for such things – a majority can understand the root of the anger that has sparked these twisted minds into action.

At the heart of this anger is America's ally, Israel. The Jewish state was created by international consensus more than half a century ago, with what now appears to be little thought to the consequences. Millions of Palestinians were displaced. Those people forced off their land, and their descendants, for the most part remain living in squalid refugee camps to this day. Their resistance has grown year by year.

This is the root of the problem between the Middle East and the West, and the cause of half a century of strife. The low-grade state of war which has remained in Israel and Palestine has cost tens of thousands of lives on both sides. Understandably, considering their isolation, surrounded by avowed enemies, Israel has traditionally been extremely heavy-handed in dealing with acts of aggression against it. But a succession of Israeli governments has squandered the few genuine opportunities to make real peace, while growing ever-more violent in their attempts to show their strength to the Arabs.

The United States, the only country to have remained in full support of Israel, has backed it strongly, even through some of the more ignoble moments in the history of mankind. While Osama has supported the Palestinian cause only when it suited his purposes, others throughout the Arab world never wavered.

In September 1982, Israel invaded Lebanon. Led by her then Defence Minister Ariel Sharon, later prime minister, Operation Peace for Galilee was planned as a speedy exercise to enter the country, force the Palestine Liberation Organisation resistance fighters out of their quarters in Beirut, and then depart. Sharon misjudged the strength of the PLO however, and it was an operation that cost thousands of Lebanese civilian lives.

Sharon then gave direct orders for the Israeli army to chaperone Lebanese Christian militias, themselves involved in a civil war split on sectarian lines, allowing them to enter the Palestinian refugee camps of Sabra and Chatilla. Prominent Palestinian writer Said K. Aburish later wrote: 'What happened there did not involve any fighting and was simply the slaughter of civilians. Nor was the entry of the Christians [militias] in to the camps a secret; they were ushered in by the Israeli troops . . . At some points [during the massacre] the Israelis were within 600 yards of the camps and therefore able to hear the gunfire, if not the shrieks of the victims who included babies, pregnant women and old men . . . the bayoneting of pregnant women was commonplace . . . the butchering did not stop until some of the Israeli army officers tired of hearing the screams and ordered an end to it all.' For thirty-six hours, the Israeli army also blocked any attempt on the part of the international media to gain access to Sabra and Chatilla.

Another event in Israeli–Palestinian relations came on April 18, 1996, when Israeli 155 mm howitzers shelled a United Nations base situated in the village of Qana a couple of miles south-east of Tyre, Lebanon. Around 800 civilians had taken refuge there. Israelis targeted the base in retaliation for the Hezbollah attack on one of their special forces groups, who were laying landmines outside of the Israeli occupied 'security zone'. On this occasion between 91 and 105 people, mostly Lebanese civilian refugees, died. An official body count was not possible as the human remains had been blasted into small pieces.

The United Nations conducted its own investigation. Major-General Franklin van Kappen, UN Secretary General Boutros Boutros-Ghali's top military advisor, submitted a six-page report that was highly critical of the Israeli Defence Force. While conducting his eight-day investigation, van Kappen made a detailed study that found that at least 36 Israeli shells had landed in or near the UN camp. The shelling was concentrated on two specific areas. The first was 120 yards south of the compound. This area was hit almost entirely, except for one round, by impact-fused shells – shells that explode when they hit the ground. They are mostly used to destroy equipment and ordnance. A second area that was struck was the UN compound itself. The camp was hit by a large number of proximity-fused shells. These shells are designed to detonate above the ground, in order to widen the radius of impact and maximise casualties.

These examples offered by Osama bin Laden to justify himself are not isolated incidents: there are many more. While it would be wrong to suggest that groups such as Hamas, Palestinian Islamic Jihad and Hezbollah have not done their part to kill, main and provoke their enemy, Israel's 'iron fist' and crippling economic policies have created a great swell of regional bitterness that has had no outlet. A desperate economic underclass of poor, angry Palestinians has been cannon fodder to extremist groups in their recruitment of men. Thus, the circle of death has been perpetuated.

Behind it all was the United States, supporting Israel economically and politically. Ordinary Muslims believe that if the United States had used its tremendous influence with Israel to press for peace, a satisfactory conclusion to the conflict could have been reached decades ago. However, even when Israel had gone too far in its offensives against the Palestinians – highlighted by the examples of Sabra, Chatilla and Qana – the US used its diplomatic muscle instead to dampen international rumblings of disapproval and veto resolutions in international bodies such as the United Nations.

For Osama to hijack the Palestinian struggle in order to broaden support for his own jihad was opportunism, pure and simple. Not once had he shown any inclination to support the Palestinians or any interest in their plight. But the fact remains that there was a rich vein of resentment and hatred towards the United States for him to tap to popularise his cause. Those who reject this observation state that Hamas, Palestinian Islamic Jihad and Hezbollah would never be satisfied until they wiped Israel off the map. To some extent this is true. But would these extremist groups enjoy the same level of support amid widespread peace? Or if the economy were able to supply jobs to the young men who make up their membership? Or if the Israeli military stopped killing with impunity? Common sense says no.

If these Middle Eastern terror groups were weakened at their source, by definition the green shoots of peace would bring more stability throughout the region. For organisations such as Al-Qaeda, this would be like turning off their oxygen.

Gradually, Osama's public pronouncements and explanations of his cause grew to include more references to the Palestinian struggle. Encouraged by al-Zawahiri, there was also a noticeable evolution in the defined targets. He had told one relative: 'We use military means against their military . . . ' but later implied the contrary in the interview quoted above: 'The crusaders continued their slaughter of our mothers, sisters and children . . . Every action solicits a reaction. It is a punishment that fits the crime.'

With almost every interview given after 1996, the hand of al-Zawahiri is distinguishable on Osama's shoulder. His definitions of those who could be targeted became wider. In one television interview Osama stated: 'With regards to reports among Muslims that Osama is threatening to kill civilians, what are they killing in Palestine? They are killing children, not only civilians, but children as well. The United States has an advantage media-wise . . . that varies its standards according to its needs. Our enemy, the target – if God gives Muslims the opportunity to do so – is every American male, whether he is directly fighting us or paying taxes.

'You may have heard these days that almost three-quarters of the US people support Clinton's strikes on Iraq. They are a people whose president becomes more popular when he kills innocent people. They are a people who increase their support for their president when he commits some of the seven cardinal sins. They are a lowly people who do not understand the meaning of principles.'

The timing of the 'Declaration of War' also offered a sign of Osama's underlying desire for acceptance; a nagging fear of rejection he had carried with him since his troubled childhood. His statement was issued on August 23, 1996, just days before he was due to head an Al-Qaeda delegation to a meeting of Hezbollah International.

The Iranians had declined to stage the meeting in Tehran, fearing repercussions from the US coming so soon after the Khobar Towers bombings. Instead, the conference venue was switched to Mogadishu, capital of Somalia. Osama had never been there, and might not have considered going had he not been contacted by Mohammed Farrah Aidid, his old warlord ally, with a personal plea to attend.

The conference was attended by leaders of the Islamic fundamentalist world – Shiia and Sunni. Senior figures from around the world arrived in Mogadishu and, to a man, stood in the conference chamber and paid glowing tributes to Osama and his achievements. Sitting quietly in his seat on a long, oval conference table, Osama looked at the floor piously, appearing to be embarrassed. But inside he must have been glowing at the praise being lavished upon him. In Mogadishu, he was surrounded by his adopted family, a family that showed its appreciation for his efforts and achievements.

But aside from talking up the achievements of their most-celebrated member, the constituents of Hezbollah International had serious business to attend to in Mogadishu. Emboldened by the success at Khobar Towers, their campaign was ready to go into overdrive.

CHAPTER SEVENTEEN

African Smoke Screen, World Cup Soccer

In any global industry, results rely heavily on planning. Microsoft did not become a global giant because Bill Gates woke up and went to the office; Pepsi, McDonalds, Nike or Ford did not become global brands by accident. Osama bin Laden applied the same logic to global terrorism.

Not until the birth of Al-Qaeda and its alliances with state sponsors of terrorism such as Iran and Sudan did the export of Islamic fundamentalism become a realistic possibility. This is where Osama and his allies were unique.

As the struggle against the Soviet Union in Afghanistan unfolded, Osama had time to apply the principles of professional management to organising his Maktab al-Khidamat network. His financial muscle and organisational ability created a force that was more effective than any of its counterparts in the mujahideen resistance.

After the end of the Soviet occupation, Osama returned to normal life for only a brief period. He felt he had become rusty after a decade away from a commercial environment. He later admitted to a relative that he had benefited greatly from his experience in the family firm, where he had worked with the most modern management systems. He took in what was going on around him and went to great lengths, away from his ordinary duties, to learn about the functions of the company. At the time, some of his brothers also working in the company thought this a charming habit. Little could they have guessed his sinister purpose.

Between 1991 and 1996, Osama took the opportunity to put into

217

practice what he had learned on two levels: organising a fighting force in Afghanistan, and establishing a commercial empire that sucked in millions of dollars of profits both for Al-Qaeda and his political sponsors in Sudan.

He applied many of the principles to Al-Qaeda that he had learned elsewhere, and evolved a terror group that had a far greater sense of organisation than any in existence. Under his guidance in the role of chief executive, four distinct departments operated independently. Subcommittees were put in place to coordinate activities between each of the four departments, but the only forum to which a department reported formally was within the Al-Qaeda board of directors, which met as often as once a week. Directors and department heads met informally with the chief executive almost daily.

This system worked well within Osama's chosen industry. All four departments functioned, as much as possible, as separate entities. And within them, separate work units did likewise. This meant that while disruption could occur due to discovery or capture, Al-Qaeda would be extremely difficult to put out of business. For example, when ordered out of Sudan in 1996, Osama and his directors had several months in hand to manage an orderly departure of the bulk of his military establishment to Afghanistan. Meanwhile, his religious committee worked on as normal. The finance department remained largely in Sudan, as working from Afghanistan would have been difficult. Al-Qaeda was a fully functioning multinational.

The same principles of compartmentalisation applied, to a lesser extent, within departments of Al-Qaeda. The military committee was heavily influenced by Dr Ayman al-Zawahiri, Osama's closest confidante and ally. The two trusted each other but no one else. The military wing was broken up into small units, each reporting not to a committee but briefing al-Zawahiri and/or Osama independently. In this way, only these two knew exactly what was going on, or could see the overall picture.

The reason Osama needed to construct the most professional and evolved terrorist organisation in the world was simple. Early during his Sudan years, Osama had evolved his master plan. He wished to hit the United States directly, at home, in its own back yard. But even for an organisation such as Al-Qaeda, with its tentacles spreading all over the world, this was a mammoth undertaking and would take years of planning and careful nurturing. During the intervening period Al-Qaeda would not go quiet; it could not for fear of losing all-important support from financial donors, government sponsors and the hearts and minds of its fighting men. But there was also another reason. Osama had grasped the lessons of armed struggle. He understood that if he were to build toward his grand design, the period between initiation of this plan and its final execution would expose him to a long period of preparation during which he would be under the close scrutiny of the West's intelligence community.

It was sometime in late 1993, in Khartoum, when the groundwork for the Al-Qaeda that Osama wished to create was in place. Around him was a functioning board of directors, various departments and a full complement of staff. In the field he had established sleepers and cells of men. He was also busy placing himself at the heart of various international Islamic fundamentalist coalitions, a network that would offer his group new expertise and skills. The time had come to build a smoke screen for his master plan.

In many ways the story of Osama bin Laden – as far as the world is concerned – begins here. Everything that went before was simply a prelude to the mid-1990s. This was the starting point for his ability to bring his madness to the world.

By definition, the military wing of Al-Qaeda had to differ in nature from departments in normal corporations, even though the whole was surprisingly corporate in structure. While other departments within the organisation grew out of a central entity, the military wing was made up of a handful of smaller groupings. Men would be assigned tasks within a single project, Khobar Towers for example, working for the most part in ignorance of the tasks of other groups. As much as possible, Osama ensured that these remained separate, even during the planning stages. Coordinators of these plots were often based in separate countries, or at least in camps at separate ends of Sudan.

He would go to great lengths to guarantee that there was no crossover or dissemination of information. In the rear of his office in Khartoum, he kept a small security safe, the type many householders buy to store their valuable papers or family jewels. It was no high-security device, but nor did it need to be: his office was permanently guarded day and night by intimidating militiamen. Only Osama knew the combination, and for good reason. Inside was nothing of intrinsic value, just a few papers. Only when the documents were examined did the reason for their storage become apparent. Each document detailed the progress of one of Osama's terror projects.

The reason for the internal security was leaks. Not that Osama mistrusted his men. On the contrary, prior to his departure to Afghanistan several years later, he felt completely at ease among a group of people who, he believed, were as passionate about this cause as he himself. Instead, the need for security stemmed from Osama's realisation that many of the men he thought of as comrades in arms would in fact be sacrificed for the cause, one way or another. Those who were not to be called upon to sacrifice themselves during the battle ahead had every chance of falling into the hands of the authorities. The less they knew, in case of interrogation or torture, the less they could tell.

Khobar Towers was a first example of the smoke screen that Osama would now begin to throw up in the face of his enemy. These were terrible acts that would draw the wrath of the world against him, yet while the international community raged, Osama considered them simply stepping stones. All were designed as blows against the United States to show the emerging power of Al-Qaeda. Yet all were significantly smaller in ambition than his 'big picture' and required him only to tip a small part of his hand in terms of operational ability. By comparison to the main event he was planning, they were primitive, and perhaps even helped to lull his enemy into a false sense of security.

As early as mid-1994, Al-Qaeda began sending small numbers of men from bases in Sudan to cities in east Africa. The so-called Africa project was managed from London by a high-ranking member of Al-Qaeda, Khaled al-Fawwaz, a Saudi dissident living quietly in a family home in north London and ostensibly running an organisation devoted to war relief work.

Al-Fawwaz dealt almost exclusively with cell leaders in Africa, while he remained in regular contact with operational commander, Ayman al-Zawahiri, and Osama bin Laden, as phone records subsequently proved. In this way, there was no discernible contact between Sudan and cells in Africa.

After his subsequent arrest, British court documents suggested al-Fawwaz may have been directly involved with the terrorist cell that carried out the bombing of the American embassy in Nairobi.

Documents supplied by Barclays Bank show that he was the signatory on the account for the Advice and Reform Committee, an organisation that British and American officials believe is a front for Al-Qaeda. His credit card statements show Fawwaz used the account to pay hundreds of pounds for stationery bought from a Huddersfield company, apparently to print thousands of copies of one of Osama's *fatwas*. His mobile telephone records show he was in frequent touch with Sudan, Yemen and Saudi Arabia – all countries where Osama had growing numbers of supporters. Calls to New York and Washington suggested that he also had links there.

Central to the operation was Kenya, where cells were created in Nairobi and Mombasa. Kenya was chosen as a venue for an attack for two reasons. Considered at low risk by the United States government, the embassy there had only light security. Secondly, Osama, like many in the Islamic fundamentalist world, were hostile to the Kenyan government for allowing Israeli troops to refuel in Nairobi during the raid on Entebbe Airport in Uganda in 1976 to rescue hostages from a hijacked aircraft. In 1980, a bomb had flattened the Norfolk Hotel in Nairobi, killing 20 people and injuring 80 more. Responsibility for the attack, said to be in retaliation, was claimed by a little-known group.

Osama's men were inserted into the country under the cover of employment within a cleverly-constructed front of several charitable groups, opening branch offices in Kenya around this time. The most significant was Help Africa People, established in Germany. The Kenyan office of Help Africa People was opened by Wadih el-Hage, born a Lebanese Christian, later to become a naturalised American citizen and convert to Islam. The group went to great lengths to ensure that, for all intents and purposes, its cells were constructed around a legitimate base; this was to become a trademark of Al-Qaeda.

The humanitarian relief and aid work done by Help Africa People was legitimate. Each month, Osama's financial maze would pay into Help Africa People's bank accounts a generous sum of laundered money, via a German bank. Other smaller donations were also paid in. If the Kenyan authorities ever, for any reason, had opportunity to doubt the credentials of Help Africa People, their accounts looked entirely plausible.

So did the men involved. El-Hage never actually did any charitable work himself, but employed several Kenyans who were responsible for donating a little money to poor families – Muslims only was the rule – and also raising money locally through street collections and soliciting donations from businesses.

In time, Help Africa People came to employ several Arabs, including Haroun Fazil and Muhammed Sadiq Odeh, who would later play key roles in the bombings. Odeh, a Jordanian, had joined Al-Qaeda in 1992. Other men were also set up in small businesses. For several years, these men and some bit-players immersed themselves in everyday Kenyan society. There was nothing remarkable about them, nothing to indicate they were anything other than charity workers, small merchants or fishermen. Headed by Arabs, these organisations employed many Kenyans. The government understandably welcomed such investment.

In Tanzania, another cell was being created in the city of Mwanza. Abu Ubaidah al-Banshiri, an Arab-Afghan from the old school who was particularly close to Osama, headed this. Al-Banshiri moved to Tanzania and invested in several tracts of farmland. Later he opened several successful import and export businesses. Again, he was welcomed by the authorities in this poor African state – a man creating jobs and willing to invest in the country.

Al-Banshiri had fought alongside Osama in Afghanistan and was a trusted member of the inner circle. As such, it is believed that he was head of the overall east Africa operation until May 1996, when he died in a ferry accident on Lake Victoria.

Probably as early as 1994, Osama's sleepers were living normal lives in Kenya and Tanzania. They occasionally collected intelligence on certain targets, but otherwise did nothing to attract attention to themselves.

Osama's plans almost came to nothing however. In the wake of the Khobar Towers tragedy and a number of smaller incidents, the United States Justice Department quietly convened a grand jury in New York to investigate Osama and Al-Qaeda as early as 1996. The FBI and CIA were both involved, and it is believed that the investigation into his activities reached even higher than this in the US political and investigative hierarchy.

During the course of this investigation, at least two sources indicated to the grand jury that something was afoot in Kenya. One was from a Saudi businessman named Sidi Tayyib who was married to a distant relative of Osama. Tayyib had been arrested in Saudi

Arabia and offered a wealth of information regarding Al-Qaeda operations, most damagingly of all, financial. A number of Osama's personal bank accounts were discovered as a result, and several of these left a trail to Kenya.

By August 1997, this information bore fruit. Investigations showed that el-Hage had been identified as someone with ties to Osama, and this led to a joint FBI/Kenya police raid upon his home under the pretext of searching for stolen goods. El-Hage was living what seemed to be a quiet life. His neighbours suspected nothing.

But, on a laptop computer belonging to him, investigators discovered several highly-disturbing documents. Put together, these provided an outline of an Al-Qaeda cell based in Kenya. The documents included a letter written by Fazil Abdullah Mohammed, that gave a vague picture of some of the intelligence that had been collected. The letter was addressed simply to 'Haj', believed to be a code word for Osama bin Laden. In the wake of this, the FBI told el-Hage and his family to leave the country. He took flight to the United States with his family in September 1997. But incredibly, the agency itself did little to counter the threat that was now becoming obvious. And its ineptitude only got worse.

Towards the end of 1997, an Egyptian national, Mustafa Mahmoud Said Ahmed, walked in to the US embassy in Nairobi. He asked to see someone from the intelligence services. Later he informed a CIA agent that he knew of a plan to detonate a truck bomb in the parking garage of the embassy. He was interrogated a second time, by Kenyan police, and admitted that he had taken part in an ongoing program of surveillance of the embassy, including taking photos. Despite the specific nature of testimony before them, the CIA did not take Ahmed's statements seriously and he was deported. He was arrested later in connection with the bombing.

According to intelligence sources, the US ambassador to Kenya, Prudence Bushnell, and her staff were briefed. Bushnell was reported to be constantly arguing with the State Department about finding the budget for a new building, or to upgrade security at the existing premises. Tragically, the State Department did not consider Nairobi a high-risk location.

In the unlikely setting of France, danger was growing inexorably. Al-Qaeda was also participating a wide-ranging plot, along with its major associates within the international terror business, to hit the

1998 World Cup soccer tournament in France. Over five weeks, a cumulative global television audience of 37 billion people watched 62 games, while hundreds of thousands more attended matches between the 32 national teams that qualified. Most watched in ignorance of the security risk posed by terrorism, and how close the terrorists came to laying waste to this festival of sport.

The world's second biggest sporting event, it was already highly politicised by the media, with the United States and Iran in the same qualifying group and set to play a match in Lyon on Sunday, 21 June. US star Alexi Lalas put the hyperbole in perspective when he commented sarcastically: 'This is a game that will determine the future of our planet and possibly the most important single sporting event that's ever been played in the history of the world. So we're dealing with that.'

While Lalas was, of course, making a different point, his actual sentiment was not far off the thoughts of those who sought a soft American target and a world stage on which to perform. Planning toward France '98 had begun several years earlier.

However, in May 1998, Abu Hamza, a senior operative within Algeria's Armed Islamic Group, was arrested and, to save his skin, he was only too willing to cooperate with the authorities. On May 16, armed with what French police claimed was evidence that 'preparations were underway to mount terrorist attacks during the World Cup', French, Belgian, German, Italian and Swiss police staged dawn raids on known and suspected supporters of the Algerian terrorist group, Group Islamic Army (GIA) and the Armed Islamic Group (AIG). Nearly a hundred people were taken into custody for questioning, including Sheikh Abdallah Kinai, an Arab-Afghan close to all the GIA leadership, and Tayeb al-Afghani, formerly one of Osama's lieutenants in his al-Ansar base in Afghanistan.

Just under 3,000 Algerians were estimated to have served among Osama's MAK Arab-Afghans. Many returned home to join myriad resistance movements against the Algerian government. These included the Armed Islamic Group (AIG) and the Islamic Army Movement (MIA). Later, the most radical elements from the AIG and MIA formed the GIA. Since 1992, at least 70,000 people have died in Algerian violence, with the GIA taking a large proportion of these lives.

France, Algeria's former colonial ruler, was used to being the focus of GIA activities and had infiltrated the group. In a 1994 airliner hijack, the GIA allegedly tried to command the pilot to fly over metropolitan Paris and then crash the plane into the city. The plane landed to refuel and before it could take off again French troops stormed it.

With its close leadership contacts to Osama, the GIA sheltered within the Al-Qaeda umbrella during the Khartoum years. In addition to being supplied with arms and funds by Osama, GIA men were trained at his camps dotted around Sudan.

The opportunities provided by France '98 seemed too good to miss. In Afghanistan at this point, Osama had funded and help organise the plan when it was presented to him, and agreed to offer additional funding and arms, in addition to the GIA sending key personnel for expert training in Al-Qaeda camps.

From the Arab world, Saudi Arabia, Tunisia and Morocco had also qualified for France '98, providing what looked like perfect cover for any number of GIA operatives entering France and Europe. However, this was an eventuality the authorities not only expected, but had planned for. Years in advance the French government had inserted moles within the Algerian's Islamic fundamentalist community and had paid informers on their payroll.

The key dates of the plot were Monday, June 15; Sunday, June 21; and Thursday, June 25, when the US national team was scheduled to play group matches against Germany, Iran and Yugoslavia respectively. This would mean a large body of American supporters together in one place, and the movement of the United States squad could be predicted. Either would be an ideal target for terrorism.

Even before many of the GIA operatives had left Algeria for Europe, Interpol was coordinating a continent-wide sweep and the GIA plan was smashed. Though no bomb-making materials were found, a police spokesman said: 'We confirmed that attacks were being planned, and were able to nab the people who were planning all this, both here and abroad.'

Official comment from the rest of the world remained muted and little information was made available. The reason for this is the public panic that would have resulted from knowing just how close *Football Mondial* came to disaster. If the full extent of the plot to attack the 1998 World Cup were to have become clear, a commercial disaster would doubtless have resulted.

★

225

The collapse of this extraordinary plan to disrupt the World Cup was a blow to the leadership of the Islamic fundamentalist world. An effective attack would have stopped the event in its tracks and showed the power of the fundamentalist movement. As so often happened, the fundamentalist movement suffered a great deal of petty squabbling and infighting when the jackals that led the industry had nothing to focus on. Once again Osama emerged as the saviour of the entire movement.

In the spring of 1998 the cells he had laid down years before in Kenya and Tanzania came to life. Internally within the Al-Qaeda network and externally through expertise obtained through Hezbollah International, a handful of men had been prepared at Al-Qaeda's camps in Afghanistan. Many passed through a transit base established in San'a, the capital of Yemen. The intelligence community believes that, at great risk to himself, Osama left Afghanistan to visit the Yemeni outpost, meeting with cell leaders from both countries.

In May 1998, Haroun Fazil, an employee of Help Africa People, rented an estate home in a high-class residential neighbourhood outside the centre of Nairobi. The building was isolated by high walls, making it nearly impossible for any passerby to observe activity within its confines. Another feature was a gated driveway, large enough to accommodate large trucks, as was the garage. Subsequent reports on the bombings indicate that the bomb used to destroy the US embassy in Nairobi may have been constructed and stored there.

In June, a 24-year-old Tanzanian Al-Qaeda member, Khalfan Khamis Mohamed, rented a large detached home in the Ilala district of Dar es Salaam, capital of Tanzania. Once again, the property was secluded, surrounded by high walls and had a garage large enough for a truck.

Subsequent investigations served to finger the point men on the entire plan. Abdullah Ahmed Abdullah is described as the mastermind of both the Nairobi and Dar es Salaam attacks. Help Africa People employee Muhammed Sadiq Odeh was the explosives expert. He had received training in explosives in Afghanistan.

Also now in place in Kenya, working diligently in civilian employment for a time so as not to arouse suspicion, were the two men on whom Osama had bestowed the greatest honour. Mohammed Rashed Daoud Al-Owhali, a 21-year-old Saudi Arabian, and Jihad Mohammed Ali had met privately with the Al-Qaeda leader in Afghanistan before their departure to Africa. They were the individuals nominated to give their lives – the suicide bombers – or, as Islamic fundamentalists came to know them the world over – martyrs.

As the plot progressed, Osama could not resist his day in the sun, showboating for the media. While travelling from his base in Kandahar to Peshawar for a meeting of Islamists, he used the opportunity to stage a press conference with sympathetic members of the media. With al-Zawahiri sitting smugly at his side, Osama reaffirmed his anti-US agenda, reaffirmed his call for jihad, and said: 'The Islamic world is facing a period of trouble; we are entering a period of danger. I refer to the presence of Christian forces in Arab lands. The Christians are attempting to establish full control over our region.

'For the first time since the rise of our Holy Prophet Muhammad, peace be upon him, we see a situation where the sacred places of our religion – the Kaabah (in Mecca), the Nabvi Mosque (in Medina) and the Al Aqsa Mosque (Jerusalem) – are under the open and covert power of non-Muslims. It has now become obligatory for Muslims, wherever they are in this world, to begin the struggle to oust the infidels from our sacred places.'

The Al-Qaeda leader went on to blame the House of Saud for allowing the Americans to take effective control of the country. He announced that Muslim scholars had issued a *fatwa* calling for a jihad, stating: 'Muslims should sacrifice their lives and resources . . .' and then went on to announce an all-out war.

The press conference was then opened for questions. Osama was at his most lucid and during the next 30 minutes went as close as he ever has to admitting his hand was behind the Khobar Towers bombing. 'In Saudi Arabia we have modern arms that are used against the United States. An incident happened in Riyadh and then in al-Khobar. We killed 19 Americans in these bomb blasts . . .'

Finally, Osama stated: 'By the grace of God, we have established an organisation named Islamic Front with the help of jihad organisations all around the world. The purpose of the Islamic Front will be to fight America and Israel. An important leader of this organisation is here with me, Dr Ayman al-Zawahiri.'

Finally, one journalist present asked Osama how long he believed it would be before the Islamic Front would begin its campaign. He replied: 'Within weeks . . .' It was then late May.

On August 4, 1998, Abdullah Ahmed Abdullah and Mohammed Rashed Daoud Al-Owhali reportedly conducted a reconnaissance of the US embassy in Nairobi. As cover, they claimed to be working for a company that sold fresh fish to city hotels. The same day a party of men also discreetly checked the premises of the US embassy in Dar es Salaam.

After a brief inspection of the surroundings in Nairobi, they decided to aim the truck toward rear of the building, instead of attempting to drive it into the embassy's underground garage or place it in the front of the embassy building, both of which had greater fields of security. This decided, a day later the bomb was primed and installed in the passenger side of the cabin of the bomb delivery truck.

On August 7, two light-coloured vehicles exited the villa in Nairobi. The first was a pick-up truck driven by Fazil Abdullah Mohammed. The second, a truck, contained the suicide bomber Mohammed Rashed Daoud Al-Owhali and was driven by Jihad Mohammed Ali toward the US embassy.

Al-Owhali had been given a dual role in the plot. He was armed with a pistol and a number of stun grenades. When the truck containing the bomb was parked, his job was to scare as many Kenyan civilians away from the site as possible, before himself setting off the bomb manually if the detonator malfunctioned. Either way, he was giving up his life.

In practice, however, Al-Owhali fell apart under pressure and his ineptitude cost the lives of dozens of innocent people who might otherwise have been spared, many of them fellow Muslims, the constituents on whose behalf he believed he was giving his life. He exited the truck without his pistol, and then weakly threw a grenade at a US embassy security guard. He then panicked and ran away.

With only one option open to him to rescue the mission, Jihad Mohammed Ali manually detonated the bomb instantly. The blast not only damaged the embassy building but tore through the nearby Cooperative Bank and reduced the seven-floor Ufundi Cooperative House to a pile of rubble.

Around 450 miles away, four minutes later, Hamden Khalif Allah

Awad, also known as Ahmed the German, was killed instantly as a result of a bomb detonation in his truck, which was outside the US Embassy in Dar es Salaam. The force of the blast was so strong that the top half of his body, still holding on to the steering wheel, was slammed into the embassy building.

In Nairobi, 213 people were killed in the blast. Witnesses described gruesome scenes in the moments after the explosion: of passengers on a bus outside the embassy incinerated in their seats; of shattered cars smouldering in the street with passengers draped out the windows; of dazed and bleeding survivors lying on the ground pleading for help. Scores of people were cut by flying glass as the blast shattered windows in office buildings five blocks away. As night fell, rescue workers were frantically trying to dig their way into the rubble of the Ufundi building to reach people that authorities feared were trapped inside. For all Al-Qaeda's efforts, only a handful of victims were American, including five embassy employees and a child. The remainder were mostly Kenyans, among them many Muslims.

In Dar es Salaam, 11 people died, including three Tanzanian guards and two locally-hired embassy staff members. The explosion destroyed the entrance to the embassy, blowing off a wall on the right side of the building, snapping trees like matchsticks and setting cars ablaze in a scene that witnesses said looked like a war zone. The nearby French and German embassies were damaged by the blast, but no one in either building was injured, authorities said.

Armed US Marines tried to maintain order among the crowds of Tanzanians that quickly gathered at the scene, cordoning off the area as they helped evacuate people from the building. Smoke rose over the compound's buildings as cranes were rushed to the scene to tear apart collapsed walls in a desperate search for survivors.

President Clinton was awakened in the White House at 5:30 a.m. with news of the attacks. In a statement he later said: 'These acts of terrorist violence are abhorrent. They are inhuman.' He ordered security to be tightened at US installations around the world and dispatched disaster-relief units and anti-terrorism specialists to the two East African capitals. Later the same day Clinton interrupted a bill-signing ceremony in the White House Rose Garden to condemn what he called 'the cowardly attacks'. He vowed that the United States would bring the bombers to justice 'no matter what or how long it takes'.

UN Secretary General Kofi Annan angrily described the blasts as 'indiscriminate terrorism'. Secretary of State Madeleine Albright said in a statement that the administration would 'spare no effort to use all means at our disposal to track down and punish the perpetrators of these outrageous acts'.

Under US federal law, the FBI is responsible for investigating a number of crimes committed against American persons and property abroad. The attacks against the embassies in Nairobi and Dar es Salaam fell under this mandate. Within hours of the bombings, FBI personnel were dispatched to East Africa where they were assisted closely by the Kenyan Criminal Investigative Division (CID) and Tanzanian CID. Understandably, considering that much information had been passed on to the FBI and CIA prior to the bombings, but not been acted upon, the plot was quick to unravel.

The investigations of these three organisations – with much international cooperation – ultimately lead to the arrest and trial of four men closely linked with the plot and the arrest of a further six currently in custody in the US or abroad. A further 13, including Osama himself, are still fugitives. The US government has public indictments against 26 members of Al-Qaeda.

In January 2001 a trial began at the US District Court in New York City. Four defendants were charged with conspiring in the bombing of two American embassies in East Africa in 1998 and in other acts of terrorism as part of Al-Qaeda. All of the defendants pleaded not guilty. The most pathetic was Al-Owhali. He had dedicated himself to entering the kingdom of God directly as a martyr for the cause, but had run away from the scene of the bombing when the attack diverged from the original plan. He was injured in the blast and was arrested in the hospital where he sought treatment. He had been extradited to the United States on August 27, 1998.

A second man charged was Khalfan Khamis Mohamed, a Tanzanian citizen who rode in the truck that carried the bomb to the embassy in Dar es Salaam. He had been responsible for leasing the house where the bomb was made and helped to build the bomb and load the truck. After fleeing to Cape Town, South Africa, in October 1999, he was arrested and made a full confession. A third was Jordanian Mohammed Sadiq Odeh, named in court as a 'technical advisor' to the Nairobi bombing cell. He left Kenya just before the bombing and was arrested trying to enter Pakistan with a fake Yemeni passport. He was interrogated by Pakistani officials, and eventually admitted being part of the embassy bombing conspiracy. Odeh was also implicated in the 1993 murder of American soldiers in Somalia. Finally came US national Wadih el-Hage who, at the time of the bombings, was living in Arlington, Texas, with his wife and seven children. He defended himself by saying that he only worked for Osama bin Laden in legitimate businesses and had had no contact with him since 1994. He was charged with conspiracy to murder Americans.

Over four months, the court heard an overwhelming body of evidence. This was highlighted by the testimonies offered by a pair of defectors from inside Al-Qaeda – Jamal Ahmed Al-Fadl and L'Hossaine Kherchtou – who had both entered the Witness Protection Program after their flight from the organisation.

The American government's understanding of the Al-Qaeda network was also aided by another man who did not testify publicly, but provided key intelligence behind the scenes. Ali Mohamed, an Egyptian former US Army sergeant, was the first person to plead guilty to charges resulting from the embassy bombings. It was Ali Mohamed who provided the most damning evidence of Osama's personal involvement in the embassies plot, not just as a remote head of the Al-Qaeda organisation but as a direct participant.

Ali Mohamed testified that he delivered pictures, diagrams and a progress report to Osama in Khartoum. He said that Osama had looked at a photograph of the US embassy and pointed to the place where a bomb truck could be driven through. There was no direct evidence presented at the trial that Osama himself ordered the bombings, although the prosecution did establish the links between him and the four men on trial. They also established through phone records and wire-tap transcripts that there was satellite telephone contact between the Nairobi cell and Osama.

All four defendants were convicted in May 2001. Although some could have received the death penalty, the court declined to condemn the men to death to avoid creating martyrs.

Osama was indicted by a federal grand jury on November 4, 1998, in the Southern District of New York, on charges of conspiracy to murder and murder of US nationals outside the United States and attacks on a federal facility resulting in death. He was named along with a number of aliases: 'Usama Bin Muhammad

Bin Ladin, Shaykh Usama Bin Ladin, the Prince, the Emir, Abu Abdallah, Mujahid Shaykh, Haij, and the Director'.

On June 7, 1999, Attorney General Janet Reno and FBI Director Louis J. Freeh announced that Osama had been placed on the FBI's list of the 'Ten Most Wanted Fugitives.' The Department of State also offered up to $5 million for information leading to his capture, the largest amount ever offered for a fugitive wanted by the US government.

Osama was the 456th person to be placed on the FBI's Most Wanted list, which was started in 1950. Of that number, by the end of 1998, 427 fugitives had been apprehended or located, 133 of them as a result of citizen assistance. In due course Osama would advance to the number-one position on the list, a dubious 'honour'.

CHAPTER EIGHTEEN

Putting Atta to Sleep

Even in death, Mohammed Atta continued the pretence that he had lived a pious life, a big lie that had brought him to the attention of Osama bin Laden and then into infamy. The suspected leader of the September 11 tragedy left behind a will that contained specific instructions about what was to happen to his earthly remains.

His will, obtained by the German magazine *Der Spiegel*, was discovered in a suitcase at Logan Airport that never made it into the doomed American Airlines Flight 11. In it Atta wrote: 'Those who will sit beside my body must remember Allah, God and pray for me to be with the angels. I don't want pregnant women or a person who is not clean to come and say goodbye to me because I don't approve of it. I don't want women to go to my funeral or later to my grave. I only want to be buried next to good Muslims. My face should be directed east toward Mecca. A third of my money should be donated to the poor and needy. My books, I will give to one of the mosques.'

Atta had had time to plan for his death in the certain knowledge of when he would die. He went on to pilot American Airlines Flight 11, crashing 91 other souls into the north tower of the World Trade Center. Whatever grand notion drove Atta, his leader thought of the men he sent to America as nothing more than pawns in a game of chess with the western world. A good Muslim had been martyred for the cause. Atta would go directly to the kingdom of God for his sacrifice, while the United States had been dealt a blow on home soil that was unparalleled.

Or so Osama – and the rest of Al-Qaeda – thought.

233

Had Osama and Atta ever sat down to talk, they would have discovered many similarities in their lives. Both were born into comfortable conditions, both suffered because of childhood timidity, both were overshadowed by their fathers and both drifted until they found a cause to commit themselves to.

There were differences too, the most striking being their inner torment. Osama put his wild days behind him after his 1977 revelation, remoulding himself as a defender of the faith and Islam's staunchest fighter of western decadence. By contrast, despite having the extraordinary depth of conviction to fly an airliner into the World Trade Center and murder thousands, Atta remained a heavy-drinking, sexually deviant young man, who, to satisfy himself, beat the prostitutes he regularly hired.

To fly himself into oblivion on September 11, Atta must have believed his twisted version of Islam, but he certainly never lived it.

Born in Kafr El Sheikh, a large conurbation on the Nile delta, Atta lived much of his early life in the Abdeen quarter of Cairo, the capital of Egypt. People who knew him during those years remain unable to connect the boy they knew and the actions of the man. 'If he could do something like that . . . then I could suspect anyone, even my brother, or my own hands,' Mohamed Hassan Attiya, a former classmate told an interviewer. He insisted Atta was polite and 'on the right path' toward his goal of becoming an engineer.

Mohamed Kamel Khamis, who ran an automobile repair shop below the apartment where the Atta family lived prior to 1992, said Atta was very introverted but was considered a good boy in the neighbourhood. His family gave nicknames to children and Atta was dubbed '*bolbol*', meaning little singing bird, reflecting his timid nature. Atta's father was a lawyer and a political animal, although without overt leanings towards fundamentalism. He shared his views of the world with his son over drawn-out games of chess, although today the father says his son was 'a moderate in his adherence to his faith like me and his mother'.

Atta graduated from Cairo University with a degree in architectural engineering. He was an average student, but was nevertheless accepted at the Technical University of Hamburg-Harburg (TUHH) and joined the facility in the last quarter of 1992, apparently first taking a degree course in shipbuilding and later urban planning.

The Technical University of Hamburg-Harburg is one of the youngest universities in Germany as well as one of the most successful. It is situated in Harburg, once a small town that is now one of the most cosmopolitan suburbs of Hamburg; nearly a third of the population, a large proportion of these being Arabs, were not born in the country.

With an average of 4,000 students, the Technical University of Hamburg-Harburg offers a uniquely high ratio of staff to students. The facility attempts to provide an environment that is 'ideal for the development of new ideas in engineering', while priority is given to research, interdisciplinary studies and innovation.

Atta settled well into life in Hamburg. His family paid for a nice apartment at Marienstrasse 54, little more than 200 yards from the TUHH campus. For some time he dutifully followed his studies and regularly attended lectures. However, he was absent for large stretches of course work, and when confronted about this defended himself, stating that he was writing his thesis based upon the city of Aleppo in the north-west of Syria, exploring conflict between Islam and modernity as reflected in the city's planning.

In part, this story holds true. One news agency tracked down Volker Hauth, a friend of the young Egyptian, who joined him on trips to Syria. 'I knew Mohammed was a guy searching for justice. He felt offended by this broad wrong direction that the world was taking,' recalled Hauth.

During school holidays, when not visiting Syria, Atta sought part-time work in a consultancy firm. Staff there, like his colleagues in university, saw only a normal man. Some believe that he went on Hajj in 1995, but aside from this, he was not overtly religious, and co-workers heard him condemn terrorist attacks on tourists in Egypt.

For a man training himself in urban planning Atta was similarly passive about his surroundings, making only passing reference to the grandeur around him in Hamburg, a modern city built out of the ashes of an old that had been destroyed by Allied bombing in 1943.

The city was going through a heady renaissance when Atta joined a pattern of social evolution in Hamburg. About 15 per cent of the population, German and immigrant, had arrived in the last decade. With 1.7 million inhabitants in the second largest city in the Federal Republic of Germany, and with a large immigrant community, it was easy for a young Egyptian to mingle.

Atta is recalled as someone who did not show much interest in anything and had no hobbies. One facet of city life, however, for which Hamburg was well known, was its peep shows, porn cinemas and sex shops. Here, Atta, the future Islamic martyr, spent much of the spending money his parents sent him from Cairo. Hamburg is almost as synonymous with sex as it is with international trade, and the focal point of the city's second biggest industry is St Pauli, the old red-light district, and Herbertstrasse. The latter has been called the 'Champs-Elysées of sex', bristling with neon-emblazoned side streets and clubs that hawk every type of sex show imaginable. Prostitutes solicit business openly. One street is a cordoned off, a men-only block where the girls sit in illuminated windows, negotiating prices with passers by.

Mohammed Atta all but disappeared for one year between the summers of 1997 and 1998. He informed the school that his absence was for family reasons, but did not return home. When he was actually in Germany he was given to disappear almost overnight and not appear again for anything up to two months.

What is believed is that, by this time, Atta already had a foot in the Al-Qaeda network. Some have pointed to his friendship with a Syrian businessman alleged to have ties to Osama, but this has never been proven. What does seem clear is that Atta had fallen under the influence of more radical Islamic thinkers during his visits to Syria, and this was his stepping stone into the murky world of international terrorism. With his rather weak and impressionable personality, Atta was an ideal candidate.

At that time, in the middle part of 1997, Al-Qaeda and Osama bin Laden were in vogue among Islamic radicals. The Khobar Towers bombing had been like a massive recruitment advertisement. Those disaffected with society, bearing a grudge against all manner of things, suddenly had a standard bearer. Osama was the Arab world's Che Guevara, a symbol of the struggle against all the wrongs that afflicted the Middle East. He raged at the status quo, and this attracted anyone with a chip on their shoulder. From its position in the shadows, Al-Qaeda's recruitment network suddenly had massive credibility and its reach grew throughout the Middle East, more powerful than ever before.

It was a world that attracted the directionless, angry student Mohammed Atta. Invited by an associate at the mosque to join a study group, Atta was slowly indoctrinated with the seeds of hatred and religious extremism. Much to his handler's delight, Atta absorbed everything he was told with ease.

Soon he was flying from Damascus, the Syrian capital, to Islamabad, and was then spirited across the Pakistani frontier to Afghanistan. It was here that Atta joined training at an Al-Qaeda mountain base. He was taught the art of terrorism and physical fitness, but also indoctrinated further in the thinking of Islamic fundamentalism.

It is unclear whether he met the Al-Qaeda leader during this time, but what is certain is that Atta was noted as a potential star. He had legitimate roots in the West and had immersed himself in the way of life in Europe. What was more he was gullible, easily led, yet technically knowledgeable. Young men like Atta were indispensable to Osama's network.

Atta was back at his desk at the Technical University of Hamburg-Harburg when the school year opened in September 1998. Just a month earlier the world had been shocked by the attacks on two US embassies in East Africa. Atta returned to school sporting a long beard. He was more serious now, quoted the Koran and prayed five times each day. But this was the extent of his change. Atta, the future martyr, continued to drink with western colleagues in the university bar and was a known 'face' in the seedy part of town where more depraved sexual services were on offer. Atta's interest lay in violence. More than once he was cautioned by police for going too far while beating up one of his hapless call girls.

If they had known about their recruit's deviant behaviour, it is doubtful that officials at Al-Qaeda would have cared. They had recruited, indoctrinated and trained a man of reasonable intelligence and a technical background, and then replanted him back in the West. He was an ideal sleeper and would continue living quietly in Germany until called upon to work on Al-Qaeda's behalf. He had a valid residency permit through enrollment at university, although now the religious Atta seldom attended lectures. Instead much of his time was spent trading in second-hand cars.

Later, in 1999, university officials granted Atta's request to open an Islamic student group, where Muslim students at the Technical University of Hamburg-Harburg could meet and pray. It was a perfect cover. Over subsequent months two younger students,

Marwan Al-Shehhi and Ziad Samir Jarrah, joined the group. Later they would travel to America with him.

But for now the mature Egyptian student went about his business as normal, awaiting instructions on his next move.

CHAPTER NINETEEN

The President's Nemesis

Immediately following the East Africa embassy bombings, American, Kenyan and Tanzanian investigators unravelled the plot at indecent speed – as well they might: twice a warning or blueprint of the plot had been handed to the US security services on a plate, ahead of the bombing.

A year earlier, in August 1997, a joint FBI/Kenya police raid on the home of Wadih el-Hage, the Al-Qaeda point man in East Africa, had thrown up a wealth of evidence, including information in a laptop computer and a letter believed to have been written to Osama bin Laden. At the end of the same year Mustafa Mahmoud Said Ahmed, an Egyptian, gave a CIA agent the details of a plan to detonate a truck bomb in the parking garage of the embassy. He was dismissed as a crank. After the event, needless to say, these two sources of information were quickly revisited. Using them as starting points, Al-Qaeda was quickly proven to be behind the plot.

As a result of this undeniable linkage, on August 20, 1998, the US Navy fired between 70 and 80 Tomahawk cruise missiles at targets in Sudan from ships in the Red Sea, and six targets in Afghanistan from vessels stationed in the Arabian Sea.

The targets in Afghanistan were training camps run by Al-Qaeda located in areas south of the town of Khost and opposite the Pakistani border towns of Thal and Miran Shah. Several of the sites hit were part of the Aswa Kali al-Batr headquarters, a support complex and four training camps used by Al-Qaeda, the Armed Islamic Group and the Egyptian Islamic Jihad.

Other reported targets for the US missiles were the village of

Khorbuz, close to the Pakistani border; a military training camp in Jawur, used by Al-Ansar Islamic Movement; Al-Qaeda bases at Salman and Tora Bora, south of Jalalabad; and Khost Airport.

Media speculation that President Clinton was firing Tomahawks in the hope of killing Osama was plainly ridiculous. The head of Al-Qaeda was far too careful to be around any potential targets in the wake of the embassy bombings. Indeed, just as Osama headed for the isolation of remote mountain caves in Afghanistan, his people were similarly evacuated within hours of the bombings. One intelligence official was quoted as saying there was 'a disbursement of people away from Bin Laden's bases of operation within Afghanistan in the aftermath of the explosions'.

President Clinton had been enjoying what the media described as a 'post-Lewinsky holiday' in Martha's Vineyard, Massachusetts, and was briefed there by his national security advisers about the simultaneous US attacks in Afghanistan and Sudan. Clinton interrupted his vacation and returned to Washington for meetings with national security advisers, and then addressed the nation. 'Today, I ordered our armed forces to strike at terrorist-related facilities in Afghanistan and Sudan because of the threat they present to our national security,' he said. 'Today, we have struck back.

'The United States launched an attack this morning on one of the most active terrorist bases in the world. It is located in Afghanistan and operated by groups affiliated with Osama bin Laden, a network not sponsored by any state, but as dangerous as any we face.

'I ordered this action for four reasons. First, because we have convincing evidence these groups played the key role in the embassy bombings in Kenya and Tanzania. Second, because these groups have executed terrorist attacks against Americans in the past. Third, because we have compelling information that they were planning additional terrorist attacks against our citizens and others with the inevitable collateral casualties we saw so tragically in Africa. And fourth, because they are seeking to acquire chemical weapons and other dangerous weapons.'

The missile strikes against Sudan hit the Al-Shifa Pharmaceutical Industries factory outside Khartoum and destroyed it. The plant was believed to be manufacturing a prototype for deadly nerve gas. But the *New York Times* of August 29 made the case that the

Khartoum plant was not the highly secretive, tightly secured military-industrial facility that US intelligence officials claimed. Quoting US and European engineers and consultants who helped build and supply the factory in the early 1990s, the daily asserted that the plant made both medicine and veterinary drugs and was not equipped to produce a precursor of the deadly VX nerve gas, as the US government claimed.

Sudanese president Omar Hassan al-Bashir, who had given a home to Al-Qaeda for five years as part of his country's sponsorship of Islamic fundamentalist terrorism, gave a press conference to announce that his nation would protest through diplomatic channels. Al-Bashir also showed he was well-versed in American tabloid journalism, adding that the attack was a crusade against Islam, carried out 'to cover up for the Monica scandal'.

Even more brazen was Sudan's parliamentary speaker and power broker Dr Hassan al-Turabi. The man who pocketed millions of dollars of government money, much-needed by his starving people, through crooked contracts with Osama's construction company in Khartoum stated: 'You allow a single person simply to divert your attention from his own affair, simply to go and attack these "niggers" in the Southern Hemisphere or fundamentalist Muslims like that . . . '

Osama's words on the matter were delivered courtesy of Abdul Bari Atwan, editor of the London based newspaper *Al-Quds al-Arabi*. A known channel of communication for the Saudi dissident, Atwan was contacted soon after the attack by a close aide of Osama. 'The battle did not start yet,' Atwan quoted Osama as saying. 'The answer is what you see and not what you hear.'

An Al-Qaeda spokesman claimed that their casualties included six Arab-Afghans: two from Egypt, three from Yemen, and a Saudi citizen from Medina. Seven Pakistanis and fifteen Afghanis were killed in the attacks. More than fifteen Pakistanis were severely injured, and so were five Arab-Afghans.

Al-Qaeda concurred with assertions by US intelligence that the attacks were timed to coincide with a meeting of the organisation's board of directors, scheduled for the Zhawar Khili Al-Badr training camp near Khost that same day. Among others, Osama and his deputy, Ayman al-Zawahiri, would have been present. However, information had reached Al-Qaeda well in advance that most US diplomats in Pakistan were being evacuated with some urgency.

This, of course, indicated that an attack was imminent and that the US feared reprisals. While Tomahawk missiles were raining down over the heads of innocent Afghans, Osama was watching the drama around him unfold on television, in the safety of a command bunker high up in the isolated Hindu Kush mountain range.

Osama has survived to see the early years of the millennium because he is a fox. He has remained several steps ahead of the combined might of the Soviet Union, and later the United States, for two decades. Both would have dearly liked to remove him permanently. But Osama continues to think like the freedom fighter he once was. Even those who would like to see him dead must agree that his instincts are sound. Cancelling a board meeting on the eve of this Tomahawk attack typifies his instinct for survival – an instinct backed up by a strong intelligence network watching his enemies.

Osama was still establishing himself and strengthening his position during this period, both within Afghanistan and the world of Islamic fundamentalism. In keeping with the sheikh-like image that he enjoyed projecting, part of his methodology in building alliances was through marriage. His first marriage came as a mere 17-year-old, when he was betrothed to a Syrian girl who was a relative on his mother's side. Much later he married a Filipina who is a cousin of Abu Sabaya, head of the extremist Islamic group in the Philippines named Abu Sayyaf.

Some time after 1996, in order to entrench himself in Afghanistan, Osama took a third wife, Fatima, the eldest daughter of the country's leader, Mullah Mohammed Omar. Little is known about her, especially as Mullah Omar prefers to keep women virtually imprisoned at home and well-covered. Osama added a fourth wife in 1998, the daughter of a senior figure within the Pashtun tribes that make up the majority of the Afghani population. These two unions underlined Osama's status as part of the community. He was still technically an outsider, but in a society that values family ties above all else, his marriages had further added to his personal integration and therefore his safety.

Osama's precautions are not signs of paranoia. As long ago as the beginning of 1995, the United States had begun to make its first serious efforts to close down Al-Qaeda, under the stewardship of President Clinton. On January 23, 1995, Clinton wrote to Congress regarding 'the freezing of Bin Laden assets'.

'In light of the threat posed by grave acts of violence committed by foreign terrorists that disrupt the Middle East peace process, using my authority under, *inter alia*, the International Emergency Economic Powers Act, I declared a national emergency and issued Executive Order 12947. Because such terrorist activities continue to pose an unusual and extraordinary threat to the national security, foreign policy, and economy of the United States, I have renewed the national emergency declared in Executive Order 12947 annually, most recently on January 21, 1998.'

Clinton added: 'Osama bin Ladin and his organisations and associates have repeatedly called upon their supporters to perform acts of violence. Bin Ladin has declared that killing Americans and their allies "is an individual duty for every Muslim . . . in order to liberate the Al-Aqsa Mosque and the Holy Mosque". These threats are clearly intended to violently disrupt the Middle East peace process . . . I have authorised these actions in view of the danger posed to the national security, foreign policy, and economy of the United States by the activities of Osama bin Mohammad bin Awad bin Laden.'

As intelligence reports reached the White House of Al-Qaeda's growing power and of the emergence of Hezbollah International, the United States government sought to place a noose around Al-Qaeda. CIA Director George Tenet called Osama 'the world's No. 1 terrorist'. 'The threat from terrorism is real, it is immediate, and it is evolving,' Tenet informed a Senate Select Committee on Intelligence. 'Osama bin Laden and his global network of lieutenants and associates remain the most immediate and serious threat.'

In 1998, President Clinton issued another order to freeze his assets. In the three years following this, incredibly none were found, so none were frozen. Strict banking privacy laws worldwide provided a perfect cover for a terrorist network seeking to hide its funds within the legitimate banking system. 'We've encountered terrorist organisations that have had rogue-state funding before, but we've never encountered an independent terrorist organisation like this,' said Matthew Devost, founding director of the Terrorism Research Center. 'He can inflict a tremendous amount of damage with the wealth that he has.'

By the second half of the 1990s cash was rolling into Al-Qaeda coffers in ever-greater quantities. Commercial interests in Sudan and other parts of Africa continued to be worth hundreds of millions of dollars in profit each year. More millions filtered in through donations from wealthy supporters, while Al-Qaeda was also raking in additional funds from its tax collections from the heroin and opium industries in Afghanistan.

Another reliable method of raising money was extortion. So great was this source of dollars that Secretary of State Madeleine Albright discussed the issue with Prince Sultan ibn Abdul Aziz Al Saud, the Saudi defence minister, during a visit to Washington. A Saudi government audit acquired by US intelligence named five of Saudi Arabia's top businessmen who had allegedly ordered the National Commercial Bank (NCB), the kingdom's largest bank, to transfer personal funds, along with $3 million diverted from a Saudi pension fund, to New York and London banks. The money transfers were discovered in April 1999 after the royal family ordered an audit of NCB.

The money was deposited into the accounts of a number of charities that serve as Al-Qaeda fronts. The businessmen, who are said to have personal assets of more than $5 billion, were handing over 'protection money' to stave off attacks on their businesses in Saudi Arabia. It is believed that Al-Qaeda raises tens of millions of dollars each year though this form of blackmail against Muslim businessmen, mostly from the Gulf.

Increasingly brazen in his financial dealings, Osama never stopped bragging about his financial reach. In a 1996 interview, he boasted: 'To put it simply, the Bin Laden establishment's aid covers 13 countries, including Albania, Malaysia, Pakistan, the Netherlands, Britain, Romania, Russia, Turkey, Lebanon, Iraq and some Gulf countries.' By this time, his UK concerns allegedly included three companies, among which were a construction firm and the Qudurat Transport Company, based in London's Notting Hill. In 1997, he even purchased a successful travel agency business based in Peshawar that could handle more efficiently the transportation needs of his organisation.

All this was fed into a financial maze that, as hard as the United States try, has proven unbreakable even to this day. Large amounts were bounced around the Middle East using a tangled web of sympathetic businessmen. Charities all over the world, such as Islamic Relief and Blessed Relief, fronted Al-Qaeda and provided untraceable movement for cash. In the case of a field operation, such as the several thousand men Al-Qaeda sent to Bosnia, funds were funnelled to fighters through several sham Islamic charitable organisations working on the ground there.

The *New York Times* reported: 'According to current and former intelligence officials and other policy-makers, the United States has been trying to kill Bin Laden and destroy Al-Qaeda for years, as the terrorist organisation has become more ruthless and ambitious in its efforts to attack American interests around the world.

'There have been an array of unsuccessful attempts to target Mr Bin Laden and disrupt or destroy Al Qaeda . . . The Clinton administration even considered mounting a secret effort to steal millions of dollars from the bin Laden terrorist network . . . but discarded the scheme because of objections from the United States Treasury about the implications for world finance.'

One must wonder about the advice given to President Clinton when he was in office. He repeatedly attempted to use a financial stick to try and beat the Afghan authorities into handing over Osama, but failed miserably, despite attracting worldwide support. British bank accounts held by the Taliban, for instance, were frozen in 1999 after the regime's refusal to hand him over. Reportedly two accounts were discovered at the National Westminster Bank, now owned by the Royal Bank of Scotland.

Only after September 11, 2001, did news surface publicly that the CIA believed Osama provided an estimated $100 million in cash and military assistance to the Taliban after his arrival in Afghanistan. The CIA concluded that he 'owns and operates' the Taliban, highlighting the pervasive influence that Osama and his terror network exert within Afghanistan. Considering this, it is hardly surprising that Mullah Omar was content to let the Afghan people suffer while zealously protecting his guest.

On several isolated occasions, however, President Clinton did sanction attempts to kill or arrest the head of Al-Qaeda. Speaking to reporters in New York after September 11, Clinton admitted: 'I authorised the arrest and, if necessary, the killing of Osama bin Laden and we actually made contact with a group in Afghanistan to do it. We also trained commandos for a possible ground action but we did not have the necessary intelligence to do it in the way we would have had to do it.'

According to intelligence sources in August 1997, a large

operation was planned by the US that would have seen American special forces enter Afghanistan and attempt to snatch him in a commando-style operation. The plan was practised in the Pakistani desert and active preparations were being made as the intelligence services attempted to locate him. But, inevitably, the presence of US troops in Pakistan could not remain secret. Osama was reportedly tipped off by sympathetic elements in the Pakistani military and a story appeared in London's *Al-Quds Al-Arabi* newspaper.

Other plans have since surfaced. The *New York Times* reported that the CIA has, for several years, been sending teams into areas held by anti-Taliban forces led by Ahmad Shah Masood to seek Masood's help in finding or assassinating him. The report stated: 'The CIA's clandestine efforts to deal with Mr Masood were among the most sensitive and highly classified elements of a broader long-term campaign, continuing unsuccessfully through the end of the Clinton administration and into the Bush administration, to destroy Mr Bin Laden's terrorist network.'

Under Clinton's instructions, by 1999 the CIA had also begun to train and arm a crack, secret platoon of Pakistani commandos. At the same time, stringent efforts were made by the intelligence community to locate Osama, and a short list of potential targets had been finalised. The mission called for up to 60 elite Pakistani soldiers to stake out several bases or command bunkers and wait for their target to arrive. Their orders were then to capture him dead or alive.

The plan had been developed jointly with Nawaz Sharif, the Pakistani prime minister hoping to curry favour with Washington and have trade sanctions lifted. With just weeks remaining before the plan was to go into affect, however, Sharif was swept away in a military coup headed by General Pervez Musharraf. The plan was quickly terminated by General Musharraf, fearful of provoking his own constituency in Pakistan. Once again, without even knowing it, Osama's incredible luck had saved his skin.

Even if General Musharraf had not come to power, or had supported the United States and allowed this plot to continue, discovering the whereabouts of America's Most Wanted fugitive in order to carry out the exercise could not be guaranteed. He seldom stays in the same place for two consecutive days, and much of his time is spent in the vast mountain ranges of Afghanistan.

His method of travel also varies. Sometimes he moves by four-wheel drive vehicle, other times on horseback. Every few days, just in case a net is closing in, a helicopter can easily whisk him under cover of darkness to a separate part of the country.

Surprisingly, living this fugitive, nomadic existence is no impediment for a man who uses the most modern technology to remain in contact with the world and run his terror network. For non-operational calls he uses a portable Inmarsat phone that transmits and receives calls via satellites owned by the International Maritime Satellite Organisation. Satellite phones can be used anywhere on earth, as long as they are within the footprint of their carrier's low-Earth orbiting satellites.

After a long period of use of the Inmarsat system, Osama learned that this system is open to interception, both for covert observation and possibly for homing in on the signal. Satellites 22,500 miles above the Indian Ocean could easily determined his location with pinpoint accuracy within seconds of the beginning of a call. After he became aware of this, he used the system only periodically for calling his mother. Other times he would call an unknown recipient at a call box somewhere in the world, using the freedom that this allowed to taunt the men he knows are listening. Doing this, he loved to throw the US security services into a panic by speaking of imminent assassination plots on public figures and of bombs planted in major buildings.

For the same reason, Osama only infrequently used telephones belonging to the failed Iridium network – ironically a venture that the Binladin Group of companies backed heavily.

Osama could not have chosen a more remote or difficult area of the world for his refuge. The central highlands of Afghanistan, which account for 64 per cent of its landmass, are part of the Himalayan mountain range. The Hindu Kush ridge is over 21,000 feet high. Evidence suggests that he maintained homes in and around the village of Farm-e Hadda, close to Jalalabad. He also has homes in and around the city Kandahar. But while wives and children are known to remain in these, Osama himself is far more elusive and it is rare for him to even visit.

One vast area Osama is known to operate in regularly is the Sheikh Hazrat mountain range, around 50 miles north of Kandahar, the former Taliban stronghold. His other favourite refuges have been the provinces of Uruzgan, which has largely inaccessible mountainous terrain and thousands of caves in which to shelter, and Nangarhar, where the Tora Bora base is located.

Throughout the parts of the country in Taliban control, Osama secretly and systematically made and enlarged dozens of caves to accommodate mini-command centres. These have drawn comparisons with the 'bat cave' used by comic book superhero Batman and, indeed, this is an apt analogy.

Among the small entourage that travels constantly with Osama is his technology/communications advisor. Probably western-educated in IT, this person provides the Al-Qaeda leader with international communications links, patching Osama into the Internet via a hub elsewhere in the world. He also ensures that his leader is fully connected to the outside world through fax and telex machines and through illicit taps into foreign telephone systems that are virtually untraceable.

Osama is clearly computer literate, and evidence has shown that he maintains contact with cell leaders around the world via the Internet. He uses the latest in encryption technology and stenography to disguise the messages – technology that has, so far, outwitted his pursuers.

The FBI is fighting back with advanced online surveillance technology, including a highly secret satellite-based espionage network capable of monitoring worldwide communications. But despite such ground-breaking technology, Osama's lines of communications have never been discovered, much less cut.

General Mike Hayden, head of the National Security Agency (NSA), has admitted that his organisation was finding it difficult to crack Al-Qaeda electronically. 'We are behind the curve in keeping up with the global telecommunications revolution,' he told reporters.

Throughout his years as president, Bill Clinton's time was progressively dominated by this extraordinary and unparalleled foe. For more than half a century, his predecessors in the Oval Office had faced the predictable Soviet bloc in a cold war that rarely warmed. Clinton meanwhile found himself handling the attentions of a completely different beast. The security services at his disposal were clearly having problems dealing with a shifting threat that, like an iceberg, remained mostly hidden. Al-Qaeda mutates continuously.

During Clinton's first term, Al-Qaeda was still gathering steam. But as his second term went on, Clinton saw the situation with Al-Qaeda dangerously gathering momentum. His attempts at being more assertive came to naught due to Osama's luck, and mistakes by foreign governments. In the cold light of day, the disasters that later befell the United States at the hands of terrorist Islamic fundamentalists were preventable, had the intelligence been properly processed.

Throughout his two terms, information flowed into Clinton's office, courtesy of the FBI and CIA, illustrating that Osama was becoming increasingly ambitious in his attempts to arm the organisation he had built. A flood of studies indicated that a desire to build nuclear weapons would not seem as far-fetched as one might like to think. Credible proof came that he was working in this direction. A report produced by the International Task Force on Prevention of Nuclear Terrorism in 1986 stated that a team of former US nuclear weapons designers has established that 'crude nuclear bomb-making, while not as simple as once supposed, can be accomplished with a sufficient quantity of reactor-grade plutonium or highly enriched uranium . . .'

A decade later the Department of Energy, Office of Arms Control and Nonproliferation stated: 'At the lowest level of sophistication, a potential proliferating state or sub-national group using designs and technologies no more sophisticated than those used in first-generation nuclear weapons, could build a nuclear weapon from reactor-grade plutonium that would have an assured, reliable yield of one or a few kilotons (and a probable yield significantly higher than that). We believe that this goal could be achieved.'

Evidence clearly suggests, at the very least, attempts on the part of Al-Qaeda to obtain nuclear materials. Asked about reports on his attempts to develop or purchase nuclear of chemical weapons, Osama commented to *Time* magazine: 'Defence of Muslims is a religious duty. If I indeed have these weapons then I thank God for enabling me to do so. I am carrying out a duty. It would be a sin for Muslims not to try to posses the weapons that would prevent the infidels from inflicting harm on Muslims.'

The threat of Al-Qaeda obtaining nuclear or chemical weapons must be considered very real considering the wealth of the organisation and its global network of contacts. One of the key witnesses in the trial of those convicted of the US embassy bombings in east Africa, Jamal Ahmed Al-Fadl, described a 1994 effort to buy uranium for $1.5 million. He said the uranium came in a two to three-foot cylinder with engravings indicating the source as South Africa. Whether the transaction was completed was left unanswered.

Perhaps one of the most worrisome connections between Al-Qaeda and nuclear materials was provided by the Chechnya conflict. Al-Qaeda was an active participant in the struggle for independence from Moscow, providing fighters, arms and funding for the struggle. In a rare interview, Chechen resistance leader Chamil Bassaev stated: 'We have no nuclear weapons in Chechnya. But in 1993 I was offered . . . a nuclear explosive for $1.5 million.'

One Arabic publication claimed that Osama had offered the Chechen resistance an infusion of $30 million in cash and two tons of opium in exchange for Chechen criminal contacts and gangs operating in Russia obtaining nuclear material or a warhead. While this amounts to unsubstantiated speculation, what is clear is that the Chechen mafia is large enough and has enough criminal reach to be directly involved in the trade.

Several years later, in 1998, a close aide of the Al-Qaeda leader was arrested in Munich and accused by German authorities of 'acting to obtain nuclear materials'. On another occasion, a year later, the Bulgarian press agency, BTA, reported that Bulgarian businessman Ivan Ivanov met Osama at a religious festival close to Peshawar. Osama voiced his interest in the nuclear waste from the atomic power plant in Kosloduj. The antiquated Soviet-style reactor, situated along the Danube River, is being slowly wound down by the government in Sofia. The Bulgarian, who was employed by a company linked to Al-Qaeda ownership, voiced his concerns to the Bulgarian government. He reported that Osama personally initiated a conversation about the Kosloduj plant and had indicated a special interest in uranium 235, which is used as a fuel for nuclear plants and can be adapted for use in nuclear weapons.

But while building a nuclear arsenal is a project that costs tens of millions of dollars, for a result that is difficult to guarantee, waging biological war is another matter. To underline this fact, the most effective non-military chemical attack ever was carried out by the Aum Shinrikyo cult on the Tokyo subway in 1995. Aum Shinrikyo attempted to produce bulk amounts of sarin gas, recruiting scientists and spending at least $10 million on the project. The delivery method was crude: cultist members dropped concealed plastic bags of sarin on a subway platform and in trains, and then pierced them with umbrella tips. Although the amounts used were relatively small, a dozen people died and thousands needed medical treatment. It was a frightening illustration as to the effectiveness of chemical weapons in a packed urban environment.

In more recent times, evidence of Al-Qaeda operatives attempting to buy and lease crop dusters in the United States illustrates clearly that Osama now has this capability, even if the subsequent anthrax mail attacks prove not to be his doing.

The clearest early evidence of his desire for these weapons was provided by a chemical named ethylmethylphosphonothioic acid, or EMPTA in abbreviated form. During the furor surrounding the President Clinton-sanctioned attack on the Al-Shifa Pharmaceut-icals factory in Sudan in 1998, tests on the destroyed factory and its immediate vicinity came up positive in one soil sample for EMPTA. Osama has been linked as an owner of Al-Shifa Pharmaceuticals and EMPTA is an essential ingredient in the production of the deadly nerve gas VX, which is considered an ideal weapon for terrorist attacks, as it is relatively easy to transport and difficult to detect by conventional security devices.

'We know that bin Laden's organisation has attempted to develop poisonous gases that could be fired at US troops in the Gulf states,' said John Gannon, chairman of the CIA's National Intelligence Council, following the hit on Sudan. '[There is] an ominous pattern we had been piecing together against Bin Laden and his network.'

The production of biological weapons can be carried out virtually anywhere – in simple laboratories, on a farm, even in a home. And security officials in the United States admit in private that they have had mounting evidence that Osama has concentrated a great deal of effort in this direction. Even during his Khartoum years, Osama followed this line of development, attempting to recruit technicians familiar with chemistry. But suspicion was first raised that he was closing in on his objective during the second half of the 1990s.

By this time the United States was actively searching out Osama's whereabouts and seeking to locate Al-Qaeda bases and training camps using spy satellites. During these efforts, evidence first emerged of the testing of such weapons. Satellite images showed fields in which dozens of animals lay dead, although not from any discernable injury. Experts believe that this indicates Al-Qaeda was testing the effectiveness of their bio-weapons as their development progressed.

Aside from Al-Shifa Pharmaceuticals' dabbling with one of the building blocks of VX gas, little evidence was gathered as the emphasis of the Al-Qaeda research. Anthrax, a disease originating in livestock, has long been a focus of biological warfare research and development programs because it comes from relatively tough spores that can be sprayed over a battlefield or a city. Anthrax is most effective as a weapon when converted to a powder, which can be inhaled.

Also involved in many research programs before the international banning of the development of biological weaponry were ricin, one of the most toxic naturally occurring substances known; botulism and smallpox, the latter obliterated fully as a naturally-occurring disease in 1980. Anthrax is not communicable, whereas smallpox can be transmitted with ease from one person to another. As part of its own programme, Iraq was said to be working on camelpox, classified as among the riskiest foreign animal pathogens.

All evidence points to the fact that as long ago as the early 1990s Osama pursued a campaign to arm Al-Qaeda with weapons of mass destruction and bio-weaponry. During the second half of the decade, the little information that reached the public indicated that he was actively testing chemical elements, and that serious attempts were being made to obtain the building blocks that could be used to forge a crude nuclear weapon.

It was a program that President Clinton and the international community consistently attempted to foil, with limited success. Unless Al-Qaeda and Osama were stopped, it was highly unlikely that they would not eventually succeed in manufacturing or purchasing weapons of mass destruction.

During the intervening period, Al-Qaeda's conventional terrorist capacity was growing alarmingly. During the late 1990s he had hit the United States with Khobar Towers and the Africa embassy bombings. Before Clinton was due to step down from power and make way for a new president, his nemesis would deliver yet another blow.

CHAPTER TWENTY

Tweaking the Nose of the Enemy

'This was an act of terrorism . . . a despicable and cowardly act. We will find out who was responsible and hold them accountable. If their intention was to deter us from our mission of promoting peace and security in the Middle East, they will fail utterly.' President Bill Clinton was visibly shaken and angry when he spoke to the press in the Rose Garden at the White House. It was October 12, 2000. Hours earlier Osama bin Laden had claimed his latest victory in the battle against the US. Two suicide bombers had detonated their explosives-packed boat next to the USS *Cole* as it refuelled in the harbour at Aden on Yemen's southern tip, killing 17 sailors and wounding 39.

By the time of the bombing of the USS *Cole*, there was little doubt within the Clinton administration that the terrorist threat they were now facing was serious and credible. In briefings with national security advisors, Clinton was kept informed about developments. On his desk in the Oval Office was photographic evidence that Al-Qaeda was testing biological weaponry on animals in Afghanistan. Alongside these were research papers detailing Osama's huge investment in attempting to obtain either a stolen nuclear warhead or to build one of his own.

Nor was Osama reticent about what he was doing. He rejected accusations that he was upping the ante, telling one interviewer: 'We believe that the right to self-defence is to be enjoyed by all people. Israel is stockpiling hundreds of nuclear warheads and bombs. The Christian West is largely in possession of such weapons. Hence, we do not regard this as a charge, but rather as a right . . .

It is as if you were accusing a man of being a courageous knight and fighter. It is as if you were denying him this. Only a man who is not in his right mind would level such accusations . . . We regard this as one of our rights, of Muslim rights.'

Unfortunately, the domestic scandals that dogged President Clinton's eight years in office, which ended on January 20, 2001, served to obscure the clear dangers abroad to the future of America. Mismanagement by the US intelligence services allowed the threat posed by Osama and his network to grow inexorably.

The United States had survived several near misses on the road to the USS *Cole* bombing, and Al-Qaeda operatives were foiled in a multiple-venue series of attacks as late as January 2000. The planned January 3 'day of rage' would have seen USS *Sullivans* attacked in a similar hit to that sustained by the USS *Cole*. Other targets included American interests in Jordan and busy sites in the United States such as the Seattle Space Needle, Los Angeles International Airport and Disneyland.

The man who pleaded guilty to a failed plot to bomb Los Angeles airport during the millennium celebrations claimed that he was trained at a camp in Afghanistan run by Osama. Ahmed Ressam was a former member of the Armed Islamic Group in Algeria, an organisation closely tied to Al-Qaeda. In the early 1990s he had taken the course of many Algerian economic migrants and shifted to France. Later, in 1994, he moved to Canada as an Al-Qaeda sleeper.

Those who later investigated his life in Canada believe that he was a good one. There was no discernible contact with the world of Islamic fundamentalism, although he did pray at several mosques regularly. There was no illicit funding either. Instead Ressam supported himself with odd jobs. In 1998, however, he took a trip to Afghanistan. There he was 'prepared' at an Al-Qaeda camp at Khaldan, trained in the use of handguns, machine guns, and rocket-propelled grenade launchers, and in bomb-making. He returned to Canada in February 1999 with $12,000 in funding for his 'project' and did not attract any attention until the latter part off the year. After spending time at a hotel in Vancouver – rarely leaving his room as, inside, he was making bombs – he attempted to cross the border into the US, a border proudly described by both countries as the longest undefended border in the world. Border checks are minimal.

Ressam would have succeeded in crossing except for the professionalism of one guard whose suspicions were roused. The weather was freezing, but Ressam was sweating profusely. He was arrested when a search of his car revealed the bombs.

'What if January [of 2000] had started with 1,000 Americans dead at six or seven locations around the world?' wondered Richard Clarke, then President Clinton's top adviser on counter-terrorism. The USS *Sullivans* plot 'was pretty poorly run', he said. Intelligence exchange among several countries led Jordanian authorities to arrest suspects who confessed to planning attacks on the Radisson SAS Hotel in Amman and two Christian pilgrimage sites. Arrests were also made in Yemen, foiling the USS *Sullivans* plot.

On October 12, 2000, the USS *Cole* docked in Aden. The vessel and its complement of 350 crew was scheduled to stay for only four to six hours during a routine refuelling stop, and its presence in the port had not been advertised. As was standard practice, the Yemeni government had been notified of the *Cole*'s visit 12 days in advance, allowing for the provision of food, fresh water and fuel. An Arleigh Burke-class DDG 67 guided-missile destroyer, carrying sophisticated Aegis weaponry, the USS *Cole* had travelled to Yemen via the Suez Canal and Red Sea, en route to the Arabian Gulf. There it was scheduled to join the US-led maritime interception operations in support of United Nations sanctions imposed against Iraq after Baghdad's 1990 invasion of Kuwait. It was part of the USS *George Washington* battle group.

Unbeknownst to the USS *Cole* or American authorities, a low-key observation of the port of Aden had been going on for several weeks. From a hilltop apartment with a roof commanding a sweeping view of the harbour, two men had binoculars trained on foreign ships that stopped to refuel. Sometimes other men were seen.

Elsewhere, in the Madinat ash-Shaab district close to the waterfront, in an innocuous small compound, the same pair had been hard at work. Their glass fibre boat was being modified, with welded metal pockets inside. These were designed to carry a load of explosives. The men hardly talked to their neighbours. But they spent a lot of time on the beach, grilling fishermen about the comings and goings of ships in the harbour.

A few days before the attack, the two men unusually went out of their way to speak to neighbours in friendly terms, informing them that they were going to Saudi Arabia on a pilgrimage and planned to return in late December after the holy month of Ramadan. This appears to have been an attempt to built a cover for their subsequent disappearance, as neither was seen again.

In other locations, others in the Al-Qaeda cell had been working hard. In a pair of rented apartments they constructed the bombs that would blast a hole in the USS *Cole*.

The US had received a vague warning the previous month that there was the possibility of an attack on an American warship. No detail was given or even the country in which this could be expected. Later it also emerged that the previous May, US intelligence had unearthed reports that an Egyptian Islamic group was in the final stages of preparing an attack against an American target.

Aboard the USS *Cole*, the crew was watchful, but not unduly worried as no specific threats had been passed on. The crew had extensive training in repelling an overt attack by a small boat and additional armed seamen were on watch on the deck.

On October 12, the two men launched their small boat, laden with explosives. From among the many small vessels being watched that day, one small, fiberglass boat, piloted by a couple of inconspicuous looking locals, received nothing more than a passing observation by those on deck. The small boat looked as though it was involved in helping the USS *Cole* with mooring lines and certainly did not appear to be a threat.

But after securing one line on a buoy, the men steered their boat to the port side of the USS *Cole*. As the guards on deck looked on, perhaps unsure, the pair stood to attention. Seconds later, 500 lbs of explosives ignited, blowing a hole 40 feet by 40 feet in the destroyer's hull. The hole in the side of the 505-foot ship, near the engine and electrical rooms, caused extensive flooding along the waterline but no fire. The explosion destroyed an engine room and nearby mess area where sailors were eating lunch. Those killed were working in the engine room area amidships on the port side of the USS *Cole*. The destroyer USS *Donald Cook*, the frigate USS *Hawes*, and the fast combat support ship USS *Camden* were already on the scene and scrambled to help.

Thousands of miles away in the White House, President Clinton was informed of the attack – and briefed that this was almost certainly a product of Al-Qaeda or an organisation attached to

Osama bin Laden. The president's nemesis had struck again. He immediately ordered the Department of Defense, the FBI and the State Department to send officials to Yemen to begin the investigation. He also ordered US ships in the Middle East to pull out of port, in case of similar attacks elsewhere, and US land forces to increase their security.

An FBI team of about 100 agents quickly assembled in Yemen from all over the world, and the Pentagon deployed its Fleet Anti-Terrorist Support Team – a group of about 70 specially-trained marines, based at the Navy's 5th Fleet headquarters in Bahrain, the independent island state in the Arabian Gulf. These specialist groups were backed by a complement of some 1,400 marines.

After initially rejecting that there was a terrorist dimension in the USS Cole attack, when Yemeni president Ali Abdullah Saleh was presented with the evidence he then offered the complete cooperation of his government. A number of joint US/Yemeni task forces were created to lead the investigation. The Yemeni government asserted that those who carried out the bombing belonged to al-Jihad, a small, loose grouping of Islamist Yemenis and other Arabs. The Americans also looked closely at the likes of Hamas, Hezbollah, Palestinian Islamic Jihad and Egyptian Islamic Jihad.

But even as the plot unravelled on the ground, strong circumstantial evidence pointed to Al-Qaeda. As normal, Osama denied all involvement, but was apt to throw the media a bone that would keep him being talked about and publicised. At his base in Afghanistan, he would greedily devour parcels of newspaper clippings speaking about him and Al-Qaeda, and he spent evenings flicking between satellite channels taking in reportage of his latest 'alleged' atrocity. This obsessive indulgence leads many to suspect that it is the publicity, rather than Islamic fervour, that drives him.

In the case of the USS *Cole*, the talking point that Osama fed to the media was a videotape, recorded before the attack, which was quickly circulated. This 'starred' the head of Al-Qaeda himself and his second in command, Ayman al-Zawahiri. In it, neither Osama nor al-Zawahiri made reference to the USS *Cole* by name, but made specific statements regarding the plot, ahead of the attack. Al-Zawahiri also said: 'Enough of words, it is time to take action against this iniquitous and faithless force [the United States], which has spread its troops through Egypt, Yemen and Saudi Arabia.'

Within days, investigators in Yemen discovered both the hilltop apartments where observers had studied the coming and goings of US military vessels, and the two mid-town apartments where bombs were constructed. Bomb-making materials were found in one flat, which was rented by two non-Yemeni Arabs, at least one of whom, according to local residents, had a Gulf accent. The same men kept a fiberglass boat parked nearby.

These discoveries led to the arrest of plotters who had remained in Yemen. Chief among them was the Al-Qaeda point man in Yemen, Jamal al-Badawi. An Arab-Afghan, al-Badawi had remained within the Al-Qaeda sphere since the end of the Afghan conflict, based most of the time in Yemen. As a sleeper, he had lived what was considered by those who knew him to be a normal life. He was not noticeably political and while Yemeni authorities were aware of those involved in recruitment and fund-raising for the likes of Hezbollah and Hamas, he was never identified as a supporter of any illicit group.

But during 2000, al-Badawi had been activated by his masters in Afghanistan. Little is known of his activities other than that his Al-Qaeda handler, a man unknown to him called Mohammed Omar al-Harazi, was contactable on a telephone number in the United Arab Emirates. Al-Harazi has been identified as a Saudi Arabian national with Yemeni roots, not unlike Osama himself. Finance for the Yemen cell, and later equipment requests, were handled through al-Harazi.

US and Yemeni investigators interviewed several hundred people. They built up a body of circumstantial evidence that the Al-Harazi connection led directly to Al-Qaeda, backing up strong suspicions generated by the earlier video release by Osama. By January 2001, the Yemeni authorities were ready to begin the trial of three to six suspects in the case, but agreed to delay it in a bid to get more information and net more suspects.

Experts were by now piecing together evidence surrounding the central explosives used in the attack. This comprised an estimated 272 kilograms of 'shaped' high explosive, placed within a metal container to channel the blast and penetrate the armoured hull of the warship. The device was a significant 'technical advance' on the crude bombs used on the US embassies in Kenya and Tanzania.

President Clinton said: 'The idea of common humanity and unity amidst diversity . . . must surely confound the minds of the hate-filled terrorists ... They envy our strength without understanding the values that give us strength. For them, it is their way or no way. Their interpretation, twisted though it may be, of a beautiful religious tradition. Their political views, their racial and ethnic views. Their way, or no way. Such people can take innocent life ... but they can never heal, or build harmony, or bring people together. That is work only free, law-abiding people can do.

'We will find you, and justice will prevail. America will not stop standing guard for peace or freedom or stability in the Middle East and around the world.'

His sentiments were moving and heartfelt. But behind the scenes, Clinton had worrying proof that his adversary was getting stronger. The Bin Laden millions had been well invested and money was thus flowing around the terror network. Al-Qaeda had also used its contacts with other major Islamic fundamentalist groups to gain specialist knowledge and expand its arsenal of weaponry. The Al-Qaeda of 2000 was a far cry from what had gone before.

While the US was reconsidering harbours for its navy, Osama was more concerned with his own safe harbour. He believed he had found this in Afghanistan. Not since his early days in Sudan had his roots been so entrenched and secure. 'The safest place in the world for me is Afghanistan. There are several places where we have friends and close brothers – we can find refuge and safety with them,' he said.

In the years following his arrival in Kandahar, Osama had been given a free hand to develop the organisation as he pleased, unhindered by the chaos and social problems in the country. His significant share of the Afghan opium and heroin industry was a significant boost for funds. Al-Qaeda went to great lengths to encourage the cultivation of opium among peasant farmers, even going to the extreme of burning fields of food crops and forcing the sowing of poppy seeds. Maulvi Abdul Kabir, number two in Taliban hierarchy, was a partner in several poppy-growing businesses, an 'insurance policy' to protect his interests should anything happen to Mullah Omar.

It is small wonder then that Osama bin Laden was able to respond in such an off-hand manner to Clinton's determination to claim retribution for the USS *Cole*. 'The dream to kill me will never be completed,' he boasted in a statement issued to *The Jang*,

Pakistan's largest circulation Urdu-language newspaper. 'I am not afraid of the American threats against me. As long as I am alive there will be no rest for the enemies of Islam. I will continue my mission against them.'

Much of this mission concerned the unification of Islamic fundamentalist groups worldwide, one of Osama's strategic aims. However, three years earlier in 1997, he had suffered a setback in this effort. The election of Hojjatoleslam Seyed Mohammad Khatami as president of the Islamic Republic of Iran in a landslide victory on a reformist 'civil society' platform proved the undoing of the Iranian-backed Hezbollah International.

Khatami was a moderate and promised wide political and social reforms. More disturbing to Osama was that his election held out the hope of a thaw in relations between Iran and the West. Khatami's election sent Osama into a fury. In a rare late-night phone call to a member of his family in Jeddah, Osama stormed: 'We [the Muslim world] are going backwards . . .'

Khatami however faced his own trials and tribulations. As president, he ranked second in the hierarchy behind the supreme religious leader, Ayatollah Ali Khameini, a dogmatic conservative who was a staunch supporter of Hezbollah International. Nevertheless, his election ended an era of massive support for Islamic fundamentalism and sounded a death knell for Hezbollah International. He spelled this out in a landmark interview with CNN on January 7, 1998.

Osama, sitting in a command centre in the mountains around Kandahar watching television – which was officially banned in Afghanistan – was one of the millions who tuned in to watch. He was horrified. From the start, Khatami made his position clear: 'In the name of Allah, the Beneficent, the Merciful. At the outset, I would like to congratulate all free and noble women and men, especially the followers of Jesus Christ, peace be upon him, on the occasion of the New Year. I take as a good omen the concurrence of the Christian New Year with the Islamic month of Ramadan, the month of edification and self-restraint that has been the goal of all divine prophets.'

Such a sentiment would normally leave Osama gasping; coming from a president of the Islamic Republic of Iran, it was too much to bear. From his perspective, there was worse to come as Khatami commented: 'The American civilisation is worthy of respect . . .

The American civilisation is founded upon vision, thinking and manners . . .

'Today we are in the period of stability, and fully adhere to all norms of conduct regulating relations between nations and governments. With the grace of God, today all the affairs of country are being conducted within the framework of law. And as I have stated, both in domestic and foreign affairs, we shall endeavour to strengthen the rule of law in every respect.'

A key question was asked by interviewer Christiane Amanpour on Iranian support for terrorism. The Iranian president replied: 'We believe in the holy Koran that says: "slaying of one innocent person is tantamount to the slaying of all humanity". How could such a religion, and those who claim to be its followers get involved in the assassination of innocent individuals and the slaughter of innocent human beings . . . the logic of history has proven that violence is not the way to achieve desired end. I personally believe that only those who lack logic resort to violence.

'Terrorism should be condemned in all its forms and manifestations; assassins must be condemned. Terrorism is useless anyway and we condemn it categorically. Those who level these charges against us are best advised to provide accurate and objective evidence, which indeed does not exist.'

Osama's response to a loosening of ties with Iran was to attempt to construct his own replacement for Hezbollah International, the much heralded Islamic Front for the Struggle against the Jews and the Crusaders (the Front), or Al-Jabhah al-Islamiyyah al-'Alamiyyah li-Qital al-Yahud wal-Salibiyyin. Unveiled before journalists during an interview in Khost, in Afghanistan, in May 1998, Osama tried to use this new organisation to further his existing ties with Dr Ayman al- Zawahiri's Egyptian Islamic Jihad, Rifa'i Ahmad Taha of the Armed Islamic Group, and others.

Legitimising the struggle was also easy, courtesy of Mullah Omar, who arranged a religious rubber stamp. On May 14, 1998, the London based *Al-Quds Al-Arabi* newspaper reported that clerics in Afghanistan had issued a *fatwa* stipulating the necessity to remove western forces from the Gulf region. The Afghan Ulema (the college of religious leaders) said: 'The enemies of Islam are not limited to a certain group or party; all atheists are enemies of Islam, and they take one another as friends.' They urged Islamic governments to perform the duty of 'armed jihad against the enemies of Islam. If

Muslims are lax in their responsibility, the enemies of Islam will occupy the two holy mosques as well.'

It was great publicity, but nothing else. The Front was simply a regrouping of organisations that had functioned under the Al-Qaeda banner for a long time.

However, while both events – organisation and *fatwa* – were window dressing to overcome the loss of the Iranians, they did have an effect. The *fatwa* and Osama's statements became a rallying call to thousands of disaffected individuals throughout the Middle East and further afield. Within weeks, this pan-Islamic call had attracted Kashmiris, Pakistanis, Indians and Muslims from the Soviet Republics who contacted fundamentalist leaning institutions in their own countries to seek ways of joining the Front.

From an operational standpoint, the Front also sought to replace Hezbollah International as a driving force for cooperation and modernisation within the worldwide fundamentalist struggle, and worked to achieve that goal over ensuing years. A measure of its success came at the end of January 2001, when an extraordinary three-day meeting was held in Beirut in association with the ever-accommodating Imad Mughniyah of Lebanese Hezbollah. Organising such a gathering underlines both the bravado and confidence of Osama bin Laden today.

Although Osama could not risk travelling to Beirut himself, Al-Qaeda was heavily represented and indeed he helped to cover the costs involved in staging this mammoth event. Hamas, Egyptian Islamic Jihad and Algeria's GIA were just a few of the groups represented among a list of delegates said to number more than 400. Representatives came from as far afield as Algeria, Egypt, Jordan, Pakistan, Qatar, Sudan and Yemen.

The groups present agreed to put aside old rivalries in order to develop a common agenda aimed at destroying Israel and freeing the region of US influence. This new alliance was named the Jerusalem Foundation. Ramadan Abdullah Shallah, head of Palestinian Islamic Jihad, and senior Hamas official Musa Abu Marzouq were named to head this new grouping. Despite the fury of the Lebanese government, which protested that it knew nothing of the conference until it was over, the Jerusalem Foundation also said that it would maintain an office in Beirut.

An end-of-meeting communiqué reported that the 400 delegates had rededicated themselves to the jihad aimed at reclaiming

Palestinian land from the Israelis and winning full Arab sovereignty over Jerusalem. 'The participants are firm that the strategy that should be adopted in dealing with the Jerusalem issue cannot be based on co-existence with the Zionist enemy . . . but rather by uprooting it from our land and holy Islamic–Christian shrines. The only decisive option to achieve this strategy is the option of jihad in all its forms and resistance.'

The communiqué also betrayed a growing sense of hatred for the United States, stating: 'America, today, is a second Israel.'

CHAPTER TWENTY-ONE

Preparing for War

'This war will not only be between the people of the two sacred mosques and the Americans, but it will be between the people of the Islamic world and the Americans and their allies because their war is a new crusade led by America against the Islamic nations.' These were the words of Osama bin Laden.

On January 20, 2001, George W. Bush was inaugurated as president after winning a bruising and at times farcical election battle with Clinton's vice president, Al Gore, which ended with the Supreme Court deciding the matter. Watching this on his satellite television in a den deep in the mountains of Afghanistan, Osama had to have been delighted to see Americans battling themselves in this domestic squabble. Perhaps seeing the fiasco even strengthened his belief that the project he was working on would bring the entire country down.

Bush entered the White House labelled a lightweight by the media. But while the American electorate showed during the campaign that they cared little for issues of foreign policy, on entering the Oval Office Bush had a great deal to think about in this direction.

Americans comprise only about five per cent of the world's population, but State Department statistics indicate that during the 1990s, thirty-six per cent of all worldwide terrorist acts were directed against US interests and citizens. A dangerous trend was emerging. When it came to large-scale attacks, the percentage was even higher. What was more, Bush's newly-appointed foreign policy hawks advised him that there was trouble brewing over the horizon in Afghanistan.

Osama watched the convoluted American political process with obvious glee. This was evidence, he said, 'that the lumbering superpower is crumbling'. He felt he could afford to be glib and self-satisfied: he had outfoxed and sidestepped the might of America for more than half a decade.

Al-Qaeda had also gone from strength to strength: each hit demonstrating a degree of evolution, greater organisational and technical ability. Along the way those groups under its umbrella had been dragged into the twenty-first century. All now posed a far more potent threat.

His confidence was to no small degree reflected in Al-Qaeda, which had grown into an international enterprise. According to a report by the House Republican Research Committee's Task Force on Terrorism and Unconventional Warfare, Osama bin Laden was 'working behind closed doors [to] prepare a second generation of Arab-Afghans charged with installing fundamentalist regimes in several Arab and Islamic countries'.

To achieve this he had continued to build upon a basic corporate structure. Arabic newspaper *Al Watan Al Arabi* reported: 'His returns represent a huge financial resource to the radical religious factions [that he supports]. It is said that Bin Laden's financial and accounting department consists of 17 staffers headed by a Sudanese called Abu-al-Hasan. Yemeni sources say that Bin Laden owns commercial firms in Kenya that deal in electrical appliances and make a great deal of profit that is transferred to his financial department that is spread in several European capitals, including Rome.'

Despite the fact that much input has come from those around him, particularly the influential al-Zawahiri, Osama apparently considers himself a genius. He is without doubt a symbol, one that the United States and others would like to remove permanently in the hope that this would degrade Al-Qaeda as a functioning unit.

If this were to happen, it is thought by those familiar with the group that al-Qaeda is capable of elevating a new leader or command structure. Before his reported death in December 2001, it was assumed this would have been al-Zawahiri. Nevertheless, within a grouping numbering thousands of men, it is unlikely that the loss of Osama's presence would make a great operational difference. But the image he has carefully moulded for himself is a powerful one and no one within Al-Qaeda hierarchy has anywhere near the charisma to replace him.

It has long been recognised within Al-Qaeda that a tremendous amount of effort has had to go into protecting Osama. Over the course of the five years between his arrival in Afghanistan and the beginning of 2001, a massive protective umbrella was constructed in secret. Central to this is a network of command posts dotted around Afghanistan. These are camouflaged bunkers, dug into mountains in remote locations. For the most part they are all but invisible, with only a small, unobtrusive entrance set among miles of barren, mountainous rock face and light foliage as camouflage: nothing that would show to observers hunting him, or attract attention if caught in a satellite sweep. They were designed as hiding places. Only a handful of people know the whereabouts of each, and only Osama himself knows where all his refuges are situated.

Inside these command bunkers, Osama is at home and in comfort. He has central heating, provided through a system of hot water pipes. He has his own room, a library of books, an arms store, barracks for his guards and access to a supply of canned food and fresh water. One design feature included in all is a communications centre. Using this he can remain in contact with the world via the World Wide Web. He has boasted of keeping e-mail accounts under the noses of his enemy. 'I am using their own networks to undermine them,' he mockingly told one relative in a surprise e-mail that appeared in his mailbox half a decade ago. 'I know they will probably be reading this. But what can they do? If they close this account down I will open another through some other country.'

But while he baits the US intelligence services, Osama sits before his computer using the Web for far more sinister purposes. The Internet has given him international reach: instant communications with the rest of the world from an isolated mountain in Afghanistan. His 'office' includes a scanner. Here he scans in pornographic photos from magazines, ready for posting in obscure websites. This is not for kicks, but part of an illicit communications system with cells all over the world using stenography, a method of hiding messages inside other files that is virtually impossible to spot and even more difficult to decipher.

The technologically-aware Osama spends a great deal of time alone in his communications centre, preparing messages and encrypted blueprints of attack plans, inserting them into photographs, and posting them on the Internet on pre-arranged Web pages. It is a simple, yet effective system that allows him to talk to his worldwide network instantly, without Al-Qaeda either maintaining its own network or using more traditional forms of communication that are open to eavesdropping. 'It's brilliant,' Ahmed Jabril, spokesman for the militant group Hezbollah in London, told *USA Today*. 'Now it's possible to send a verse from the Koran, an appeal for charity and even a call for jihad and know it will not be seen by anyone hostile to our faith, like the Americans.'

The use of such technology for fundamentalist purposes was pioneered by Al-Qaeda after Osama recruited a number of Muslim IT professionals during his Khartoum years. They were political radicals themselves, of course, but were drawn to Sudan by generous packages that could compete with the lure of Silicon Valley. One is identified as Fazil Abdullah Mohammed, an explosives and computer expert. He was recruited from the Cormoros Islands in the Indian Ocean and participated directly as a bomb handler in the embassies bombings. He is still at large. The US government has offered a $2 million reward for his apprehension.

When Al-Qaeda switched from Sudan to Afghanistan in 1996, several IT experts moved with Osama and continued to serve him there, putting in place networks in the remotest mountain bunkers, advising him how to avoid being detected and bringing the latest computer technology into the country. No expense was spared, and through organisations such as the Iranian-backed Hezbollah International and later the Islamic Front for the Struggle against the Jews and the Crusaders, Osama spread the word about the advantages of e-terrorism among other groups.

Sheikh Ahmed Yassin, the founder of the militant Hamas group, has also alluded to the technology. 'We will use whatever tools we can – e-mails, the Internet – to facilitate jihad against the [Israeli] occupiers and their supporters. We have the best minds working with us.'

But the Internet is not just a tool of terror for Osama. The information superhighway has been a valuable source of just that – information. While the Taliban regime banned television as the work of Satan and imposed the death penalty for possessing one, Osama not only flouted this rule but also had satellite television, bounced from somewhere in Pakistan to a portable dish. He argued that it was not possible to keep abreast of international events without CNN, BBC and ABC. The informational value of American soaps is questionable, but it is obvious that he has seen them, judging by references to the godlessness of *Baywatch* as an illustration of the collapse of western society.

VHS video players in his bunkers enable him to watch tapes of himself sent by sympathetic media monitors elsewhere in the world.

Abdul Bari Atwan, editor of *Al-Quds Al-Arabi*, visited one such command centre, in a cave outside the city of Kandahar in 1996. He described a library of 'richly bound Islamic books'. Regional newspapers were sent in almost daily, and at least once a week a batch of international newspapers, such as *The Times* of London, the *New York Times* and *Washington Post*, were flown in.

Well over a dozen of these command bunkers were built and equipped, enabling Osama to run Al-Qaeda's worldwide cells effectively, even under fire. Even in peaceful times, without people actively hunting him, he rarely stayed in these for more than one night, not wishing to alert people to his presence. Instead, he moved between a network of remote homes and camps in a solitary vehicle, as a convoy would attract too much attention in the war-ravaged land. As he moved around the country – usually in a Toyota Land Cruiser, reportedly his favoured four-wheel drive vehicle, as it is not produced by a 'western' corporation – a chief of security would have four teams in the surrounding area. As night fell, four camps were established, far apart, and only at the last minute would Osama choose in which direction to go. In this way, he increased his personal security while ensuring his freedom to travel among various Al-Qaeda bases. Of course, with his liberty being challenged following the rout of the Taliban, such easy movement is a thing of the past. This is difficult for Osama, who believes it is important to be seen by commanders and ordinary men in the organisation, a figurehead around which the loyal can rally.

It is believed that upwards of 100 training camps were established in Afghanistan and remote areas of northern Pakistan, by the time of the United States–led attacks on the Taliban and Al-Qaeda. All were small to reduce the chances of detection in satellite sweeps and, in case of discovery, easy to move. Propaganda videos released by Al-Qaeda show masked men training with machine guns and heavy weapons, using pictures of enemies such as former president Clinton as targets.

Many bases were shared with allies such as Hamas, Islamic Jihad and Hezbollah, who sent men for expert training under Al-Qaeda instructors. Also believed to be a part of this network is Harakat al-Mujadhideen, a Pakistani group, several of whose men were killed when the US launched attacks on Afghanistan in 1998. Harakat is believed to be responsible for the hijacking of an Air India plane that was flown to Afghanistan at the end of 1999.

Osama was in the habit of visiting many such bases each month. He would tour a site, sometimes appear before a video camera as part of a public relations exercise, and sit with his commanders. Usually he would carry with him the same battered Kalashnikov rifle that he claims to have taken off a dead Soviet soldier during the 1980s. In more recent times he has been seen carrying a thin walking cane, a good prop for the consummate actor.

Before the American-led campaign, Osama often met with Mullah Omar in Kandahar, shoring up support with the Taliban and taking tea with others within the organisation's leadership. It is an important duty and Osama has never tired of it. Over the years he 'invested' tens of millions of dollars in the Taliban, its fighters and leaders. As we have witnessed, he bought their loyalty to such a degree that Mullah Omar would sacrifice his grip on the country before he handed over Osama to the United States.

The Taliban needed Osama as much as he needed them. His military and financial support was vital both to offset the Northern Alliance and to maintain a firm grip over a disillusioned population weary of the regime's social terrorism. Only the intervention of the international community following the events of September 11 finally swung the military balance of power in favour of the Northern Alliance. Mullah Omar, formerly recognised as head of state by just three countries – Pakistan, Saudi Arabia and the United Arab Emirates – is now recognised by none. Though divested of much of his power, he continues to go to great lengths on behalf of Al-Qaeda to deceive enemies as to the capabilities, intentions and whereabouts of his most infamous guest.

The area around Kandahar, the one place in Afghanistan where support for the Taliban has remained almost until the bitter end, is also the one place where the Al-Qaeda hierarchy could always operate safely. From different parts of the country, the men Osama considered part of his board of directors would arrive discreetly. At a remote house they sat on the floor, majlis style, and discussed the latest developments. Al-Zawahiri always sat next to Osama, while around the room ranged the heads of various departments of Al-

Qaeda. Attempting to keep his unusual organisation together and operating in a coherent form, Osama tried to stage a board meeting at least once a week despite the abundant risks to himself. However, the freedom of movement enjoyed by Al-Qaeda in Afganistan is, of course, a thing of the past. The impact of the loss of communications between its various divisions is unknown.

Greater coherence was needed during the early months of 2001. Aside from Osama, perhaps only al-Zawahiri knew of the impending storm that would soon be heading for Al-Qaeda.

But there was time for frivolity, mixed with a little official business. On occasion Osama made brief stops to see his wives and 17 children at one of their many homes, but family life has mostly had to be lived vicariously by radio telephone, such were the risks. His unwieldy family is far too large to haul around Afghanistan with him and would attract attention. Instead, they live an isolated existence, moving between homes in remote villages.

One extraordinary event that did come to world attention was the wedding of one of his sons to the 14-year-old daughter of one of his close aides. It was a political match, brokered by Osama with Mohammad Atef, an Arab-Afghan who remained a key part of Al-Qaeda senior management from the 1980s until he was killed by American bombs in November 2001. A video of the wedding, staged in Kandahar, was acquired and shown by the Arabic Al-Jazirah satellite television channel. Nineteen-year-old Mohammed bin Laden, named in honour of his grandfather, was pictured wearing a traditional white Arab headdress, seated on a carpet between his father and al-Masri.

Rumours had been circulating that Osama was unwell, that he was having trouble with his kidneys and had liver disease. With his finger ever on the pulse, this gossip may have been the reason Osama allowed a supposedly private family event to be so stage-managed and a video be leaked to the media. The video showed him looking healthy and smiling broadly at guests, among them the ever-present al-Zawahiri.

One of the speakers at the event was ten-year-old Hamza bin Laden, another of Osama's sons, who had written a poem which read: 'I am warning America that its people will face terrible consequences if they chase my father. Fighting Americans is the base of faith.' His father's poetic tribute to the newlyweds, clearly referring to the United States, read: 'She sails into the waves flanked by arrogance, haughtiness and false power. To her doom she moves slowly . . . your brothers in the East readied themselves. And the war camels are prepared to move . . . '

Instead of camels, Osama should have used packhorses as a more accurate analogy, for by the time of the wedding video his human packhorses were carrying equipment into the United States. All the meetings and quiet plotting of 2000 and 2001 had come together. The smoke screen of the Khobar Towers, the African embassies and the USS *Cole* bombings had mired the FBI and CIA in vast time- and manpower-consuming investigations. These 'events' had also lulled Osama's enemies into the false believe that, while he was the most advanced terror advocate in the world, Al-Qaeda was nothing more than an above-average terrorist group with run-of-the-mill capabilities.

While the FBI and CIA were tied up elsewhere, from his command bunkers, Osama had set about orchestrating the activities of long-dormant cells in the United States and Europe. Principal among these operatives was the Egyptian, Mohammed Atta.

Early in 1999, the faculty of the Technical University of Hamburg-Harburg had given permission for Atta, one of its students, to open an Islamic Student Group. Here up to 40 Muslim students would meet each day for prayers and discussion. Atta, fancying himself as a zealot after his training and indoctrination by Al-Qaeda in Afghanistan, led discussions and organised the group conscientiously.

But the Islamic Student Group had another use. Through its doors Atta would meet several of the men sent to him by the Al-Qaeda network who would come under his command in the future assignment he had been promised he would lead. The university was a superb cover for a handful of sleepers. Both Marwan Al-Shehhi and Ziad Samir Jarrah, participants in the events of September 11, 2001, entered Europe through this route, spending their time learning western ways and immersing themselves in the culture.

Attempting to avoid raising suspicions through unexplained absences, all three had repeatedly travelled to Afghanistan during holidays. On one such visit, Atta had been ushered into the esteemed company of Osama and al-Zawahiri. It was a singular honour. Osama explained to Atta that he had been chosen to lead the cause of Islamic fundamentalism into a new phase of the war. He had been honoured with what people in the West would regard as a death sentence. But in the world of fundamentalism, sacrifice is seen as martyrdom. Atta was immersed in this thinking and accepted his fate without question.

At the end of 1999 Atta, Al-Shehhi and Jarrah reported their passports stolen. Passports marked with entry stamps from Pakistan were troublesome, even more so those that indicated a journey to Afghanistan. With fresh travel papers quickly issued, the travellers had a clean bill of health as far as US immigration was concerned. Atta used his new passport to gain a tourist visa for the United States, granted on May 18, 2000.

Less than a month later, he flew to Prague, in the Czech Republic, where he stayed for twenty-four hours before leaving for the United States. Investigators have since claimed that, in Prague, Atta had his first of two meetings with Iraqi intelligence officers operating undercover as diplomats. One was named as Farouk Hijazi, the Iraqi ambassador to Turkey. A second meeting was held in April 2001.

Despite media attempts to link Iraq to the September 11 bombings, US intelligence sources play this down, indicating that the Iraqis knew that they were under surveillance and therefore would be unlikely to knowingly meet with Atta. However, this does not answer the question of why he took the trouble to fly to Prague.

There are also indications that subsequent flights Atta took to Spain were at times when senior Iraqi intelligence officials were in the country. Iraq has repeatedly denied having anything to do with the plot, and we have since learned that members of possibly two Al-Qaeda cells in Spain may well have had prior knowledge of the September 11 attacks, and thus may have conspired with Atta.

From Prague, Atta arrived in New York on June 3, 2000, apparently his first visit to the country. Subsequent intelligence gathering failed to turn up sightings of the bearded Atta. Instead, he arrived in America thoroughly westernised. Clean-shaven, Atta wore clothing heavily branded with fashionable logos.

Despite being in the US on a tourist visa, he showed a marked interest in agriculture. At one point he visited a Department of Agriculture office in Florida to request information on government loans for buying crop-dusters. He also made repeated visits to a Florida crop-dusting airfield, according to Willie Lee, the chief pilot and general manager of South Florida Crop Care in Belle Glade. Lee identified Atta to the FBI. Lee recalled that he had asked many questions about crop-dusters, including how big a load of chemicals they could carry.

Several weeks later, Atta showed up at the Airman Flight School in Norman, Oklahoma. He requested details for a professional pilot's course, offering qualifications for a commercial pilot's licence for a single- and multi-engine landings.

But for the most part, preparations went ahead in the Florida area. There, Atta and the others took flying lessons from July until December 2000. 'They apparently were good pilots,' says Rudi Dekkers, who owns Huffman Aviation, where the pilots trained. Aside from regular visits to Huffman Aviation they kept a low profile, living in several short-term rental apartments, opening e-mail accounts and buying cellular phones.

Atta travelled to Spain several times for visits possibly linked with Iraqi intelligence. He also made several trips to Las Vegas. At one point, in August 2001, he rented a car and travelled some 3,000 miles, although where he went is the subject of speculation.

Then, on August 28, Atta used the Internet to purchase a ticket on American Airlines Flight 11. Soon after, Atta's rental car was recorded on closed-circuit video at Boston's Logan Airport, where Flight 11 originated.

Atta was there checking the landscape. Osama's sleeper was now fully awake.

CHAPTER TWENTY-TWO

One Day in the Sun

On September 10, 2001, Osama bin Laden visited Kandahar where he met with Mullah Omar. The men sat alone for about half an hour, quietly discussing their plans, out of the earshot of others in the mullah's large, walled compound. Unusually, observers noted, as the meeting ended the pair embraced. It was deep warm hug, a clinch shared by friends who, perhaps, were going their separate ways.

Around lunchtime the same day, Osama took the short journey by car from Mullah Omar's compound to a home in which his wives, many of his children and various servants and armed retainers were staying. A small and unassuming whitewashed villa set away from Kandahar city, the residence was nevertheless grand by Afghan standards where, after more than two decades of war and civil struggle, most people had been reduced to conditions akin to the Middle Ages.

At the family home, surrounded by his sons and daughters, he bid the same adieu to his family as he had shared with Mullah Omar. Something big was going to happen, he explained. They would be taken care of and moved to a safer place later that day, broken into smaller units and smuggled into Pakistan, away from what he believed would soon become a war zone. He was heading for a more remote location. The Americans were sure to come looking for him. His family would not see him for a while.

Reports that a similar message was relayed to Osama's mother Hamida via satellite telephone are almost certainly false. He knew that such calls were easily monitored and would never have risked operational failure through a careless word that alerted the United

275

States. His mother had all but cut off her son by this point, anyway, after he repeatedly refused to give her custody of her grandchildren so that they could be released from a life on the run.

With his farewells over and after a few brief meetings with senior Al-Qaeda officials, later that day Osama, Ayman al-Zawahiri and a small entourage of aides and militiamen set out from Kandahar in three or four Toyota Land Cruisers. The convoy was small to avoid observation by satellite. Their destination was the Hindu Kush mountains, a chain running about 600 miles through Pakistan to western Afghanistan. About two dozen summits in the chain rise to more than 23,000 feet. The highest point is Tirich Mir, at 25,230 feet.

By dusk this small party had travelled far into the mountains, almost to the limits of their vehicles in the rugged terrain. More men were waiting for them at a makeshift camp. After a few hours of sleep, just before dawn, the party set out on horseback. It was an uncomfortable ride, but with every passing minute they entered territory more isolated.

Based on informed speculation, we can assume that the party arrived at their destination before lunchtime. High in the mountains, away from roads, villages or the watchful eyes of the people Osama knew were hunting him, was a cave. The entrance was rough and crude, untouched, but inside, down a narrow passage, the cave opened out into a larger area that had been shaped by miners and fitted out to his personal specification. It was one of a string of caves and command bunkers that run the length of the Hindu Kush and beyond.

With all the comforts of home there, the men settled in while Osama sat glued to CNN and watched news sites on the Internet. It was a tense time. Discovery of his plans was always a possibility, especially at this late stage.

At two minutes to eight in the morning Eastern Standard Time, 5:28 p.m. Afghanistan time, United Airlines Flight 175 took off from Logan International Airport bound for Los Angeles. Not even half full, it carried 65 passengers and crew. A minute later, American Airlines Flight 11 took off from Logan, also bound for Los Angeles. At the controls was Captain John Ogonowski, a US Air Force veteran. There were 92 people on board.

Eleven minutes later, American Airlines Flight 77 cleared the runway at Washington's Dulles Airport, heading to Los Angeles.

Sixty-four people were on board this flight. Thirty-one minutes later, after delays on the ground, 45 passengers and crew took off aboard United Airlines Flight 93 from Newark International Airport bound for San Francisco.

Almost halfway around the world, the head of Al-Qaeda was glued to his television and the Internet watching for something indicating discovery of his men. He knew that, by now, at least several of the aircraft he had so carefully targeted were airborne. His men were off the ground.

Aboard American Airlines Flight 11, 29 minutes after take-off, Mohammed Atta and his gang enter the cockpit brandishing knives and box cutters and take over the plane.

'Nobody move, please. We are going back to the airport. Don't try and make any stupid moves,' says one unidentified voice.

A pilot deliberately leaves his radio microphone open; passengers, crew and air traffic controllers can hear something untoward happening. The transponder, which allows controllers to identify the plane, is turned off by someone in the cockpit.

'We have some planes. Just stay quiet and you'll be okay. We are returning to the airport,' they hear someone say.

With Atta in charge, a man calling himself Abdulaziz Alomari and a Wali M. Alshehri are now at the controls, while also on board are Wali's younger brother, Waleed, a former airline pilot and another Saudi, Satam M. A. Al Suqami. The aircraft makes an unexpected hard left turn. Now it is on course for downtown New York, not Los Angeles. Panic erupts in air traffic control.

United Airlines Flight 175 is now also uncontactable. At the controls is Fayez Rashid Ahmed Hassan Al Qadi Banihammad, a man linked with the Lackland Air Force Base Defense Language Institute in San Antonio, Texas. Team leader in the hijack is Ahmed Alghamdi, an experienced Al-Qaeda militiaman with experience fighting for the cause in Chechnya. Also on board are Hamza Alghamdi, Marwan Al-Shehhi and Mohand Alshehri.

American Airlines Flight 11 is now heading almost due south toward New York. Two fighter jets are scrambled from Otis Air Force Base, but they are too distant to reach a position where they could intercept or even shoot down the aircraft, which is hurtling in the direction of Manhattan at 400 miles an hour.

Nothing can be done. At 8:46 a.m. the aircraft, 92 souls and 10,000 gallons of highly inflammable fuel hit the North Tower of the World Trade Center between the 94th and 99th floors of the 110-storey building.

Minutes later, CNN breaks into its regular programming to beam live coverage worldwide of the appalling accident that has befallen the World Trade Center. Thick black smoke is billowing from the tower, symbol of US economic power, of international commerce and the capitalist system. This picture reaches Afghanistan and the isolated command bunker deep in the Hindu Kush. Osama knows that he has struck an unprecedented blow. But while the world watches in shock and disbelief, he also knows that there is more to come.

Seventeen minutes later, at 9:03 a.m., United Airlines Flight 175 crashes into the South Tower, between the 78th and 84th floors. This is carried live on television networks the world over. Hundreds of millions of people are watching in horror. As the implications of the double tragedy becomes clear – that this is a synchronised act of evil – in one isolated Middle Eastern spot there is euphoria. Al-Qaeda has succeeded in the most astonishing act of terrorism perpetrated in the world.

And there is more satisfaction to come for Osama. President George W. Bush is in Sarasota, Florida, speaking on education. As news of the second hit is related to presidential aides, Bush is on the podium. His chief of staff, Andy Card, interrupts Bush's address and whispers the news. There is no doubt now. While some terrible catalogue of failures could have explained a single accident, a double hit makes it abundantly clear that something is terribly wrong and that the World Trade Center has been the focus of a terrorist assault.

A determined Bush finishes his address on education and is immediately asked by a reporter if he has comments on the situation in New York. 'I will talk about that later,' he states, heading off to be briefed by his national security advisor Condoleezza Rice on the emerging situation.

Osama must have watched in joyous disbelief as, at 9:30 a.m., a grim-looking president returns to the podium. He says the country has suffered an 'apparent terrorist attack'. News is filtering through that the Federal Aviation Administration (FAA) has ordered the shut-down of all New York City area airports and that the Port Authority of New York and New Jersey ordered all bridges and tunnels in the New York area closed. Osama has closed down New York.

Nearly 40 minutes after the South Tower of the World Trade Center is hit, American Airlines Flight 77 swings round, loops 270 degrees and comes in low over Washington. Shortly before reaching its final destination, the aircraft picks up speed dramatically before slamming into the west side of the Pentagon, the symbol of American military power

Aboard are Yemeni Khalid Almihdhar and Chechen campaign veteran Nawaf Alhazmi, both of whom had gained flying experience at Sorbi's Flying Club in San Diego. Another with flying experience is Saudi Arabian Hani Hanjour, who received a commercial pilot's licence in 1999 from the FAA. Also aboard are Salem Alhazmi, another Chechen fighter, and a Majed Moqed.

The plane is almost fully loaded with fuel that ignites and sparks off an inferno that quickly spreads 300 yards each side of the impact site. CNN cuts to the Pentagon just seconds later to hear a correspondent describing an appalling scene. Pictures show the Pentagon belching plumes of black smoke.

Minutes later it is announced that the FAA has halted all flight operations at all US airports, the first time in history that air traffic nationwide has been frozen. At 10:24 a.m. the FAA diverts all inbound transatlantic aircraft flying toward the United States to Canada.

Osama has not only closed New York, he has shut down the United States as a whole.

High above Pennsylvania, meanwhile, another drama is afoot. Hijackers aboard United Airlines Flight 93 from Newark to San Francisco are not having things go their way. Four men are attempting to take over the aircraft. They are headed by Saeed Alghamdi, who received electronics, communications and intelligence training, intended for members of foreign military services, at installations in Florida, Maryland, Illinois and Virginia. He is accompanied by Ahmed Ibrahim A. Al Haznawi, Ahmed Alnami and Ziad Samir Jarrah, who studied aeronautical engineering in Hamburg, Germany from 1996 to 2000 while project leader Mohammed Atta was also in Hamburg.

Their target is apparently the White House. But word has already reached the cabin of the disasters that have befallen the World Trade Center. Several passengers on board use their cell

279

phones to make final, agonising calls to their loved ones. Realising that the men among them are part of a wider plot, and realising that they have nothing to lose, passengers and crew resist. The aircraft flies an erratic course, as though different pilots are at the controls, or the hijacker is unsure of himself. In the passenger cabin, one man is dead, felled while resisting the hijackers. The passengers 'engaged in a fight for their lives with their four hijackers', comments FBI counter-terrorism director Tim Caruso later. 'And most likely, as a result of their efforts, saved the lives of unknown individuals on the ground.'

Around 80 miles south-east of Pittsburgh the aircraft crashes in a wooded area. All on board are killed instantly. But the plane has missed its target, possibly saving thousands of lives.

News of this has not yet reached CNN, leaving Osama unaware of a failure. Elsewhere his men aboard another aircraft, United Airlines Flight 23, see their mission aborted at the last minute. Four men 'of Middle Eastern origin' are on the flight, which is standing on the runway at New York's John F. Kennedy airport waiting for permission to take off when news of the FAA airport closure is relayed to the pilot. The four engage in animated discussions in the cabin and then bolt when the aircraft's door is opened back at the terminal.

The FAA's quick decisions saved another disaster in the form of United Airlines Flight 23, and later evidence suggests that several other cells had their plans foiled by the speedy closure of United States airspace. But these successes mean little.

At 9:59 a.m., Osama watches as incredible scenes unfold in New York live on television. Tower Two of the World Trade Center suddenly collapses. Eleven minutes later a section of the Pentagon goes, but this is hardly mentioned on CNN, which continues to focus on the scene of cataclysm in New York. Twenty-nine minutes after its companion, Tower One of the World Trade Center buckles and collapses too.

Al-Qaeda has delivered utter devastation to the heart of America and the western world that Osama so despises. Years of planning, a multi-billion dollar investment (with an estimated $200,000 spent on the September 11 attacks) and the careful construction of a massive smoke screen has borne fruit in a way that he could only have dreamed.

★

As the day wore on, the master terrorist must have found himself watching in disbelief and joy as events unfolded. For over a decade he had been the hunted. President Clinton had hounded him out of Sudan, unleashed the CIA and FBI upon Al-Qaeda and attempted on numerous occasions to assassinate or snatch the organisation's leader. Throughout this, Osama had survived.

He had missed the opportunity to wreak such havoc upon the United States during the Clinton presidency, something he would dearly have liked to have done, but on September 11, 2001, Osama turned the tables. Now it was George W. Bush who looked like the hunted.

Hearing news of the attack in Florida, Bush wished to return immediately to the White House. Close aides, fearing for the safety of the president with unknown numbers of civilian airlines still in the air, counselled evasive action. More than nine hours later, having criss-crossed the country, he returned to Washington. Thousands of miles away, Osama was enjoying the theatre being played out on his television screen.

Osama knew that retribution would come sooner or later, that US investigators would quickly link evidence to Al-Qaeda and by definition to his door. At four in the afternoon US time, the icing on the cake was provided by CNN National Security Correspondent David Ensor. Ensor appeared on the network to report that 'US officials say there are "good indications" that Saudi militant Osama bin Laden, suspected of coordinating the bombings of two US embassies in 1998, is involved in the attacks, based on "new and specific" information developed since the attacks.'

It was already morning Afghan time, and 8:30 p.m. at the White House, when Bush made his first major statement on the crisis. The United States had not faced such a crisis since December 7, 1941, when Japan attacked the US naval base at Pearl Harbor on the island of Oahu, Hawaii. A day later President Franklin D. Roosevelt delivered his famed 'Day of Infamy' address. Sixty years later, it fell to President George W. Bush to draw the country together. He went on television to say:

'Today, our fellow citizens, our way of life, our very freedom came under attack in a series of deliberate and deadly terrorist acts. The victims were in airplanes or in their offices – secretaries, businessmen and women, military and federal workers. Moms and dads. Friends and neighbors. Thousands of lives were suddenly ended by evil, despicable acts of terror . . . These acts of mass murder were intended to frighten our nation into chaos and retreat. But they have failed. Our country is strong. A great people has been moved to defend a great nation.

'Terrorist attacks can shake the foundations of our biggest buildings, but they cannot touch the foundation of America. These acts shatter steel, but they cannot dent the steel of American resolve . . .

'Our military is powerful, and it's prepared . . . The search is under way for those who are behind these evil acts. I have directed the full resources for our intelligence and law enforcement communities to find those responsible and bring them to justice. We will make no distinction between the terrorists who committed these acts and those who harbor them . . .

'This is a day when all Americans from every walk of life unite in our resolve for justice and peace. America has stood down enemies before, and we will do so this time.'

Epilogue

Ariel Sharon, the hawkish Israeli prime minister, is not everyone's idea of a world saviour. But in the history books of the future it could be Sharon, not President George W. Bush or British prime minister Tony Blair, who is the man ultimately credited with putting an end to the reign of terror of Osama bin Laden and Al-Qaeda. It seems an unlikely prospect as we view the cauldron of hate that is the Middle East today, and doubly unlikely that Sharon would accomplish this by becoming a dove. But it is entirely plausible, as the fate of the struggle against Osama and all he stands for is in Sharon's hands . . .

Al-Qaeda was ready for America's wrath even before the events of September 11, 2001. Osama had proved he would never be caught unprepared. He had weighed the possible scenarios of September 12, 2001, the day the United States would inevitably wake up angry. It did not take a genius to anticipate that they would come looking for him.

During the early summer of 2001 Al-Qaeda bases around Afghanistan had come alive with activity. Training programs were speeded up in order to complete as much preparation as possible. Equipment and supplies were shifted away from bases to remote locations, to be stored in caves or buried. All this was done gradually so as not to attract attention. Groups of men were also dispatched into the mountains, to caves that had been stocked with winter clothing, firewood, ammunition and enough food and water to last months.

Osama knew that few countries anywhere in the world provided such excellent cover in its remote areas for his men and organisation as Afghanistan. His men now did what their hosts had done for centuries. Natural limestone caves became their home, where they could base themselves almost indefinitely and from which they expected to strike out almost with impunity should the Americans make the same mistake as the Soviets and commit ground troops.

Anyone who believes that Osama bin Laden went to ground in an Afghan cave without a carefully prepared escape plan has not seriously considered who they are dealing with. It is a distinct possibility that he has already taken a Hindu Kush escape route and is ensconced in a remote part of Bangladesh, Bhutan, China, India, Myanmar, Nepal or Pakistan, far from prying eyes. Osama has consistently proven himself a clever operator; he is simply not going to wait around to be captured – unless it happens on his own terms, and as part of a preconceived plan.

Every move by Osama and Al-Qaeda has been thought out, scripted and carefully orchestrated. The Al-Qaeda videos that have materialised since September 11 have verged on the theatrical, and clearly Osama and his cohorts have worked hard on their production. Osama, with his ever-present Kalashnikov in the background, sits on his knees piously staring at the floor. He's an actor, playing a role. Next to him is the ever-present Ayman al-Zawahiri, who exploited Osama's infatuation with him to further his own ends.

The two have strenuously pushed their claim as leaders of the fundamentalist world, attempting to widen their appeal by associating themselves with the Palestinian issue – a genuine grievance close to the hearts of Muslims everywhere. And there was more to come in this public relations offensive.

Osama thinks nothing of keeping his wives and children almost as hostages on the verges of his life. While content to live his own life as a renegade on the run, Osama has decreed that his long-suffering family also remains in this shadowy existence. For most of them, it is against their will. Despite the efforts of his mother, Hamida, to have his children returned to Saudi Arabia where they could at last live a normal life, their father has decreed that they live life on the run, now constantly under attack from the United States.

Another threat is bounty hunters seeking a slice of the $25 million now offered as a price on Osama's head. One son, Hamza, was injured by a bullet two years ago in a gunfight when bounty hunters ambushed the car in which he was travelling, believing Osama to be a passenger. The attackers were killed, as was one Al-Qaeda militiaman who was assigned to protect the vehicle.

Despite the obvious dangers, Osama has moved to using his children as tools to front his campaign. His youngest son, ten-year-old Ali, was used to deliver a pre–September 11 tirade against the United States on a video of the wedding of his brother, 20-year-old Mohammed, earlier this year. Then Osama's eldest son, 21-year-old Abdullah, surfaced in Pakistan after the World Trade Center attacks to deliver a carefully scripted litany of lies to the press, clouding the whereabouts of his father and denying his involvement in the attacks. The family involvement is cynical window dressing, part of Osama's public relations campaign to deflect attention from his true intentions.

It is doubtful, given his craving for attention, that September 11 will be enough for Osama. He retains the capability to murder and wreak havoc on a global scale. Almost inevitably, given his efforts to acquire them, somewhere he is also nurturing the materials and tools that present him with the opportunity to inflict other serious wounds to our society. Whether the present campaign to capture him ultimately succeeds or fails, he will certainly strike back through dozens of cells already established in North America, Europe and Asia.

While the West had failed to contain the threat of Al-Qaeda over the last decade, the organisation has significantly increased its arms capabilities and its reach. For most of the 1990s Osama pursued vigorously his dream of having a bioweaponry and even nuclear weapons at his disposal. It would take a foolhardy man to state with any conviction that he has not achieved that aim.

'Bin Laden has been trying to get his hands on enriched uranium for seven or eight years,' said former CIA director Robert Wolsey. What is more, the collapse of the Soviet Union has created a lucrative black market in stolen fissile material. Also up for sale is expertise. In the collapsed former–Soviet bloc nuclear economy, hundreds of scientists and technicians have been made jobless. Those that cling to jobs are paid a pittance.

Dozens of instances have occurred where groups of criminals have been caught in possession of nuclear materials capable of being utilised as the building blocks of a weapon. Other reports place Al-Qaeda operatives in situations where they were able to acquire these.

While Russia and the former Soviet states have retained a firm grip upon a combined strength of up to 40,000 nuclear weapons, their nuclear stockpile has sprung leaks. The so-called RA-115 and RA-115-01, better known as suitcase nuclear weapons, are top secret and no western official has ever seen one. However, one official highly placed in the Boris Yeltsin administration, environmental advisor Aleksei Yablokov, announced that of 132 of the weapons made, Russia could only account for the whereabouts of 48.

To dismiss Osama's desire and financial ability to succeed in his quest before the events of September 11 was foolhardy. Not to focus on the clear and present danger presented by a nuclear or bio-weaponry program clearly underway – now knowing exactly what he is capable of – is to invite nuclear attack by a man who has shown such a callous disregard for the sanctity of human life. This is the new front in the ever-changing battle lines being drawn up against Al-Qaeda. The fall of the Taliban in Afghanistan, or even the death or capture of Osama, will not change that.

Osama's Achilles' heel has already been shown up, however. His inflated sense of worth to the Muslim world does not match the reality. He is intelligent enough to know that, while some of the issues he has raised in public as his motivating factors have widespread and deep-rooted support around the Arab and Muslim world, his methods of carrying these issues to the world stage are sickening. A majority are offended that he invokes the name of God in his attacks. To Muslims, to suggest that God would stoop to murder and acts of violence is to suggest that the most pure of entities in the universe thinks the same way as the most twisted of mortals. It is a measure of how warped Osama and his ilk have become that they believe a serene God applauds them and condones their methods.

A tiny minority of the nearly one billion Muslims worldwide cheered the devastating acts of September 11. The majority condemned his actions and realised that the Prophet's teachings had been wrenched out of context by Islamic fundamentalists to justify their own ends.

Because of this, Osama knows that Al-Qaeda's base of support is so narrow that he cannot succeed in his long-term aim of creating a Middle East under the rule of Islamic fundamentalism, and himself. He believes that by drawing the United States and its allies into open conflict, he can energise the masses around his cause. This would lead to a collapse of governments in Saudi Arabia and Pakistan, and this in turn would leave Osama in control of the Islamic world's only nuclear arsenal as well as its holiest sights. Leveraging these, he would be able to instigate the fall of pro-Western Islamic governments such as Egypt, Yemen and the Gulf states.

Gradually, so the plan goes, Osama bin Laden would lead an Islamic revolution that would spread throughout the Middle East and, having proclaimed a unified regional Islamic state, he himself would rule as caliph.

The one sticking point in this master plan is the people of the Arab world. Osama believed that his horrendous attacks on America on its home turf would make him a caliph-in-waiting. However, the weeks since September 11 did not pan out as he and his cohorts had hoped. For in reality, while the masses may say they loathe America, they actually dream of having all things American themselves.

Happily, aside from delivering an occasional body blow to the West, Osama remains impotent and sidelined. This is why he sought to link his entirely un-Islamic campaign of hatred with the Palestinian issue, a cause that he has never shown any inclination to support.

He is correct in one regard, however. The fate of millions of Palestinians denied basic human rights, jobs, freedom, land and homes has continued to be an issue that concerns the entire Muslim world. If one topic could be used by Al-Qaeda as a rallying point to gain support, it was this. In seeking a connection with the issue, he has exposed his desperation to garner widespread support, but he has also handed the world the means to defeat him on a plate.

A raging concept cannot be beaten with bombs and bullets. Instead it must be calmed with hope and human dignity. Fundamentalism's base, its financial supporters and foot soldiers, gravitate towards the concept because of their anger and frustration with the alternative – the disastrous socio-economic and political situation that presents itself in the Middle East of today.

All the maladies that afflict the region stem from, or have been aggravated by, this one issue. It is pointless for George W. Bush to mouth platitudes such as 'there ought to be a Palestinian state, the boundaries of which would be negotiated by the parties . . . ' if he intends only to throw a bone to Islamic states whose support he needs in order to bomb Afghanistan. Nor can the United States simply press Israel and the Palestinians to tone down their conflict to avoid interfering with coalition building. This will fix nothing. Instead, the US and the West must take an active role in redressing the balance in the Middle East. This means helping Palestinians as well as Israelis realise their dreams and aspirations, and in so doing close a gaping wound that has been hurting Arabs and Muslims for half a century.

When peace is achieved, the entire complexion of the region will change. A Palestinian with a job, food on his table and a degree of basic human rights – all things missing from the lives of so many ordinary people today – will not fight Israeli troops on the streets, or join Hezbollah, or support extremist views. When men are not driven into the arms of fundamentalism, and people are not motivated by anger to give money and moral support, the diseased branch of Islamic fanaticism will wither and die. The terrorist groups that this fanaticism has spawned will fade away for want of support, just as surely as with every new clash on the streets of the West Bank and Gaza these evil groups grow in prestige and power.

And so it comes back to Ariel Sharon. The United States and its allies can bring pressure to bear, but only the Israeli leader has it within his power finally to strike a deal for lasting peace. A place awaits him in history as the statesman who achieved what his predecessors could not in silencing the guns that surround the Jewish state.

Peace will bring stability and stability will bring prosperity to a region starved of all three for more than 50 years. If this half-century old fracture in the hegemony of the Middle East can finally be mended and lives put on the road to recovery, then Osama bin Laden's support will collapse just as quickly as the World Trade Center towers after the most hideous crimes against humanity since the Second World War.

Index

INDEX

INDEX

INDEX

INDEX

INDEX